The
Complete
Spice Book

The Complete Spice Book

Maggie Stuckey

Illustrations by

Elizabeth Mason

St. Martin's Griffin ❦ *New York*

Where historical medicinal applications of spices are described, the reader should bear in mind that this book is intended as a general reference, and should not be used in place of consultation with a medicinal professional. Responsibility for adverse effects or unforeseen consequences of the applications, preparations, or recipes contained in this book is expressly disclaimed by the author and publisher.

Library of Congress Catologing-in-Publication Data

Stuckey, Maggie.
    The complete spice book : from allspice to vanilla—the ultimate companion to the ancient and everyday wonders on your spice rack / Maggie Stuckey ; illustrations by Elizabeth Mason.
    p.   cm.
  ISBN 0-312-20131-1
  1. Cookery (Spices) 2. Spices I. Title
  TX819.A1 S884   1999
  641.6'383—dc21
                                                98-49822
                                                    CIP

First St. Martin's Griffin Edition: February 1999

10   9   8   7   6   5   4   3   2   1

❧ Contents ❧

❧ Acknowledgments ❧

Please allow me a few moments to extend thanks to:

The good people at the American Spice Trade Association, McCormick & Co., and Specialty Foods (Spice Islands), for background information and permission to use some of their recipes.

Renée Shepherd, owner of Renée's Garden and author of two "From the Garden" cookbooks, for graciously allowing me to share some of her lovely recipes with you.

Elizabeth Mason, for her wonderful drawings. I stand in awe of your talent, Liz.

Sandra Schleppy, for her computer wizardry, intelligence, and good cheer shining through the clouds.

Heather Jackson, at St. Martin's Press. All authors should be so lucky.

Maggie Stuckey
Portland, Oregon

⊰ Foreword ⊱

Spices are magical.

They're not much to look at. Most of them resemble dried twigs, tiny pebbles, or a small pile of dirt. They come in ordinary little glass jars, not exactly impressive in size or demeanor. Yet the richness of flavor they add to our food is a quiet miracle.

But that is only the top layer of their magic. The same unremarkable substances also enlivened the foods of our ancestors, and enriched their lives in many other ways. As far back as we have records of human history, spices have been used in medicinal formulations to treat and prevent disease. They have served as practical household aids, cosmetics, dyes, elements in religious ritual, and protection against plague and evil spirits.

And there is more. It is not an exaggeration to say that the intercontinental trade in spices was the reason, and also the mechanism, for opening up the world as we know it. For many hundreds of years, spices—those simple, humble substances—were the single most important force driving the world's economy. At first, caravan merchants and Arab traders brought goods from the East to the West, and took Western goods back with them; at the same time, they were exchanging cultures and expanding horizons. Later, fierce and bloody competition among European nations to control the spice market led to the great Age of Exploration, and the discovery of the New World. Their motivation may have been avarice, but the consequences were, nonetheless, momentous.

Finally, at the most fundamental level, it is possible to view spices as threads linking human experiences across all dimensions, including the dimension of time. Hot chili peppers, so important to the Aztecs in the 1400s, are fearlessly chopped into soups in modern Vietnam. Nutmeg, which we casually sprinkle on our holiday eggnog, was so precious in the 1600s that its thieves were executed. Cardamom, which originated in tropical Asia, was traded in Constantinople to Vikings who brought it home to Scandinavia; today it flavors coffee in Morocco, bread in Sweden, fruit salad in Canada, and curry in India.

This I think is the most profound magic of all: that each time we measure out a spoonful of spices in our kitchens today, we are dipping into the rich reservoir of human tragedy and heroism that brought them ultimately to our tables. And we are, in a sense, sharing our meal with people in other lands who have also spooned out that same spice today.

It is my hope that, after spending some time with this book, you will never again look at a simple jar of spice in quite the same way.

The
Complete
Spice Book

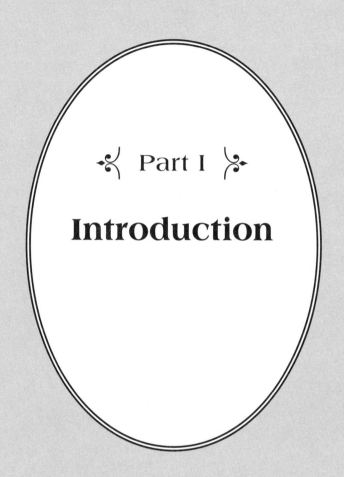

Part I

Introduction

How This Book Is Organized

The core of this book is the Encyclopedia section, in which thirty spices are described, each in its own chapter. The spices are arranged in alphabetical order, by their common names. The chapters describe the plant that produces the spice, the history that surrounds it, the medicine that is (or once was) made from it, in some cases crafts projects that incorporate it, and the ways in which it is used in cooking. At the end of the book there is an Appendix listing mail-order sources for buying spices and obtaining information about them.

But first come two foundation chapters. The first is this Introduction, which you are reading now. In it are short pieces on some general characteristics of spices that I believe you would do well to have under your belt before we move into the individual spice chapters, including a little chemistry and a little botany. The second chapter is a recounting of the amazing history of spices—brief, informal, and, of necessity, simplified.

You can, if you wish, skip these two chapters, and still find answers to most if not all of your questions about spices. From just the chapters in the Encyclopedia section, you can learn everything, or practically everything, you ever wanted to know about these thirty spices, along with some things you didn't know you wanted to know.

However, this course is not without risk. If you do decide to skip these early chapters, you will (1) not have as full a grasp of the big picture, (2) miss out on some interesting stuff, and (3) hurt my feelings. Up to you.

1

Spice Basics

The Difference Between Spices and Herbs

It's not as significant as, say, the issue of whether or not there is a God or whether money can buy happiness, but there is in some circles an ongoing debate over the difference between spices and herbs.

According to the traditional definition, if the plant from which cometh the whatever-it-is grows in the tropics or subtropics, it's a spice. If the plant grows in the temperate zone (the milder climate zone between the tropics and the poles, which includes most of Europe and the U.S.), it's an herb.

As a general rule the traditional definition works as well as any other general rule, which is to say: What do we do with the exceptions?

- What about coriander? Most people would consider that a spice. Yet it comes from the exact same plant that produces cilantro, which practically everyone considers an herb.
- What about plants whose seeds we use to flavor food—dill, for example? The leaves, commercially marketed as "dill weed," you would probably describe as an herb. But are dill *seeds* an herb? My guess is that most of you would say no, it's a spice . . . well, sort of a spice.

Furthermore, the traditional definition somewhat begs the question. The goods brought in by caravan from the tropical islands of southern Asia were called *species* by the ancient Romans, meaning "wares, assorted trade goods." Much of our language derives from Latin, and so the word *species* became *spice* in English. Now, what if, by some quirk of geography and plant evolution, the ancient civilizations of Greece and Rome had come to depend on other types of plants that grew elsewhere? Would *those* products now be called spices? To say they are spices because they come from the tropical zone, and anything from the tropics must be a spice, is an exercise in circular logic. And in the end not terribly important, in my opinion.

Some people, not overly concerned with definitions, separate them by color: if it's green it's an herb; if it's brown, red, orange, black, or anything other than green, it's a spice. That's easy to understand and easy to remember and it almost works, but it presents a few anomalies also.

Ultimately I concluded that, for the purposes of this book, spices are (1) any aromatic part of a tropical plant customarily used to flavor food, *plus* (2) the dried seeds or fruits of temperate-zone plants used the same way. Then, some things that would ordinarily fit this expanded definition (such as achiote, lemon grass, and tamarind) were omitted because they are neither widely used nor readily available. (This was a difficult decision, because I wanted to introduce you to everything, but alas there isn't room for everything.) Finally, I decided to include three products that are actually blends of several spices: chili powder, curry powder, and five-spice. There are other blends on the market (pickling spice, pumpkin pie spice, lemon pepper, etc.), but these three are in a class by themselves because they are frequently misunderstood as being "*a spice*"—and besides, you have to draw the line somewhere.

In this admittedly arbitrary way, I settled on these thirty spices:

allspice	five-spice powder
anise	ginger
caraway	horseradish
cardamom	juniper berries
cayenne	mace
chili peppers	mustard
chili powder	nutmeg
cinnamon	paprika
cloves	pepper
coriander	poppy seed
cumin	saffron
curry powder	sesame seed
dill seed	star anise
fennel seed	turmeric
fenugreek seed	vanilla

Why Spices Taste the Way They Do

You probably never gave plant chemistry a great deal of thought, but consider for a moment that some plants smell sweet and some smell awful, some roots are nutritious and some will kill you, some barks taste good and some taste like, well, bark. It all has to do with each plant's chemical makeup.

A Short Lesson in Chemistry

The fragrance and taste of a plant come from substances called essential oils that are carried in the cells of the plant's tissues. (*Essential* means it is the essence of the plant, not essential as in mandatory.) Sometimes these substances are spread throughout the plant and sometimes they are concentrated in just one part. Think of this: How much fragrance do you smell from the leaves of a rosebush, compared to the flower?

These essential oils are themselves made up of various chemical substances (that is why this is a chemistry lesson). These chemicals have names like benzaldehyde, neryl acetate, cineole, limonene, and zingerone. The oils of most spices contain a dozen or more constituent chemicals, which is one reason we describe their taste as complex. And many of the chemicals are present in more than one spice, although not usually in the same proportions.

For example: Cinnamon gets its principal taste from something called cinnamic aldehyde, which makes up two-thirds of the essential oil. If you could isolate cinnamic aldehyde, however, and taste a drop of it, it wouldn't taste exactly like the spice because the cinnamon tree also contains other chemicals, and the taste we recognize as cinnamon is a combination of all its chemical parts. One of those parts, for instance, is eugenol, which is a minor constituent in cinnamon but the primary taste component of cloves. That is why we think of cinnamon and cloves together; they don't taste exactly alike, but they do belong in the same neighborhood.

Another example: The seeds of the anise plant, which is a small, annual herb, contain anethole, methylchavicol, and anisaldehyde. Star anise, the dried fruit of an evergreen tree, contains those same three chemicals. And that is why anise and star anise, which have absolutely no relation in any botanical sense, produce spices that taste so similar they are used interchangeably.

Why do you need to know this? Because knowing how they work helps you understand how to work with them. The presence of these chemical substances in the cells of the plants is the reason behind the common advice that you cook with whole spices whenever possible, rather than those already ground into a powder. To release the oils that are in the spices, the cell walls must be ruptured. Cooking does this, and so do grating, grinding, and pounding. However, there is a catch-22: Essential oils are volatile at room temperature, meaning they will eventually evaporate. Once spices are ground, the entire structure is exposed to air, and the process of evaporation begins. In whole spices, on the other hand, the essential oils are locked into the interior and there they will stay until they meet up with a grater.

Essential Oils for Sale

Because essential oils are volatile, they can be deliberately evaporated and captured in the process known as steam distillation—just like bourbon. Many of our common spices are distilled this way, and food manufacturers use the oils widely to add natural flavors to their products.

In recent years, essential oils packaged in small vials have become available to general consumers; several mail-order companies that sell essential oils are listed in this book's Appendix. Note carefully whether these products are food quality. So-called "fragrance oils" contain synthetic substances, and are meant to be used with crafts such as making potpourri.

Essential oils are nice to know about. Think of them as spices in another physical form. They are, by the way, not oily in the usual sense of the word, but more like water.

Extracts are not quite the same as essential oils, but functionally similar. A solution of water and alcohol is used to pull out (extract) the flavor essence from the spice. Extracts are very stable, and have a long shelf life. The most familiar is vanilla extract, but others are also available.

Buying Spices

In supermarkets large and small all across the country, you can find small jars of spices from several major national and "store-brand" manufacturers. This is the most common source of spices for most people, and I am certainly not going to try to steer you away from them. On the contrary, these are excellent products, and decidedly convenient when you run out of something in the middle of a recipe. One new trend from these commercial companies that I applaud is smaller jars; not only are they more affordable, but they're less likely to lose flavor before you get a chance to use them.

I do hope, however, to extend your horizon slightly, to introduce you to new ways of buying spices. If your town has a natural foods store or an herb shop, the chances are good that they stock spices in bulk, usually in large containers from which you measure out as much or as little as you wish.

It is worth getting acquainted with shops like this. The selection of spices is usually large, and often they carry the more unusual or more exotic items that the supermarkets don't stock. Another advantage: You can buy a very small amount of something, just to experiment with; if you don't care for it, you haven't invested much. On the other hand, if you have need for a large quantity of a certain spice (at pickling season, for instance), you'll find it more economical to buy in bulk than to purchase several of those small commercial jars.

In my neighborhood (in a midsize city in the Pacific Northwest), there is a store like this, and I absolutely love shopping there. The spices are in one-gallon jars that remind me of a country general store from forty years ago, and just looking at the range of colors and textures spread out on the wall gives me pleasure. When I'm trying a new recipe I often buy just the amount of spices I need, and it costs only pennies—literally. Then if I don't like the dish, I don't have to keep looking over my shoulder at the spice rack, wondering how I'm going to use up the rest of that spice.

Sometimes I take children with me when I shop at this store, and they are invariably enchanted by the multicolored display of spices. We have fun dipping out the right amount and writing up the labels on the little plastic bags, with maybe a small geography lesson snuck in here and there. (I can't help it; that's what aunts do.)

So search those stores out, and patronize them; it's fun.

But even if you don't have a shop like that in your hometown, you can still have almost the same experience via mail order. In the Appendix at the back of this book are descriptions of several companies that sell spices and spice-related products by mail.

Storing Spices

No matter where and how you buy your spices, you owe it to yourself to store them properly. All ground spices should be kept in a dark, cool spot. The refrigerator is ideal, if you have room.

Second best: In a cupboard or drawer (to keep out light) and, if you have a choice, a cool corner of the kitchen.

Worst choice: Right above the stove—it's way too hot.

Some of these precautions apply more to herbs than to spices, but in real life most of us keep spices and herbs together. It's especially important to keep chili powder, curry powder, paprika, saffron, turmeric, and whole vanilla beans away from direct light.

If you buy spices via mail order or from a merchant who sells in bulk, take them out of the plastic bag and put them into some kind of airtight glass container. Several kinds are illustrated on page 9; for smaller amounts, of course, you can also recycle empty spice jars. Avoid storing spices and herbs in plastic, which has its own aroma that could interfere with the spices.

How Long Do They Last?
A long time, if they are still whole. Years, even.

You may come across a suggestion to discard spices that are more than a year old. That's probably a good idea with *herbs*, which lose flavor much more rapidly, and then start to taste rather like hay. Spices, on the other hand, keep their potency longer. If they are in whole form, some spices keep for years. Even the preground ones don't go bad in the usual sense (except mustard seeds and sesame seeds do eventually go rancid); what happens is that they gradually lose their "oomph." I don't discard old spices, for the simple reason that my ancestors were Scottish

Glass containers for spices. To maintain quality, spices should be stored in glass containers that have tight-closing lids. Keep the jars in a cool spot away from direct sunlight.

and we don't believe in waste. Just use a larger amount, taste, then add still more if needed.

Cooking with Spices

There is no better way to add rich, deep flavor to your food than with spices. And it's virtually guilt-free: One teaspoon of spice, generally speaking, has less than ten calories, only a fraction of a gram of fat, and very little sodium.

But make sure you get all the flavor that can be gotten from your spices. This is so important I'm going to repeat it: Whenever possible, use whole spices rather than preground ones. You have two options:

1. Add the whole spices, intact, to whatever you're cooking—either loose or in some kind of infuser.
2. Grind the spices just before using and add the freshly ground powder to your dish.

The choice primarily has to do with texture: Do you want the whole spice in the finished dish—crunchy fennel seeds in your apple pie, for example—or not?

In some cases, your choices are limited. Cloves are an example. It's

Several kinds of infusers. Infusers allow you to capture the more intense flavor of whole spices without having the actual spice in your dish. The bottom item, with the large holes, is for spices only (it has a screwtop, not shown in drawing). The others are actually designed for brewing tea, and their smaller holes make them ideal for smaller whole spices such as fennel and caraway seed.

not a good idea to have loose cloves floating around in your stew, because people could choke on one. So if you want the flavor of cloves without little specks of ground spice, use some type of infuser and remove it before serving.

Another limiting factor is the basic nature of the dish you're preparing. Infusers, including tea balls and cheesecloth spice bags, work in liquid; slow simmering gradually extracts their flavor. So they are a good choice with stews, soups, things like that. But if you're making a cake, or scalloped potatoes, obviously you can't use an infuser, so you'll need spices in the form of a powder that you can spread throughout the dish.

Grinding your spices just before you use them is mostly a matter of having the right equipment. And it doesn't have to be fancy, or expensive. A simple mortar and pestle has served cooks since prehistoric times.

Mechanical grinders in many shapes and sizes are widely available. Sometimes they are called pepper mills, but you don't have to limit them to pepper; many whole spices can be ground this way.

For nutmeg, use a small grater.

Electric grinders are another option. The size intended for grinding coffee beans is the most common, and works fine with spices. If you go

Making a spice bag. Use 1 or 2 thicknesses of cheesecloth, cut into a 6-inch square. Pile spice mixture into the center, bring up the edges, and tie with plain (undyed) string.

this route, you'll probably want a separate grinder for spices, not the one you use for coffee. The last time I looked, they were about $20; often you can pick up a good secondhand one at garage sales or thrift stores. In gourmet kitchen shops and catalogs you can sometimes find smaller grinders designed especially for spices.

Toast Spices First

When you add an infuser of spices to your bouillabaisse, or a bouquet garni to black bean soup, the heat of the cooking gradually breaks down the cell walls of the whole spices and the essential oils are released into the surrounding liquid. When you grate nutmeg into your special creamed spinach, the act of grating exposes the oils. But when you add whole spices to a dish that cooks quickly, and especially when you sprinkle them on at the end as a garnish, you don't always get the full richness of the taste.

To overcome that, make time for one additional step: Toast the spices before you add them. It is extraordinarily simple to do, and it makes an

Nutmeg graters. Freshly grated nutmeg is the only way to go. Any of these graters makes quick work of the task; the one on bottom left has a compartment with a sliding lid to store the whole nutmegs.

enormous difference. Heat the oven to 350°, spread the spices in a shallow, unbuttered pan (like a pie tin), and roast them for five to ten minutes, until they become very fragrant. Another way, which may be even easier: Spread them in the bottom of a heavy skillet with no oil (I use a cast-iron pan) and cook over medium heat until they begin to turn darker in color and they become fragrant.

> If you take away only one new idea from this book, let it be this: Toast spices before adding them to your cooking.

Those Weird Latin Names

Sooner or later (mostly sooner), people who read about plants run smack into the problem of scientific names. When they do, their reactions vary. Some run screaming from the room, some relish the challenge, and some blissfully ignore the whole thing (in many cases an altogether sensible approach).

It helps if you know the reason behind the names, so let's talk botany.

Every plant on the face of the earth has been given its own botanical name, in Latin; no other plant has that same name. Thus scientists, plant breeders, and gardeners all over the world, no matter what language they speak on a daily basis, can be certain they are talking about the same plant if they all use that Latin name. That one plant, on the other hand, may have a dozen or more common names, all different; you can imagine the possibilities for confusion.

The botanical name is always in two parts, somewhat like people's names when they are presented surname first: Twain, Mark.

Example: *Illicium verum* (Star anise)

The first name is the genus the plant belongs to, the second name is its species. A genus (pronounced *jean*-us) is a grouping of plants that share one or more characteristics; a species is a subcategory. So a genus can have several species; they will be different from each other in some ways, but also similar in many ways. Cousins, you might say. There may be other Illiciums, and in fact there are, but the full name *Illicium verum* designates just one plant.

Often the translation of the Latin words tells us something interesting or useful about the plant. *Illicium* comes from the Latin word for "attracting," a reference to fragrance; *verum* means "true"; in other words, the real thing. Other Illiciums are *I. floridanum*, a species discovered in Florida, and *I. henryi*, named in honor of Augustine Henry, a physician and amateur plant collector who found this species in China. (Notice that when several species in one genus are mentioned together, the genus name is abbreviated after the first time.)

To be honest, I have to tell you that occasionally glitches appear. Sometimes new names get assigned. Sometimes the defining criteria that place one plant in a certain genus and not in another get changed by those whose profession it is to worry about these things. Which is why sometimes you will see two different Latin names for the same plant, one current and one former.

Do you really need to learn the Latin names? No. The commercial spice companies must pay strict attention to all this, but as far as you and I are concerned, the botanical names of spices serve primarily as a point of interest. But when you get to the chapter on chili peppers and learn about all the different kinds of Capsicums there are, you'll be a step ahead of people who skipped this section.

The Sex Life of Plants

Some of the substances we call spices come from the bark or roots of certain plants, but the majority are berries, seeds, or dried fruits. And before they produce berries, seeds, or fruits, these plants must start with a flower. And that brings us to the last part of the botany lesson, the sexy part.

All flowering plants have a sophisticated reproductive system built into their flowers, with both male and female reproductive organs. The male part, called a stamen, produces pollen. The female organ, called a pistil, is made up of three separate parts: the ovary, tucked away in the base of the flower; the stigma, the top part of the pistil, which catches the pollen; and the style, a short, thin stalk connecting them.

When the pollen is ripe, it becomes loosened so that agents such as honeybees or the wind can move it. The flower itself, with its bright and beautiful colors, is designed to attract bees and other insects, who—so cleverly is the flower engineered—cannot help but brush against the pollen-bearing part of the stamen when they land on the blossom. Then, as they crawl around in search of the plant's delicious nectar, they transfer the pollen from their legs and wings to the stigma, which happens to be placed right where they want to go.

The stigma is usually covered with a sticky substance or fine hairs, so that any pollen grains that happen by—from a bee or a passing breeze—will stick to it. Pollen then travels down the style to the ovary. Thus the ovary becomes fertilized and a new plant embryo begins to form. The flower fades away, and the embryo grows into a full-size fruit: apple, tomato, hazelnut, or whatever. That fruit contains a viable seed, which eventually becomes another plant with flowers, pollen, and nectar. And life goes on.

Isn't Mother Nature wonderful?

2

The Amazing History
of Spices

Sometimes, when we are moving down the paths that are our lives, if we stop and turn around and stand quietly, and if the light is just right, we can see our whole life reaching back behind us, with all its critical milestones. Looking back from today's perspective, we can see that what then seemed casual, incidental, accidental, turned out to be profoundly important. People meet their mate, find their life's work, suffer or avoid life-changing accidents through fortuitous blunders and the most casual flicks of fate.

It's that way with history too—history being, after all, nothing more than the sum of all our lives. Sometimes events that we now recognize as extraordinarily significant in the development of humankind started out as humble endeavors for quite ordinary purposes.

Take spices, for instance. During the Middle Ages, spices were as valuable in Europe as gold and gems. But the plants that produced the spices grew in the Far East, and getting them to Europe was a long, difficult, and very expensive undertaking, controlled entirely by canny Arabian traders, to their enormous profit. European businessmen, heads of state, and bold-spirited adventurers began to look for ways to participate in this very lucrative business.

What if, some said, we took our best sailors and navigators and sent them to find a sea route to the Spice Islands? And thus ships under the command of Ferdinand Magellan, and Vasco da Gama, and Bartholomeu Dias set sail.

And then a young Italian sea captain had another idea. What if, he said, the way to reach those eastern areas by sea is to sail *west* instead? So, toward the very end of the fifteenth century, sailing under Spain's flag, he took off with three small ships to find the East Indies by sailing westward.

And instead discovered America. Because he thought he had landed in the East Indies, Christopher Columbus called the indigenous people he found there "Indians."

So, the search for a cheaper way to import spices from the East led to the great Age of Discovery. Eastern culture—religion, philosophy, art, literature, science, medicine—began to find its way westward. Modern geography was born. And the New World was discovered. All because of pepper, cinnamon, and nutmeg.

But we are getting ahead of our story.

3000 B.C.—The Spice Trade Begins

The Arabian peninsula—that squarish wedge of land between Africa on the left and Eastern Europe on the right—today comprises the modern nations of Saudi Arabia, Iraq, Syria, Jordan, Lebanon, and Israel. But at one time it was known simply as Arabia.

The southern end of the peninsula borders the Arabian Sea, which in turn adjoins the Indian Ocean; on the north of the peninsula lies the Mediterranean Sea, whose opposite shores touch Greece, Italy, and the rest of southern Europe.

That puts Arabia smack in the middle between East and West, between the lands where spices grow and the areas where they were in demand. From the earliest days, the Arabs operated as middlemen, buying (that is to say, trading) spices from the producers and selling to the consumers.

It is difficult to put a finger on exactly when this trade began, but we do know a few things for certain.

- The Great Pyramids of Egypt were built, around 2500 B.C., as shrines for the pharaohs, whose bodies were mummified through a process involving cinnamon and other spices.
- In approximately 1550 B.C., Egyptian physicians compiled a comprehensive record of contemporary medical practice; they described the types of surgery that were performed, the diseases that were then known, and the treatments commonly prescribed. Some eight hundred medications, most of them based on spices and herbs, were explained. This remarkable document, a scroll nearly sixty-five feet long, was discovered in the nineteenth century by an archaeologist named Georg Ebers, and today it bears his name: the Ebers Papyrus. In the individual spice chapters ahead, you will find that the Ebers Papyrus is a part of the historical record of a number of spices.
- Spices are mentioned often in the Old Testament. The Queen of Sheba came to Jerusalem to visit King Solomon, presenting him with many gifts, including spices "of very great store." Joseph, betrayed by his jealous brothers, was sold into slavery to the Ishmaelites (Arab traders) for twenty pieces of silver.

The important thing to note here is that none of these spices grew wild in Egypt or Palestine; they all had to be brought in from the Far East. And that is the story of the camel caravans.

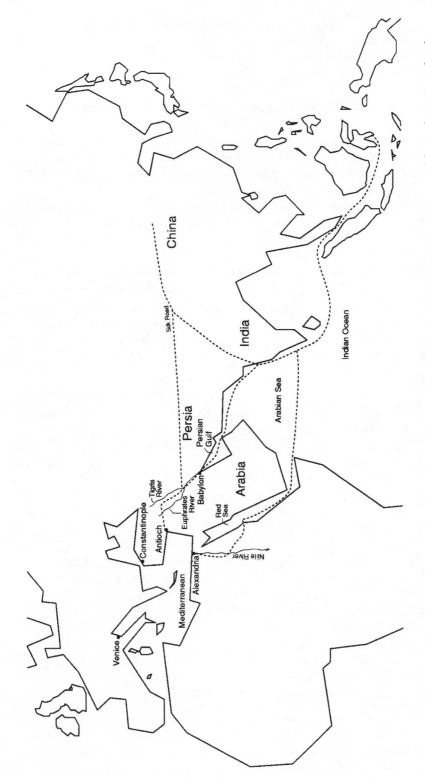

Ancient trade routes. Camel caravans came overland from China and India on the Silk Road; ships journeyed from the Spice Islands and from India via the Red Sea or the Persian Gulf. All eventually ended at ports on the Mediterranean Sea.

1000 B.C.—The Caravan Trade

Historians believe that the earliest traders used donkeys or mules. Then, starting around 1000 B.C., the lumbering, undemanding dromedary camel was brought into service. They could carry five hundred pounds apiece and cover ground at a pace of two miles per hour with little food or water, a distinct advantage in the desert terrain.

With the camel caravans, the spice trade became serious business. For the next twenty-five hundred years, Arab traders made the long trek to India and China to obtain merchandise, and the return trip to Mediterranean ports where the precious cargo was unloaded. In the process they became very, very wealthy.

There were two basic routes:

1. Overland on the Silk Road across Persia (now Iran) to the port city of Antioch (now Antakya, Turkey), on the eastern edge of the Mediterranean.
2. By sea across the Indian Ocean from the Spice Islands or across the Arabian Sea from intermediary ports in southern India, and then up the Red Sea and overland to Alexandria in Egypt, or up the Persian Gulf and overland to Babylon and then Antioch.

The trip was long, boring (we might imagine), and exceedingly dangerous. Caravaners were vulnerable to attacks by pirates and vandals, high tariffs imposed by rulers of lands they passed through, disease, starvation, and shipwreck. But for those who made it, the rewards were great indeed. At their final destination, spices were sold at many times their original cost: one hundred times, some said; three hundred times, according to others.

300 B.C. to A.D. 400: Greece and Rome

Two great civilizations of the ancient world—the Greeks and the Romans—were enthusiastic consumers of spices.

The Greeks, a culture of art, science, literature, and philosophy, used spices in many ways, both the exotic spices imported from the East and the indigenous plants that grew around them.

- Spices were burned as incense in religious ceremonies, of which there were many, for the Greeks recognized and honored many gods.
- Perfumes and body lotions, made from spices and herbs, were used by both men and women of the upper classes.
- Physicians and surgeons depended completely on spices and herbs to treat and prevent illnesses.

Except for medicine, their greatest and highest application, spices were principally important to Greeks for their fragrance; indeed, the Greek word for spices was *aroma*.

The Romans, a culture of commerce and warfare, used spices those same ways, and then expanded to others. The upper-class citizens of Rome, especially in the later years of the Roman Empire, invested much time and money in pursuit of pleasure. Now spices began to be used in cooking in a serious way. Wine was laced with spices, and some dishes were so heavily spiced that the food seemed merely a vehicle for presenting spices. In grand and formal banquets, which Romans were so fond of, small dishes of spices were passed to guests during the meal, so they could add them to the food according to personal taste.

To make their living quarters more pleasing, and to dispel the aromas from the lower classes passing by, spices were strewn on the floors and burned as incense. When high-ranking officials went out, spices and herbs were laid on the street for them to walk on. Men and women stuffed pillows with fragrant spices to give themselves sweet dreams, took baths in spice-laden water, and anointed their bodies with perfumes and fragrant oils.

The spices were very expensive, but the Romans seemed not to mind. They were very intent on living the good life and impressing others with their wealth, and so each year spice consumption grew.

The Roman Empire, at its height, stretched all across Europe. Its invading armies spread not only Roman law to the conquered lands but also many elements of Roman culture. You will see in some of the chapters ahead that certain spices and herbs now considered part of the natural landscape in Britain and other parts of western Europe were originally brought in on the food wagons of Roman soldiers.

We know what we know of spices in those days largely because learned men of the time wrote books describing their medicinal experiments, observations, and discoveries. Their goal was to keep records for themselves and the generations immediately following, records of new botanical information they uncovered and of which plants seemed to be effective with which diseases. And in that, they succeeded. At the same time, they were also creating for us a permanent record of what their lives were like.

Some of these men make appearances in the Encyclopedia section of this book, so let's take a moment to meet them:

Herodotus. 484–424 B.C. Sometimes called the Father of History, he traveled throughout much of the Mediterranean, recording the events of wars between Greece and Persia and writing his observations of daily life.

Hippocrates. 460–377 B.C. This famous doctor is known as the Father of Medicine. In addition to many works on the proper handling of medicinal plants, he also was the author of a code of ethics that is still used in medicine today, the Hippocratic Oath.

Theophrastus. 372–287 B.C. A philosopher and disciple of Aristotle, Theophrastus is mainly remembered today for his work in science. He devoted much of his time to studying how plants grow, and is now known as the Father of Botany. He was the first to note that all fruits develop from flowers. From his writings we know which plants were cultivated by the Greeks and which were imported, and how they were used.

Dioscorides. First century A.D. This Greek physician produced an amazing catalog of all the plants then known to man. A five-volume work titled *De Materia Medica*, it provides detailed descriptions of all medicinal plants and the formulas for their responsible use. So thorough is this document, and so grounded in science, it remained the authority on botany and medicine for the next fifteen hundred years.

Pliny the Elder. A.D. 23–79. This Roman scholar wrote many works of history and natural science, but only one has been preserved: the *Historia Naturalis*, a thirty-seven-volume encyclopedia of the natural world. Pliny was so intent on studying natural phenomena firsthand that he traveled to Pompeii to observe the volcano Vesuvius, and was killed when it erupted.

Celsus. First century A.D. A Roman who studied many fields—agriculture, botany, medicine, law, and military science—and wrote an extensive encyclopedia of his studies. All except eight books on medicine were lost.

Apicius. 14–37 A.D. A Roman who enjoyed life, especially food, he spent huge sums on rare foodstuffs and wrote ten cookbooks with detailed instructions on complex dishes. From him we know much about the elaborate uses of spices in cooking.

Throughout the centuries when first Greece, then Rome, dominated the West, they were dependent on Arab traders for spices and other goods from the East.

The Arabs were very astute businessmen. To protect their monopoly of this very lucrative trade, they never revealed exactly where the spices came from. If asked, they made vague reference to mysterious lands somewhere in Africa. If pressed, they invented fearsome tales describing the spice gardens and the efforts needed to harvest them.

For instance: Cassia grew in swamps protected by flying dragons with sharp claws that would rip to shreds any invader who did not know the secret approaches. Cinnamon grew in a remote mountain range inhabited by giant birds who picked the twigs from the cinnamon tree to make their nests, which they attached to the rocky slopes with mud. At great personal risk, local residents would trap the birds by putting out large pieces of meat at the bottom of the cliff. The birds would fly down and grasp the heavy meat in their talons and fly back to the nest, which, unable to support the weight, would suddenly fall to the bottom of the cliff. The workers would quickly race to pick out the cinnamon from the nest before the birds attacked them with their sharp beaks. And this, the merchants explained, is why cinnamon is so expensive.

Pliny suspected these tales were exaggerated, "invented by the natives to raise the price." Nevertheless, for the most part the stories achieved their desired effect: Few but the Arabs dared venture to the unknown regions where the spices grew.

Then, around A.D. 40, this carefully guarded secret began to unravel.

For years, the Arabs had sometimes relied on sea travel for part of the spice journey. If conditions were favorable, the sea portion was faster than overland travel. The difficulty was that often conditions were not favorable; the Indian Ocean was infamous for its awesome storms, called monsoons, which seemed to come out of nowhere. Untold numbers of ships and sailors were lost at sea.

Then in Rome a merchant named Hippalus figured out that there was a regular timetable to the monsoons. From April to October, the winds blew from India toward Arabia—and then they reversed direction for the rest of the year. Once they understood this, ship captains could reduce the length of a voyage and greatly increase its safety, simply by controlling the timing. A ship sailing from Arabia toward India would get pushed along by the strong winds if it departed in October, and ships sailing back to Arabia would also be sailing with the wind if they left India in April. Managed correctly, a ship could make both legs of the voyage in less than one year.

It was not very long before Roman ships began making this sea voyage directly. Romans were still in many ways dependent on the Arab merchants, who continued to control the land routes and the market exchanges in the main cities, and who themselves took advantage of this new understanding of the monsoons. However, the absolute stranglehold that the Arabs held over the spice trade began to crumble.

400 to 1000 A.D.: The Fall of the Empire, the Rise of Islam, and the Dark Ages

Nothing lasts forever, not even powerful countries, and slowly the Roman Empire disintegrated. Tribes of uncivilized barbarians from the north fought their way over the Alps and down toward the Mediterranean, overtaking Roman lands by sheer brutal force. These tribes have names we use in modern English to designate incivility, cruelty, and destruction: Vandals, Huns, and Goths. Our word "vandalize" comes from the Vandals; Gothic originally meant something very rough, uncouth; and Attila the Hun is used even now as the embodiment of savagery.

Soon these encroaching tribes reached Rome itself, and in 410, after three long and bloody sieges, Alaric, king of the Goths, conquered the city. The Fall of the Roman Empire had begun.

The Empire was also under attack from the south, as the followers of Mohammed gained political and economic strength at the same time their new religion was spreading across Arabia.

Mohammed, founder of Islam, was born in 570. An orphan, he was brought up by an uncle, and worked as a shepherd and camel driver while still a boy. His travels with the caravans exposed the young Mohammed to the rough living conditions endured by uneducated Arabs, and placed him on the spiritual path that culminated in his calling as prophet. Before that, however, he married the widow of the trader whose camels he had tended, a woman fifteen years his senior, and became a spice merchant himself.

By the time of his death in 632, Mohammed's disciples had, through warfare financed by the wealth of the spice trade, gained tremendous power in the Arab lands. In 641, they marched into the city of Alexandria in Egypt and took it away from the Romans. This loss of its pivotal southern port city is usually considered the final blow to the Roman Empire.

In the years ahead, the followers of Mohammed conquered much of the known world, both spiritually and militarily. In the 700s, Spain fell to a force of Muslims from north Africa known as the Moors. Other Muslims spread throughout Arabia and the ancient lands of Persia, all the way to India and China. In India Mohammed's missionaries set up shop along the Malabar Coast, largely taking over the spice trade.

Blocked by the barbarians in the north and the Muslims in the south, Europeans had only one access route to the spice market. The city of Constantinople, which had been founded by the Roman emperor Constantine in 330, became the fulcrum of a new trade route. Goods from the East were transferred at Constantinople to ships for voyages down Russian rivers to the Baltic Sea and thence to Europe—definitely the long way around. Compared to earlier days, the volume of spices reaching the West was only a trickle.

From the time of Mohammed to the time of the First Crusade, a period of some five hundred years, Mohammedans controlled most of the world south and east of the Mediterranean. The freewheeling trade between East and West essentially came to a halt, as what many have described as the Muslim Curtain descended, cutting off Europe and instituting the era that historians call the Dark Ages.

1000 to 1400: The Crusades, the Middle Ages

If history has anything to teach us, it is that nothing stays the same for long. The rigid control that Muslims held over the area south of the Mediterranean began to crack as the idea of reclaiming the Holy Land caught hold in Europe. This was the era of the Crusades: large forces of armor-clad Christian soldiers moving south, intent on taking Jerusalem and the rest of the Holy Land from the Muslims by force.

The First Crusade was in 1096, the Fourth in 1204. Jerusalem was conquered, established once again as the center of the Christian faith. For our purposes, however, the more significant outcome of the Crusades was not religious but economic.

Any observer will tell you that wars are good for business, and that definitely proved true for the so-called Holy Wars of the Crusades. The soldiers had to be transported across the Mediterranean Sea, they had to be outfitted with munitions and weaponry, and they had to be fed and clothed. The merchants of Venice, a city built on water, had long ago perfected their seafaring skills, and they became the primary beneficiary of this increased commercial traffic. Venetian ships brought in the Crusaders and their armaments, and on the return trip the ships were filled with exotic fabrics, jewels, and spices from the East.

The entire face of European commerce was changed by the Crusades, and the port cities of Italy—Venice, Genoa, Pisa—accrued fabulous wealth. Indirectly, that wealth was responsible for the accomplishments of the Renaissance a few hundred years later, for it was the financial patronage of wealthy Italians that supported the great artists, sculptors, musicians, and poets of the day.

The Crusades were a critical influence in another way as well. Those soldiers and pilgrims who spent time in the Arab lands found themselves exposed to a new culture, and acquired a taste for much of what they experienced. Here, Europeans tasted and smelled spices, many for the first time in their lives, and there was no going back. Throughout the Middle Ages, spices from the Orient were in great demand in Europe—still enormously expensive, but necessary.

It's difficult for us, accustomed to salads every day and fresh meat year-round, to imagine what mealtime was like in the Middle Ages. Because there was no way to keep hay fresh through the winter, livestock was butchered in the fall and the meat packed in salt, as a preservative. Fresh fruit and vegetables could be enjoyed only when they were in season, for there was no way to preserve them for the winter months. So for a large part of the year, the basic fare was pretty dreadful: grains, ground into a coarse meal, and dried or salted meat. Often the meat turned rancid before it was all consumed.

To make the food more palatable, large amounts of spices were added, especially to the large meat pies that were a staple in most households. Many of the spices also had a preservative quality, making their inclusion even more important.

Even so, meals were severely lacking in nutritional balance. The fatty meats were difficult to digest, fresh vegetables largely unavailable, and vitamins of course unknown. In the chapters on individual spices in this book, you will often read that this or that spice was considered beneficial to digestion. In modern times that might not seem like such a big deal; in the Middle Ages, indigestion and intestinal gas were severe problems.

In the mid-1300s, another significant event occurred in Italy and spread throughout Europe, this one tragic on a scale we can scarcely imagine: the Great Plague. In one three-year period (1347–1350), twenty-five million Europeans were killed, approximately one fourth of the total population. So swift was the spread of this disease, and so uncontrollable, it was called the Black Death.

Panic-stricken citizens searched desperately for a way to keep it from their loved ones and, when that proved unsuccessful, to cure them. In those days, the practice of medicine depended heavily on formulations made from spices and herbs, and many mixtures containing dozens of spices were assembled by physicians, both to treat their patients and to keep themselves safe in the process. People carried spices and dried herbs on their person whenever they ventured outside, fumigated sickrooms by burning spices, and wore protective clothing, including masks stuffed with spices, to bury the dead. In several of the chapters in the Encyclopedia section of this book, you will read of the spices that were used medicinally during this terrible period.

Before we leave this era, there is one other significant event we must not overlook. It started back in 1271, when a young Italian named Marco Polo, who was then seventeen years old, went with his father and his uncle on a trading journey to China. They were gone for twenty-four years. For fifteen years they traveled through the Far East as emissaries for the great Kubla Khan and then continued on their own throughout the Spice Islands, eventually returning to Genoa by ship and camel caravan with great treasure and stories no one believed.

Through all his wanderings, Marco kept extraordinarily detailed records of all he saw. Then, one year after returning home, he was put in prison in one of the many wars between Genoa and Venice. In prison, he recounted the details of his travels to his cellmate, who wrote them down and later published them as *The Book of Marco Polo*. He provided full information on the population, government structure, and customs of each place he visited. He described the islands where the spices grew, the ports of each, the distances between landings, the wind and weather patterns, the types and amounts of spices grown and traded at each landing, and the botanical characteristics of all the spice plants he saw firsthand.

At first, those who read the diaries dismissed them outright, calling

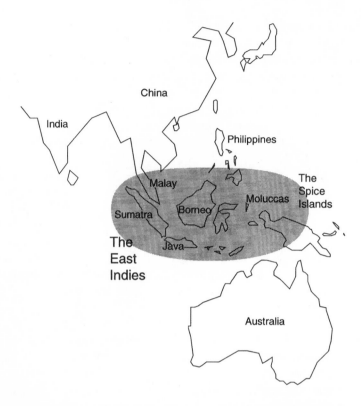

The Spice Islands. The island group called the Moluccas is generally considered the modern equivalent of the Spice Islands, although in a broader sense most Westerners used the term to include all the East Indies.

Marco "the greatest liar in Europe." But gradually, persuaded by the thoroughness and richness of detail, opinion began to change. If Marco was right, the secret land of the spices, the wondrous Spice Islands, was secret no longer.

1400 to 1900: Control of the Spice Islands

Bringing spices to Europe from the East involved several layers of middlemen, each with financial gain in mind. The goods had to be loaded and unloaded for transport through several modes of transportation; rulers along the way charged extortionate tariffs for the privilege of passing through their lands; and local officials had to be bribed. To put the matter bluntly, a lot of people were getting rich from the spice trade.

In Europe, rulers and businessmen found it increasingly hard to stomach paying such high prices for imported goods. They wanted those sums to end up in their own royal treasuries, not in the hands of foreigners. And, as Marco Polo's remarkable accounts of the true nature of spice trees began to gain acceptance, it seemed more and more possible that Europeans could travel to the spice lands and do some business on their own.

So, in a quest that in its day must have seemed as far-fetched as our goal of sending a person to the moon, Europe's leaders promoted the idea of finding a sea route to Asia, thus making the trip more quickly and, more importantly, bypassing the middlemen. With their great navies, they intended to take complete control of the spice trade.

The question was, which of the European powers would succeed first?

In Portugal in 1418, Prince Henry, not himself a sailor but a visionary leader who hoped to lead his country to economic primacy, set up a college for seamanship and navigation. Soon after, Portuguese ships set sail from Lisbon in the only direction that made sense for them: south. This represented an act of courage, for while the Equator was known and approximately understood, many people then believed that anyone passing through it would be incinerated.

In 1460, a Portuguese ship landed in west Africa and purchased a local spice called "grains of paradise," which was brought back and sold locally as a substitute for black pepper. Eleven years later, Portuguese vessels crossed the Equator. And fifteen years after that, Bartholomeu Dias sailed all the way to the southern tip of Africa, the Cape of Good Hope, and around it, thus adding an important piece of knowledge: The African continent did come to an end, and there was indeed water on the other side.

One year before Dias's discovery, in 1485, a sailor who had been born in the Italian seafaring city of Genoa but who had long been in service to the Portuguese navy applied to the crown for ships and supplies for a daring journey. He was convinced that the continent of Asia and the rich Spice Islands lay west of Europe, just on the other side of the Atlantic. Nonsense, said the Portuguese rulers.

So the sailor made his petition to the Spanish crown, which refused him many times but eventually, with reluctance, agreed to the proposal. And so on August 4, 1492, Christopher Columbus set off from the small port city of Palos, Spain, with a fleet of three small ships.

He was right, of course; the continent of Asia does indeed lie to the west of Europe and west of the Atlantic, with just one small problem: there is another continent, and then another ocean, in between.

On Columbus's first voyage, he made landfalls at several locales in what we now call the Caribbean Sea: the islands of San Salvador, Cuba, and Santo Domingo. Until the day he died, he was convinced he had landed in the East Indies. Even today, the islands in the Caribbean are frequently referred to as the "West Indies," memorializing their false link to those other islands.

Meanwhile, the Portuguese pressed on. Under orders from his king to find a sea route to India, Vasco da Gama set sail from Lisbon in 1497. His four ships swept around the west side of Africa and, following the lead of Dias a few years earlier, visited ports along the eastern coast of Africa before sailing on to India. In May 1498, after eleven months at sea, da Gama landed on India's Malabar Coast. It was the first time a European ship had sailed around Africa to the Far East, and it was a stunning victory for Portugal.

Two years later, another Portuguese explorer, Pedro Cabral, sailed into the Indian Ocean and established trading posts at two sites on the coast of India. Soon Lisbon—not Venice—was the linchpin of European commerce.

For most of the 1500s, Portugal controlled the entire spice-producing region: the nation of Ceylon, home of the cinnamon trees; and the islands collectively known as the East Indies—Java, Sumatra, Borneo, and the Spice Islands (the Moluccas). Spain had a claim to some of the same territories, by virtue of Ferdinand Magellan's historic around-the-world voyage in 1511–1514, but sold her interests to Portugal early in the century.

During this time, Portugal controlled the spice trade as a strict monopoly. Spice plantations were managed by Portuguese supervisors using local residents as slave labor, and the finished products were loaded onto Portuguese ships and shipped to Portugal. No other transport in or out was permitted; anyone attempting a bit of smuggling on the side risked death.

The other nations in Europe were no more happy to see Portugal reap all the profits from the spice business than the Portuguese had been when the Venetians were on top. England, then on its way to becoming a great naval power, formed the East India Company in 1600 with the intention of breaking into the monopoly; and Holland, two years later, followed suit with the Dutch East India Company.

Starting around 1605, almost exactly one hundred years after their first real foothold, the Portuguese began losing control of the Spice Islands. By 1621, the Dutch had managed to take over and drive the Portuguese out. Their management was, if anything, even more brutal than the Portuguese. It was the Dutch who, as a way of artificially driving up the price, ripped out and burned clove trees from all but two small islands, to the great dismay of the islanders who considered them sacred. It was the Dutch who set heavy production quotas and enforced them by beating and torturing workers who failed.

The Dutch maintained iron control over the spice trade, and the Spice Islands, for about one hundred fifty years, from the early 1600s to the mid-1700s. Then the carefully controlled monopoly was cracked by a daring raid in 1770. A French adventurer who was soon to take over as governor on an island off the east coast of Africa (an island now

The modern world. The lands once controlled by outsiders for the wealth of their spices are now independent nations, many with new names.

known as Mauritius) managed to steal away with nutmeg seeds and clove seedlings, and began a trial plantation on his island. The young trees thrived, and soon other French territories with a favorable climate were growing the spice trees. In one of history's charming ironies, that governor's name is also the name of the king of spices: Pierre Poivre (Peter Pepper).

Back in the East Indies, the fulcrum shifted yet again. The British, emerging as the leading power in Europe, began to take over the Dutch territories in the East. Finally, in 1824, the two nations signed a treaty dividing up the region; the Dutch kept Malaysia and England got India, Ceylon, and part of Borneo. And that is essentially the way things remained until World War II.

Today, the former Spice Islands are part of Indonesia, an independent republic. Ceylon is now the nation of Sri Lanka. India is no longer part of the British Empire. Spice products are grown, processed, and distributed in all those places, and more besides, but as a business— nothing more, nothing less. The descendants of the caravaners and the Arab traders have their share of troubles these days, but their troubles have nothing to do with spices.

It seems amazing now, from our supermarket vantage point, to think that so much blood was shed over such trivial, commonplace items. Perhaps a few millennia from now, when humans travel from point A to point B in a *Star Trek* instant, when the automobile is a museum relic and no one remembers what gasoline was used for, people will look back on the latter part of the twentieth century and shake their heads in amazement that wars were fought over oil reserves.

Part II

The Spice Encyclopedia

Allspice

Botanical name: **Pimenta dioica**

Part used as spice: **Berries**

Available as: **Whole berries or powder**

Some of our most popular commercial spices are actually blends of several individual spices; curry powder, for instance, and chili powder. So you might guess that a product named "allspice" would be a blend, perhaps a mixture of all the spices there are. That would certainly be a logical assumption—but wrong.

Allspice is the fruit of a specific tree that is native to the Caribbean islands (principally Jamaica) and Latin America. It's a beautiful evergreen tree, between twenty and forty feet tall when mature, with light gray bark and dark green, aromatic leaves. In the summer, the tree is covered with small whitish flowers that in turn produce small fruits about the size of peas, so small they are often referred to as berries. It is those fruits that we use as the spice.

It's called allspice because of its aroma, which smells like a combination of cinnamon, cloves, and nutmeg.

Allspice is the only spice that is grown in the Western Hemisphere and nowhere else. For a while attempts were made to cultivate the trees in the spice-producing regions of the East, but while the young trees survived, they never satisfactorily produced berries.

These beautiful trees once grew wild in the rainforests of Central American countries like Guatemala, Honduras, and Brazil, sometimes growing as tall as one hundred feet. However, harvesting fruit from a tree that is as high as a ten-story building is no mean feat, and so local entrepreneurs frequently took the course of least resistance—cut the entire tree down. Few wild trees remain.

Some allspice is now grown in Mexico and minor amounts in other parts of Central America, but the very finest comes from the island of Jamaica. Here the climate and soils are just right to produce

What's in a Name?

As anyone who has ever tried to untangle them knows, the various names by which plants are known can be very confusing. That is why each plant has one and only one scientific name—to avoid confusion. However, the Latin itself is confusing to many, and so over the years people have developed popular, or common, names for the plants they use regularly, sometimes creating another type of confusion.

Take allspice, for instance.

Sometime in the 1570s, the Spanish explorer Hernandez, in the area of Mexico called Tabasco, came upon an allspice tree. Thinking it a type of pepper plant, he named it *Piper tabasco,* "piper" being the Latin name for the type of plants that produce peppercorns. (No relation to the hot chili peppers that also grow in the same region, which flavor the commercial sauce we know as Tabasco.)

About the same time other Spanish adventurers landed in Jamaica, where they found great forests of allspice trees; also mistaking their fruit for black pepper, they named the trees Pimienta, which is the Spanish word for "pepper." This term was later modified into Pimenta, which is now the official scientific name of the allspice tree genus.

What we in the United States call allspice is known in other English-speaking countries as pimento—no relation to the canned vegetable we call pimento, which is a type of sweet pepper.

And, just to keep us on our toes, this spice that looks like peppercorns but isn't, is sometimes known as Jamaican pepper.

the most intensely aromatic berries. In carefully tended plantations, Jamaica produces the lion's share of the world's supply of allspice.

When the berries are completely ripe, they turn purple. However, by that time they have passed beyond the fully fragrant stage of their life cycle. So they are picked when they have grown to full size but are still green—a fairly tricky problem of timing, especially since they are commonly picked by hand. At one time the harvest was a family affair: Men and boys climbed into the trees, picked the sprays of berries and tossed them to women and girls on the ground below waiting to sort and clean the fruit. Today the process is somewhat more efficient but still not completely mechanized.

Any berries that have turned ripe are discarded, and the rest are spread out to dry for a week or so. When dry they are reddish-brown in color and slightly shriveled. In fact, they look like larger-than-normal peppercorns. Which partly explains the twisted history of their name (see box on page 32).

The allspice trade is serious business in Jamaica, and has been for several hundred years. Although the trees are native to the island, they are not grown in a wild jungle but in rigorously managed plantations. Land is cleared, and trees are planted and later thinned so they stand about twenty feet apart, allowing room for a full canopy of fruit-bearing branches.

Up through the end of the nineteenth century, a popular pastime was a "pimento walk"— a stroll through the parklike grounds of an allspice plantation. One British visitor, a botanist by trade, clearly enjoyed his 1755 visit: "Nothing can be more delicious than the odour of these walks, when the trees are in bloom, the friction of the leaves and small branches even in a gentle breeze diffusing a most exhilarating scent."

History and Legend

Christopher Columbus, who left Europe on a daring journey in search of spices, visited the island we now know as Jamaica and saw the evergreen trees we now know as allspice—but, in one of those small ironies of history, he didn't realize the trees were the source of a spice. That connection had to wait a few years, for other European adventurers.

Early in the 1500s, Spanish explorers discovered the aromatic trees in the West Indies and mistook them for black pepper in tree form (see box on page 32). It was nearly one hundred years before the spice was exported to Europe; the first recorded shipment was in 1601, and the spice was presented as a substitute for cardamom. In 1655 England gained control of Jamaica; by that time, allspice had

---

In Jamaica allspice has long been considered an aphrodisiac. Lovers anxious about their performance would nibble the berries at critical moments; those more interested in inflaming a partner's ardor would serve heavily spiced foods or offer a flower with an allspice berry tucked deep inside.

Does it work? In this situation, my friends, even more so than usual, perception is reality.

> The rowdy pirates who terrorized shipping in the Caribbean waters in the 1600s owe their name indirectly to this spice. In port, before setting off on a round of mischief, they would make up a supply of smoked meat by grilling it over burning allspice berries. The process was called *boucaner* (the French verb "to cure"), the grill (and also the dried meat) was called *boucan,* and the men came to be known as *boucaniers*—buccaneers.

become popular in Europe on its own merits. In 1693, almost one hundred years after the spice was introduced to England, a British botanist gave it the name by which we know it today: allspice.

But the native peoples in the areas where allspice grows had known about the aromatic berries for centuries. In Mexico, Mayans and Aztecs collected the fruit and dried them for many uses, some of which will seem to us familiar and some bizarre. They ground the berries into powder and added it to the chocolate drink they invented. Think about that the next time you go into an ultra-modern coffee bar and order a mocha or a latte and sprinkle ground allspice on top.

Another ancient use with modern ties takes advantage of the preservative characteristics of this spice. The Aztecs used the berries to embalm and mummify the bodies of their leaders. We do not know for certain, but it's a safe bet that this highly advanced civilization also used allspice to cure and preserve meat for the table. We do know that after Europeans discovered allspice and began to ship it home from Jamaica, it was commonly used to preserve meat for long sea voyages.

Once allspice was widely exported to Europe, people in many countries learned to use it as a preservative. Scandinavian and Russian deep-sea fishermen packed their catch in allspice to preserve it until they reached port. Often our tastes in food begin in practices that were originally developed as a matter of necessity, and this is an example: Scandinavians became so accustomed to associating the taste of allspice with fish that even today many fish marinades contain that spice, and pickled herring, which some consider the national dish of Scandinavia, depends on it. It is not surprising then that, on a per capita basis, Scandinavians are the largest consumers of allspice.

Medicinal Uses

The primary oil in allspice is classed as a rubefacient, meaning that it irritates the skin and expands the blood vessels just underneath it; this increases the flow of blood, making the skin feel warmer. This is undoubtedly why soldiers in frigid Russia during the War of 1812 put whole allspice inside their boots to warm up their feet. On the other hand, some people (a small minority) can have unpleasant irritation to their skin from handling allspice.

The tannins in allspice provide a mild local anesthetic; that, plus the warming effect, has led to its use as a home remedy for arthritis. It's not long-lasting medicine, but it does bring temporary relief to many. The most common technique is with a poultice, or its old-fashioned name, a plaster.

To make a poultice, crush a large handful of berries or use about ⅛ cup of powdered spice; mix in a little warm water, just enough to make a paste. Spread the paste on a clean cloth and lay it over the sore area. First, though, try a small patch to see if you're one of the few who have a negative skin reaction.

Another way to enjoy the effect of allspice on sore joints or muscles is in a hot bath. Make a concentrated "tea" by simmering ¼ cup of whole allspice berries in 2 cups of water for 10 minutes. Strain out the berries and add the allspice water to your bathwater.

Allspice also has mild carminative properties, which means that it helps get rid of intestinal gas. For a soothing drink after a heavy meal, put a few allspice berries in the water you are boiling for tea.

Crafts and Household Uses

A natural room deodorizer can easily be made from allspice. Simmer one or two tablespoons of whole allspice in a small saucepan of water on the stove, to cover kitchen odors. The warm fragrance of allspice also makes it a popular addition to potpourri mixtures (see page 126).

Project: Spice-Filled Hot Pad
A nice gift for someone who loves to cook (maybe including yourself) is a hot pad made of quilted fabric and an inner bag filled with spices. When a hot casserole dish is set on it, not only is the tabletop protected, but the heat of the dish warms the spices, releasing their fragrance.

For a time, toward the end of the nineteenth century, walking sticks fashioned from wood of the allspice tree were quite the rage in England and America, and many small trees were cut down to satisfy the demand. Fortunately, this fad passed before all the young trees were destroyed.

The one illustrated here is filled with whole allspice and whole cloves, but you could also use cardamom seeds, peppercorns, fennel, dill, or caraway seeds. Because the finished product should lie flat, it's better to use spices of the same size, rather than a mixture of small and large pieces that would create an uneven, bumpy surface.

First, make the inner bag that will hold the spices. Almost any fabric will work: cotton, linen, cotton/polyester blends. It should have a relatively loose weave, but not so porous that the spices will fall out. Stitch all around, leaving an opening to insert the spices; turn right side out, pour in the spices, and hand-stitch the opening.

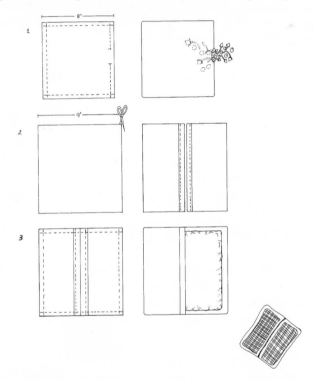

Spice-filled hot pad. Cut 2 pieces of soft fabric such as cotton; place one on top of the other and stitch all around, leaving an opening on one side. Turn seam inside, fill with spice mixture, and slip-stitch the opening closed (Step 1).

Cut 2 pieces of thickly quilted fabric 1 inch larger than inner spice bag. Cut one of those pieces in half. Bind the edges of the 2 half-pieces with bias tape (Step 2).

With right sides together, place the two halves on top of the uncut piece, with the bound edges touching. Sew all around. Trim seams and turn pad so that right sides of fabric face out. Insert the spice bag completely into the pad through the opening in back (Step 3). If the outer pad becomes soiled, remove the inner bag before laundering.

Then make the outer bag. It has an opening in the back, so the spice bag can slip in and then out when it's time to launder the outer bag.

Cut two squares from thickly quilted fabric, one inch larger than the inner spice bag. Cut one of the squares in half and bind the edges with bias tape. Lay the two halves side by side on top of the whole piece, right sides together, and sew all around. Turn right side out, and slip the spice bag into the opening.

For gifts, search out really pretty quilted fabric; buy bias tape in coordinating colors. Include a gift card explaining how to use the hot pad, pointing out the removable insert.

If you enjoy embroidery, here's a way to make the gift truly special. On the right side of the whole (uncut) piece of quilted fabric, before sewing everything together, write a message in washable marker and go over it with embroidery stitches. For instance:

"Happy Birthday"
"Allspice for You"
"Kiss the Cook"
"May 1999" (e.g., a bridal shower gift)

Cooking with Allspice

Allspice is used a great deal in commercial food preparation. It may be found in hundreds of packaged products, including:

Pickles (allspice is one of the most common pickling spices)
Mincemeat
Sausages and cured meats
Ketchup
Ice cream
Candy
Chewing gum
Liqueurs (Benedictine and Chartreuse)

In home kitchens, allspice is not as popular as the spices it resembles (cinnamon, cloves, and nutmeg) but deserves more respect than it usually gets—although in Jamaica, as you might imagine, it flavors many robust stews and soups.

Because the fragrance is sweet but not too sweet, with peppery undertones, allspice is appropriate for many meat and vegetable dishes as well as baked goods.

Use Allspice with:
- Apple pie, fruit cobblers
- Cakes, cookies
- Jams
- Sweet breads, coffee cake, gingerbread
- Pot roast and stews
- Fish marinades
- Meatballs, meatloaf, hamburgers
- Vegetables (especially beets, carrots, sweet potatoes, winter squash)
- Fruit salads, mixed fruit compotes

Allspice is very pungent, so follow recipes carefully. Too much of a good thing is bitter indeed.

⚜ Swedish Fruit Soup ⚜

1 cup pitted prunes
1 cup dried apples
2 cups mixed dried fruit (peaches, apricots, pears)
1 large can (16 ounces) pitted cherries
1/4 cup raisins or currants
1/2 cup sugar
1 stick cinnamon
1 teaspoon grated lemon peel
1/4 teaspoon mace
1/8 teaspoon cardamom
1/8 teaspoon allspice
1/8 teaspoon nutmeg
2 quarts water
whipped cream or commercial sour cream (garnish)

Combine all fruits and spices with water in large saucepan. Bring to a boil; cover, reduce heat, and simmer until fruit is tender, about 1 hour. Remove cinnamon stick; rub cooked fruit with liquid through a fine sieve or puree in blender. Chill; serve cold. Top each serving with a dollop of whipped cream or sour cream.
Makes 2 1/2 quarts.

⋇ Jamaican Red Pea Soup ⋇

1 pound boneless smoked ham cut in ¹/₂-inch cubes (about 3 cups)
2¹/₂ cups water, divided
2 cans (15¹/₂ ounces each) red kidney beans, drained and rinsed
2 cans (13³/₄ ounces each) beef broth
2 cups potatoes cut in ¹/₂-inch cubes
2 cups sweet potatoes cut in ¹/₂-inch cubes
³/₄ cup chopped celery
¹/₄ cup minced onion
1¹/₂ teaspoons dried thyme, crushed
¹/₂ teaspoon ground allspice
¹/₄ teaspoon cayenne
¹/₄ teaspoon pepper
2 tablespoons cornstarch

In a Dutch oven or large saucepan combine ham with 2 cups water, beans, broth, potatoes, sweet potatoes, celery, onion, thyme, allspice, cayenne, and pepper. Bring to a boil; reduce heat and simmer, covered, until potatoes are tender, about 25 minutes.

Combine cornstarch with ¹/₂ cup cold water until smooth. Stir into soup; boil and stir until slightly thickened, about 1 minute.

Makes 6 servings (12 cups).

—American Spice Trade Association

⋇ Beet Surprise Salad ⋇

1 3-ounce package lemon gelatin
1 tablespoon powdered horseradish
1 large can (15 ounces) diced or julienned beets
1 tablespoon brown sugar
¹/₄ teaspoon salt
6 whole cloves
1 stick cinnamon
12 whole allspice berries
¹/₃ cup wine vinegar
²/₃ cup dry white wine or water

In large bowl, mix the dry gelatin and powdered horseradish; set aside. Drain beets, saving the liquid; set beets aside. Measure the beet liquid and add enough water to make 1 cup.

In saucepan, combine beet liquid, brown sugar, salt, and spices. Heat to boiling; reduce heat and simmer 1 minute. Strain into horseradish mixture and stir until gelatin dissolves. Add vinegar, wine, and drained beets. Use a paper towel to spread a thin coat of salad oil on salad molds, either a 1½-quart ring mold or 6 individual molds. Pour mixture into molds. Chill until firm, then remove from mold. Serve on shredded greens.

Serves 6.

⭐ Twice-Baked Sweet Potatoes ⭐

4 sweet potatoes or yams
1 teaspoon ground allspice
½ teaspoon ground nutmeg
4 to 6 tablespoons butter, at room temperature

Preheat oven to 400°. Bake potatoes until very tender, about 45 minutes. Remove from the oven and set aside to cool. Reduce the oven temperature to 375°.

Cut the potatoes in half lengthwise and scoop out the pulp; make sure not to tear the skins. With a potato masher or fork, mash the pulp until very smooth; stir in the spices and the butter. A food processor, if you have one, makes this mixture wonderfully creamy and fluffy.

Spoon the pulp back into the skins. For a special occasion, you might want to use a pastry bag fitted with a large fluted tip and pipe potato rosettes into the skins. Arrange the stuffed potatoes in a shallow baking pan. (You can do this up to 6 hours ahead of time.)

Return the baking pan to the oven and bake until the edges are lightly browned and crisp, about 20 minutes. Serve hot.

⭐ Island Chicken Salad with Citrus Rum Dressing ⭐

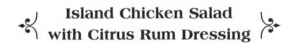

1 tablespoon soy sauce
1 tablespoon olive oil
1 tablespoon cider vinegar
1 tablespoon water
1 tablespoon minced onion
1½ teaspoons sugar
1½ teaspoons dried thyme
1 teaspoon ground allspice
½ teaspoon ground cinnamon
½ teaspoon black pepper
⅛ teaspoon cayenne
1 pound boneless, skinless chicken breast

1 head lettuce, torn into bite-size pieces
assorted fresh vegetable pieces

Combine all ingredients except chicken, lettuce, and vegetables in a large self-closing plastic bag or shallow bowl. Add chicken, tossing to coat. Refrigerate 2–3 hours.

Remove chicken and broil or grill until thoroughly cooked, about 6–8 minutes. Cut into strips and serve on bed of lettuce with vegetables. Top with Citrus Rum Dressing.

Makes 4 servings.

Citrus Rum Dressing

3 tablespoons orange juice
2 tablespoons vegetable oil
1 tablespoon lime juice
1 tablespoon water
1 tablespoon honey
1/4 teaspoon rum extract
1/4 teaspoon ground ginger
1/4 teaspoon ground nutmeg
1/4 teaspoon garlic powder

Combine dressing ingredients in a small bowl. Mix well and chill.

—McCormick/Schilling

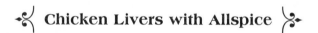 Chicken Livers with Allspice

2 tablespoons butter
1 pound chicken livers
1 small onion, sliced thin
1 cup chicken broth
1/2 teaspoon salt
1/2 teaspoon allspice
1 teaspoon brown sugar
1/2 teaspoon lemon juice
1 tablespoon cornstarch
1 tablespoon cold water
2 tablespoons minced fresh parsley
2 tablespoons chopped pimientos

Melt butter in large frying pan. Meanwhile, clean chicken livers. Sauté the livers and onion in butter until nearly done, about 3 minutes. Add chicken broth, salt, allspice, sugar, and lemon juice; simmer for about 10 minutes.

Dissolve cornstarch in water and stir into pan. Cook over low heat until liquid is clear and thickened.

Serve over rice; garnish with parsley and pimientos.

Serves 4.

Note: This dish is especially attractive served over rice made golden by cooking it with turmeric or saffron. See page 279.

❧ Baked Spiced Pork Chops ❧

Serve with plain rice, or mashed sweet potatoes; use the spicy sauce as a gravy.

> *4 pork chops, cut 1 inch thick*
> *2 tablespoons butter, divided*
> *¹/₂ medium onion, thinly sliced*
> *1¹/₂ cups chicken stock*
> *¹/₄ teaspoon thyme*
> *¹/₄ teaspoon ground cinnamon*
> *¹/₄ teaspoon ground allspice*
> *¹/₈ teaspoon finely ground black pepper*
> *peel and fruit sections from 1 orange*

Brown pork chops in 1 tablespoon butter in a heavy frying pan. Remove chops from frying pan and arrange in casserole or baking dish. In same frying pan, sauté sliced onions over very low heat until a dark golden color; arrange onions on top of chops.

Add chicken stock and spices to frying pan; scrape browned bits from bottom of pan, add spices, and simmer for 5 minutes.

Meanwhile, remove peel from orange. Use a zester, if you have one, to make thin curly strips. If not, peel orange, cut away white pith, and cut peel into strips with a sharp knife. Set the peel aside. Remove all remaining white pith from orange and divide orange into sections; arrange sections around chops in baking dish.

Pour sauce over chops. Cover and bake in a 300° oven for 1¹/₂ hours or until chops are tender. Skim off any excess fat. Garnish each chop with reserved orange peel. Serve hot from casserole or baking dish, using the sauce for gravy.

Makes 4 servings.

⋅ৰ্ঝ Mulled Cider ৡ়-

A wonderful beverage for wintertime parties.

2 quarts apple cider
1 stick cinnamon
1 teaspoon whole cloves
1 teaspoon whole allspice
1/2 unpeeled lemon, thinly sliced

Mix all ingredients in large saucepan and simmer for 10 minutes; strain and serve hot.
Makes 16 half-cup servings.

Variation: Instead of cider, brew 2 quarts of your favorite tea, either black tea or an herbal blend. You may want to add sugar to taste.

For Other Recipes Featuring Allspice, See:

Anise

Botanical name: **Pimpinella anisum**

Part used as spice: **Seeds**

Available as: **Whole or ground seeds; extract**

Anise is a rather small, delicately pretty garden plant that bears a strong family resemblance to its cousins in the spice world: dill, fennel, coriander, cumin, and caraway. All of them have at one time or another been compared to licorice in greater or lesser measure, but in the case of anise there can be no doubt—anise *is* the taste of licorice.

This is true both figuratively and literally: An oil distilled from the plant is what gives the distinctive flavor to licorice candy (not, by the way, the herb plant that is known as licorice, which has a somewhat different taste).

If you have the interest and the place to do so, you can grow anise in your garden. The feathery leaves make a very pretty garnish, and they too have the distinctive licorice taste. Then, at the end of the summer, you can harvest the flower heads and dry your own seeds.

If you'd just as soon let someone else do all that, you can buy whole anise seeds (the term "aniseed" means the same thing) or powdered spice in the supermarket. Occasionally you can also find anise extract; it comes in small bottles like lemon extract, near which it will

Star anise is not at all the same as anise, botanically speaking. One is a tree, the other is a short (eighteen-inch) garden plant. However, their essential oils are chemically similar, and therefore they taste very much alike. Star anise is described in its own chapter later in this book.

be shelved in the market. The advantage of extract over the spice is that it has a much longer shelf life; on the other hand, it doesn't crunch nearly as well as the seeds.

History and Legends

The anise plant is native to the Mediterranean region: Greece, Turkey, Egypt, Crete, and the other islands of the Mediterranean Sea. In modern times it has been cultivated throughout the world, for it grows handily in all temperate climates. But originally it grew wild in the areas of some of our earliest civilizations, which is why it appears in the writings and legends of ancient Greeks, Romans, and Egyptians.

Anise is, in fact, one of the oldest known spice plants:

- There is evidence that anise was used in Egypt as early as 1500 B.C.
- Theophrastus, the Greek scholar who studied the plant world four centuries before Christ, wrote about anise.
- In the book of Matthew in the Bible, there is mention of paying tithe with anise.
- Two men important in the history of plant studies—Pliny of Rome and Dioscorides of Greece, both of whom lived in the first century A.D.—included anise among their botanical writings.
- Also in the first century, Virgil, the Roman poet best known to us as the creator of the classic epic *The Aeneid,* wrote a description of a typical feast. What is interesting for our purposes is his mention of a sweet cake called "mustaceum," heavily laced with anise seeds and other spices. It was served at the end of the many-coursed banquet to help diners digest the heavy foods.

The people of these ancient lands used the plants that grew around them in various and sundry ways, some of them exactly the same as we use them now, and some of them bizarre indeed. For instance, it was believed that anise would:

- Act as an aphrodisiac—one writer warned that it "stirreth up bodily lust."
- Keep away nightmares if placed under one's pillow.
- Ward off the Evil Eye.
- Increase milk flow in nursing mothers.
- Cure epilepsy.
- Counteract the poison of snakebite and scorpion stings.

But the most significant use, aside from flavoring food and drink, was in many types of medical treatments. Some of them seem silly to us now—we know that anise will not cure epilepsy—but in fact many of the ancient medicinal values ascribed to anise have proved to be correct.

- Pythagoras, the Greek mathematician who lived in the sixth century B.C., recorded the popular belief that anise would prevent belching and stomach pain. Now, twenty-five hundred years later, we know that it is a carminative, meaning that it is effective against intestinal gas, and a digestive, meaning that it helps with indigestion. For the same reasons, a mild anise tea is very soothing to babies with colic.
- To ease sore throats, coughing, and chest congestion, anise was boiled in a mixture with honey, vinegar, and hyssop, and the resulting syrup was used as a gargle. Today we know that anise is an expectorant, meaning that it helps break up congestion; it is included in the formula in many cough medicines and throat lozenges.
- Even the old theory that anise was a cure for scorpion bites may not have been so far from wrong, for there is some evidence that a paste made of crushed anise seeds soothes insect bites.

As the Greeks and, most especially, the Romans spread their culture throughout the rest of Europe, they took with them seeds of familiar plants and their knowledge of how to use them. By the Middle Ages, anise was being cultivated throughout Europe. In England, King Edward I in 1305 declared it a taxable drug; any merchant who intended to bring it into the city of London was required to pay a toll when crossing over London Bridge. The tolls were used to maintain and repair the bridge.

It is recorded in the Royal Household Account of 1480 that the king's personal linen was to be stored with "lytil [little] bags of fustian [a fabric made of cotton and linen] stuffed with ireos [iris] and anneys [anise]."

The good folks who managed the household of England's King Edward VI had, we can presume, discovered that iris root, dried and ground up, has the ability to preserve the aroma of other plants it is mixed with, in this case anise. Those of us familiar with today's use of orris root (which comes from a type of iris) as a preservative in potpourri mixtures should tip our hat to them.

In the Middle Ages, the expectorant qualities of anise had already been discovered. Here is a prescription for chest congestion:

"Let the plain countryman, in a consumptive cough and stoppage of the lungs, take the following electuary: the flour of fenugreek seed [that is, ground seed], common Molossus [molasses] or treacle, oil of anise seed 6 drops; mix them and lick it often, and esteem it, though a plain thing, an excellent cheap medicine."

Shall we assume, from the self-effacing tone of this recipe, that even then there were some who disdained home remedies in favor of the services of more learned physicians? If so, the "plain countrymen" can take heart: Twentieth-century technology has verified their remedy by copying it in modern cough syrups.

Anise was one of the plants brought to the colonies by the settlers from England. In 1619, the first Assembly of Virginia announced that each family that was given a plot of land was required to grow certain plants on it as a condition of ownership, among them six anise plants; they were also required to save the seeds and plant anise again the following year.

Later, to fill the needs of city dwellers and industrial workers, the Shakers began commercial production of medicinal plants, including anise.

Medicinal and Household Uses

We have already learned some of the home remedies that anise is used for. Perhaps the most common use is to help dispel gas and aid digestion.

- For colicky babies, simmer a teaspoonful of seeds in water for about 10 minutes, strain out the seeds, and then mix some of the water into milk.
- Warm milk in which aniseed has been steeped is also a very soothing bedtime drink for grownups, especially those afflicted with mild insomnia.
- Adults suffering from gas or indigestion can make an anise tea by simmering seeds in water and using the water to brew a cup of tea. Or, if you like the taste, just drink the anise "tea" by itself, perhaps with a little honey.
- An even simpler way to get the digestive benefits of anise is to chew on a few anise seeds after a meal, to help digestion and also to sweeten the breath. This has been the custom in parts of Europe and the Middle East for centuries—and still is in many places.

Today anise is used in the manufacture of many commercial cough and cold syrups and sore throat medications. It is also added to other types of medicines to improve their taste.

One old folk remedy says that anise will destroy lice; here the distilled oil is used. If you should ever have occasion to try this, however, always remember that you should never put essential oils onto your skin full strength, but dilute them first in something like salad oil.

It is said that mice are attracted to the aroma of anise, so a few drops of anise oil on your mousetrap would probably improve your chances of catching him. By the same token and for the same reasons, some fishermen dab it on their lures; whether you believe their reports of results is up to you.

Cooking with Anise

Because we associate the flavor of licorice with candy, we tend to think of anise as a sweet taste, and so mostly it is used in cakes, cookies, tea breads, and that sort of thing. But it can also be used as an adventurous addition to nonsweet foods as well.

Use Anise with:
- Soups and stews
- Curries
- Fish and shellfish (put seeds in the poaching water)
- Cottage cheese and cream cheese for dips and spreads
- Fruit cobblers and pies
- Cakes, cookies, coffee cakes
- Applesauce and stewed fruit

> You might be surprised to learn that anise is a good source of iron. One tablespoon of seeds provides 16 percent of the recommended daily allowance for women, 25 percent for men.

Another very delicious way to enjoy anise is in the spice-flavored liqueurs produced by several European cultures. Anisette (from France), anisina (Italy), anis (Spain), and ouzo (Greece) are probably the best known. A recipe for homemade anisette is included in this chapter.

❧ Scandinavian Bread ❧

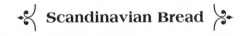

2 cups milk
2 tablespoons molasses
1/3 cup honey
1/2 cup butter or margarine, cut into small bits

1 1/2 teaspoons salt
2 packages yeast
1/2 cup warm water
1 teaspoon grated orange peel
1 teaspoon crushed fennel seed
1 teaspoon crushed anise seed
3 cups rye flour
5 cups all-purpose flour
1 egg white, slightly beaten

Scald milk and pour over molasses, honey, butter, and salt in a large bowl. Stir until butter is melted, then set aside to cool to lukewarm. Sprinkle yeast over warm water in large measuring cup, and set aside. When it is bubbly, add it to milk and honey mixture. Beat in orange peel, fennel, and anise. A little at a time, add in the rye flour and 4 1/2 cups of the all-purpose flour; mix to make a soft dough.

Sprinkle the last 1/2 cup flour onto board; turn out dough and knead until smooth (about 5 minutes). Place in greased bowl; turn dough over so that greased bottom is now on top. Cover; let rise in warm place until size is doubled (about 1 1/2 hours).

Punch the dough down, cover with the bowl and let rest for 2 minutes, then divide dough in half. Roll each half into a rope approximately 2 feet long. Fold the rope in half, then loop one half over the other twice, forming a loose braid. Place braids on lightly greased baking sheet. Cover and let rise until almost doubled (about 45 minutes). Brush with egg white. Bake in a 350° oven for 45 minutes or until a toothpick inserted into the center comes out clean.

Makes 2 loaves.

❧ Spicy Italian Pork Patties ☙

1 pound lean ground pork
1/4 cup fine dry bread crumbs
1 egg
2 cloves garlic, minced or mashed
2 tablespoons dry red wine
1/2 teaspoon salt
1/2 teaspoon pepper
1/2 teaspoon anise seed
salad oil for pan broiling

Mix together all ingredients except the salad oil. Divide into four portions and shape into patties about 1/2-inch thick. These can be cooked outdoors on the barbecue grill, in the oven's broiler, or pan broiled. To pan broil, heat 1 tablespoon salad oil in heavy frying pan over medium-low heat for 1 minute. Lay the patties in the pan and cook 6 to 7 minutes on each side or until meat is no longer pink inside. To oven broil, place patties on a broiler rack about 4 inches from the heat and cook about 6 minutes on each side. Or grill over hot coals about 6 minutes on each side.

Makes 4 servings.

⚜ Anise Cookies ⚜

¹/₂ cup butter
1 cup sugar
1 egg
¹/₂ teaspoon vanilla extract
1³/₄ cups sifted flour
¹/₂ teaspoon salt
1¹/₂ teaspoons baking powder
1¹/₂ teaspoons anise seed

In bowl of electric mixer, cream butter until fluffy; gradually add sugar and beat until light and smooth. Add egg and vanilla, mixing well. In separate bowl, sift flour, salt, and baking powder together. Gradually add dry ingredients and anise seed to mixing bowl, beating well after each addition. Roll dough into a log, cover with waxed paper or plastic wrap, and chill at least an hour.

When ready to bake, preheat oven to 400° and lightly grease a baking sheet. Cut dough log into thin slices, place on baking sheet, and bake about 8 minutes or until golden brown.

Makes about 5 dozen.

⚜ Front-Porch Lemonade ⚜

2 cups sugar
2¹/₂ cups water
1 tablespoon anise seeds
1 cup mint leaves
juice of 6 lemons
juice of 6 oranges
grated rind of 1 orange

Add sugar to water in saucepan and simmer until sugar is dissolved. Add anise, mint, fruit juices, and orange rind to the pan. Bring water to boil, then cover pan and remove from heat. Let steep for 1 hour. Strain syrup into container and refrigerate—will last about a week or so. To serve, place 1/3 cup syrup into tall glass, fill with crushed ice and water. Garnish with fresh mint leaf.

Makes 10 to 12 servings.

⤷ Espresso Granita ↶

2/3 cup water
2/3 cup sugar
1/3 cup light-brown sugar, packed
2 teaspoons anise seed
8 cardamom pods, cracked
3 lemon-zest strips, approximately 3 inches long and 1/2 inch wide
2 2/3 cups freshly brewed espresso
3 lemon-zest curls
whipped cream

In medium saucepan, combine water, sugars, spices, and the large lemon-zest strips. Simmer until sugars are dissolved, then add coffee. Bring to boil, remove from heat, and cover. Let steep 45 minutes. Strain out spices and cool the coffee mixture to room temperature. Pour into shallow freezer pan and freeze 3 hours, stirring every 30 minutes to break up ice crystals. The final texture should be slushy. Spoon into chilled dessert dishes or stemmed glasses. Decorate with whipped cream and lemon-zest curls.

Makes 3 portions.

Note: If you don't have an espresso pot or machine, make coffee in your usual way but extra-strong.

⤷ Your Own Anisette ↶

2 tablespoons anise seeds
1 quart vodka or brandy

Crush the seeds and place in a covered jar with vodka or brandy. After two days, taste; if the flavor is as you wish, strain out the seeds. If not, continue to steep the seeds until you achieve the taste you like. Vodka, which has little flavor of its own, produces an intensely licorice liqueur. Brandy will take on a licorice flavor in addition to its own taste.

For Other Recipes Featuring Anise, See:
Hungarian Goulash, p. 250
Pfeffernusse, p. 262
Spiced Chicken Livers, p. 300

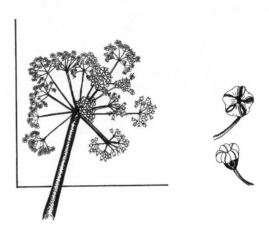

Caraway

Botanical name: **Carum carvi**

Part used as spice: **Seeds**

Available as: **Whole seeds; occasionally ground seeds**

Caraway is one of those plants that inhabit the no-man's-land between spices and herbs; depending on circumstance and the mood of the user, it can be either herb or spice or sometimes both. By "circumstance" I principally mean your level of commitment to gardening. For caraway is also one of those plants that will grow in temperate climates and so, if you have the space and the inclination, you can grow it in your backyard. This will let you enjoy all parts of the plant, including the green leafy portions that meet most people's definition of "herb."

If you decide to grow your own, you will need a certain measure of patience to begin with, for caraway is a biennial, the term for plants that require two years to go through a full life cycle. The first year, you plant caraway seeds and a small green plant grows; the second year, the plant grows taller, flowers, makes seeds, and then—its botanical destiny fulfilled—dies. Some of the seeds that fall to the ground will produce new plants for next year, and so the cycle continues.

In your garden caraway is a pretty but unspectacular plant. The frilly leaves are edible and make a pretty garnish; in appearance they will remind you of the foliage of carrots, to which they are related. The thick root, which is also edible, looks rather like a parsnip and tastes like one too, with an undertone of caraway flavoring.

However, far and away the most used part of the plant is the seeds, and since these are so readily available from commercial sources, you will be forgiven if you decide to use your garden space for something else.

The caraway plant is native to northern Africa, the Mediterranean area, and much of Europe, and grows easily in all those regions, plus North America and the temperate parts of Asia. However, it is commercially cultivated mostly in the Netherlands and Germany, two countries that use it enthusiastically in their cuisines.

In Asia, caraway has often been confused with cumin, and sometimes we still find translated cookbooks in which the confusion persists. The two seeds look similar and taste somewhat alike, for they are botanically related. Today some Far Eastern spice markets sell what they call "foreign cumin"—in other words, caraway.

History and Legends

Archaeologists exploring the site of a prehistoric culture in the mountains between Switzerland and France, a culture known to be five thousand years old, found caraway seeds among the remains of the dwellings. So we know that caraway was part of the household supplies some five thousand years ago. As far as we now know, that makes it the oldest cultivated spice.

Caraway was known and used in the great ancient civilizations of Greece and Rome, both as a flavoring for food and as a medicine. Apicius, a Roman who lived in the first century A.D., made a name for himself as a great appreciator of fine food; his detailed descriptions of Roman feasts preserve for us a record of fancy cooking of those days. He wrote of vegetables flavored with caraway and a fish sauce based on this spice. In the same century, Dioscorides, a Greek physician, prescribed a caraway tonic to bring a healthy color to pale young ladies. Julius Caesar's soldiers ate a bread made from ground caraway root mixed with milk.

During the Middle Ages, knowledge of caraway spread through the Arabian peninsula and upward into northern Europe. The Arabs called it "karawya" (also spelled "karauya"), obviously the source of our name caraway. In Europe, caraway was listed in herbals (reference books describing plants and their medicinal applications) as medicine for all manner of illnesses, and also continued to be a popular flavoring.

Among the many superstitions associated with herbs and spices, there may be none more curious than the old belief that caraway could keep people and possessions from straying. People believed that if they mixed caraway seeds in among their most important personal goods, those things would not be stolen—and if anyone tried, the thief himself would be held in place. These same magical powers would keep a lover from wandering, and so caraway was part of most ancient love potions.

Medicinal and Other Uses

Like many other herbs and spices, caraway has in the past been accorded certain powers that we now know are fictitious. It will not, as one medieval text claimed, "restoreth hair that be fallen away." However, many of its old medicinal applications have been verified by modern medicine.

The primary medical value of caraway is its beneficial effect on the digestive system. Like its cousins in the plant world, caraway is a carminative and a digestive, which means that it helps with gas and indigestion. The custom of chewing a few caraway seeds after a heavy meal, a practice as old as ancient Rome, reflects this.

Caraway gives a warm feeling to the stomach and is gentle enough for babies. Thus it has been used for generations as a remedy for colic. Simmer seeds in water or milk (1 tablespoon per cup of fluid) for 10 minutes, then strain out seeds and cool; you might want to sweeten with a little honey.

Another chemical constituent of caraway is lightly (and safely) sedative; this is another reason it is good for fussy, colicky infants.

This spice is also among the plants classed as "antispasmodic," and so it is useful to calm the stomach after taking medication that might cause nausea. A cup of caraway tea, or warm milk in which seeds have steeped, helps settle a queasy tummy in both children and adults.

In days past, caraway seeds were pounded into a paste to be applied as a poultice for bruises and cuts.

Cooking with Caraway

Caraway is a versatile spice. You may find it in recipes for:

- Breads, cakes, and cookies
- Sausage casseroles, oxtail stew, and similar dishes
- Coleslaw
- Soups (especially cabbage and potato)
- Omelets
- Rice and pasta dishes
- Cheese spreads and other canapés
- Carrots, cabbage, beets, potatoes, cauliflower, and other vegetables
- Applesauce
- Baked fruits (especially apple)

Caraway is a favorite with German cooks, who add it to breads, piecrust, and several sauces. It is an essential taste in sauerbraten and sauerkraut and quite indispensable to rye bread. In fact, it is the caraway seeds (not rye seeds) that give rye bread its distinctive flavor. In

Holland it is added to or served alongside cheese, and it is used in many countries to lighten the heavy taste of dishes like spareribs, roast pork, or goose.

Afternoon tea, that very British institution now developing fans in all countries, makes use of caraway. One very popular food served with

> Twentieth-century cooks experimenting with the interesting taste of this spice and thinking yourselves quite modern, take note. In the seventeenth century, John Parkinson, one of the best-known English herbalists, wrote this about caraway: "The seed is much used to be put among baked fruit, or into bread, cakes &c to give them a rellish."
>
> And even the acclaimed Mr. Parkinson borrows from his predecessors. In 1390 or thereabouts, the royal chefs to King Richard II put together a record of contemporary British cooking; along with garlic, pepper, and coriander, they listed caraway as an essential spice.
>
> These cooks, in their turn, may have learned about caraway from Apicius, a Roman epicure who lived more than one thousand years before them.

tea is known as seedcake; it's similar to a pound cake, spiced with cinnamon and filled with caraway seeds. Another tea treat popular with children is fingers of bread spread with rich butter, then dipped butter side down in a dish of toasted caraway seeds.

Caraway *confits*, little candies made of seeds coated with sugar, are used to garnish cakes and cookies; in central Europe they are served by themselves at the very end of the meal as a breath sweetener and digestive candy.

The popular European liqueur called kummel gets its characteristic taste from caraway.

❧ Rosy Caraway Cheese Dip ❧

Pumpernickel or other dark bread goes well with this savory spread.

8 ounces low-fat cream cheese, at room temperature
1 tablespoon butter, at room temperature
1 tablespoon Dijon mustard
1 large shallot, minced
4 teaspoons caraway seeds
4 teaspoons paprika
4 teaspoons capers, drained

Garnish:
2 tablespoons chopped chives

In a food processor or a bowl combine all ingredients except capers and chives. Process or mix until very well blended. Add capers and blend in for a few seconds. Chill. Serve in a bowl sprinkled with chives. Best if made several days ahead.
Makes about 1 cup.

—Renée Shepherd

❧ Italian Rye Bread ❧

A food processor makes quick work of this delicious bread.

3¹/₂ to 4¹/₂ cups unbleached flour
1 cup rye flour
1 tablespoon salt
1 tablespoon sugar
¹/₂ stick butter
¹/₂ teaspoon caraway seeds
2 packages active dry yeast
1³/₄ cups very warm water, divided
cornmeal
corn or vegetable oil
1 tablespoon cold water
1 egg
1 teaspoon dill weed

With metal blade in place, add 2 cups unbleached flour, the rye flour, salt, sugar, butter, caraway, and yeast to bowl of food processor. Pulse machine a few times until butter is thoroughly blended into dry ingredients. Add half the water and pulse the processor on and off 4 times. Add 1¹/₂ cups flour and remaining water. Pulse again 3 or 4 times, then let processor run until a ball of dough forms on the blades. If the dough is too sticky, add the remaining flour.

Turn dough onto lightly floured board and knead several times to form a smooth ball. Cover with plastic wrap and a towel, and let rest for 20 minutes. Divide dough in half. Roll each half into a rectangle 15 × 20 inches. Beginning at wide side, roll tightly. Place on greased baking sheets that you have sprinkled with cornmeal. Brush dough with oil, cover loosely with plastic wrap, and refrigerate 2 to 24 hours.

When you are ready to bake, remove loaves from refrigerator. Carefully uncover them and let stand at room temperature for 10 minutes. Meanwhile, preheat oven to 400°. Make 3 or 4 diagonal cuts on top of each loaf with edge of metal blade or sharp knife. Beat egg with cold water and dill weed, and brush onto surface of loaves. Bake for 25 to 30 minutes until golden brown. Cool on wire rack.

Makes 2 loaves.

Variation: You can use fennel seeds instead of caraway.

⤷ Corn and Potato Salad ⤶

1 pound boiling potatoes
1 cup cooked corn, cut from cob (one to two ears)
1/2 cup sour cream or blend of half sour cream and half plain yogurt
2 teaspoons caraway seeds (more if desired)
salt and pepper

Steam or boil potatoes until just tender. Cut into 1-inch pieces. Add corn, sour cream, and caraway and gently toss together. Add salt and pepper to taste before serving as a hot dish.

Serves 4.

⤷ Caraway Coleslaw ⤶

3 cups finely chopped or shredded cabbage
1/2 cup chopped green onions, including some green tops
1 tablespoon sugar
1/2 teaspoon salt
1/4 teaspoon dry mustard
2 tablespoons white wine vinegar
1/2 cup sour cream
1/2 teaspoon caraway seed

Mix cabbage and green onions and chill thoroughly, approximately one hour. Meanwhile, make dressing. In a medium bowl, combine sugar, salt, and mustard; whisk in vinegar and sour cream. Crush caraway seeds in a mortar and pestle or with a rolling pin between two sheets of waxed paper, and add to dressing. Just before serving pour dressing over cabbage and mix well.

Makes 6 servings.

❈ Chicken-Caraway Simmer ❈

1¹/₂ cups apple juice, divided
1 tablespoon cornstarch
1 teaspoon garlic powder or fresh garlic, minced
1 teaspoon paprika
1 teaspoon salt
¹/₈ teaspoon pepper
1¹/₂ cups sliced carrots
1 teaspoon caraway seeds
12 ounces skinned and boned chicken breasts (cutlets), cut in
*   ¹/₂-inch strips*
1 cup chopped unpeeled tart apple, such as Granny Smith

In a small bowl combine until smooth 1 cup apple juice, cornstarch, garlic powder, paprika, salt, and pepper; set aside.

In a large skillet heat remaining ¹/₂ cup apple juice until simmering. Add carrots and caraway seeds; cook, stirring occasionally, until carrots are nearly tender, 3 to 4 minutes. Add chicken; cook and stir until chicken is slightly pink, about 2 minutes.

Stir reserved cornstarch mixture; add to skillet; cook and stir until mixture thickens and boils. Add apple; cook and stir until chicken is done and apple is heated through, about 2 minutes.

Serve over steamed rice, if desired.

Makes 4 servings.

—American Spice Trade Association

❈ Turkey Pot Pie ❈

Old-fashioned goodness combined with an unusual crust; a great use for Thanksgiving leftovers.

2 cups cooked turkey, cut into bite-size pieces
1 cup broccoli pieces
¹/₂ cup chopped onion

4 tablespoons butter
6 tablespoons flour
¹/₄ teaspoon thyme
¹/₄ teaspoon crushed rosemary
¹/₄ teaspoon coarsely ground black pepper
1 cup chicken stock
Caraway Biscuit Crust (see recipe below)

Place turkey, broccoli, and onions in a buttered 8-inch square baking dish. Melt butter in small saucepan; add seasonings and cook briefly; then gradually add flour and cook until bubbly. Remove pan from heat. Add chicken stock and whisk until thoroughly mixed. Return pan to stove and cook over low heat until thickened. Pour over turkey. Place Caraway Biscuit Crust over turkey mixture, pressing down firmly around the edges. Bake in 425° oven 20 to 25 minutes.
Serves 4 to 6.

⤚ Caraway Biscuit Crust ⤙

1 cup all-purpose flour
1¹/₂ teaspoons baking powder
¹/₂ teaspoon salt
¹/₂ teaspoon dry mustard
¹/₄ cup shortening
1 teaspoon caraway seeds
¹/₃ cup milk

Sift flour, measure 1 cup, and sift again with baking powder, salt, and dry mustard. Cut in shortening with pastry blender or two knives until mixture is crumbly. Add caraway seeds and milk, and stir until dough can be shaped into a ball. Roll out on floured board to a 9-inch square.

Carefully place crust over turkey mixture, crimping edges under the edge of the baking dish to hold it in place while the pie cooks. Prick pastry with tines of fork to allow steam to escape.

⤚ Caraway Pound Cake ⤙

For a different and delicious taste, cut in thicker slices than usual, spread with softened butter, then lightly toast under the broiler.

1 package (about 1 pound) pound cake mix
1 teaspoon finely grated orange peel
1/4 teaspoon ground mace or nutmeg
1/2 cup finely chopped pecans or almonds
2 to 4 teaspoons caraway seed
powdered sugar (optional)

Prepare the cake mix as directed, adding the ingredients called for on the package. In addition, beat in the orange peel and mace. After beating, fold in the pecans and caraway seed. Pour into a greased loaf pan, 5 × 9 inches, and bake as directed.

Cool the cake in the pan about 10 minutes, then turn out of pan and let cool completely on a cake rack. At serving time, sift powdered sugar over the cake, if you wish.

Makes about 10 servings.

⋊ Cheese Spread ⋉

1 tablespoon caraway seed
1 pound cheddar cheese
2 tablespoons brandy

Toast seeds in a 350° oven until fragrant, about 10 minutes; reserve a few for garnish and crush the rest coarsely. Grate the cheese, and mix in the brandy and the crushed seeds. Let sit for 1/2 hour to blend flavors, then shape into a mound for serving, and sprinkle reserved whole seeds on top. Serve with crackers or sliced French bread as an appetizer.

⋊ Caraway Noodles ⋉

8 ounces wide noodles
1 tablespoon caraway seeds
1/4 cup slivered almonds
1/2 cup butter

Cook noodles, drain. Meanwhile, toast caraway seeds and almonds together in an unbuttered pan in a 350° oven for 10 minutes. Melt butter, stir in seeds and almonds. Stir into hot cooked noodles and serve immediately.

For Other Recipes Featuring Caraway, See:
Easy Saffron Bread, p. 278

A Shakespearean Treat

In caraway's essential oil (where aroma and taste reside), the basic flavor comes from a chemical named carvone; it is balanced in almost equal measure by another chemical, limonene, which most people identify as lemony. It is this combination of spicy sweetness with the undertaste of lemon that makes caraway such a pleasant addition to fruit desserts.

In *Henry IV, Part 2*, Shakespeare has one of his characters invite another to partake of "a last year's pippin [apple], with a dish of caraways." So the particularly pleasing combination of apples and caraway was well known in Shakespeare's day.

To enjoy this old treat, melt enough butter to cover the bottom of a baking pan and add thick slices of apple. Bake 10 minutes at 350°, turn apple slices over, sprinkle sugar on top, bake 5 minutes more. Meanwhile, spread a layer of caraway seeds in a separate, ungreased pan; roast 10 minutes, to bring out the flavor. Serve the apples with a separate dish of caraway seeds, to be nibbled along with the apple.

Cardamom

Botanical name: Ellataria cardamomum

Part used as spice: Seeds

Available as: Whole seed pods, whole seeds, ground seeds

There are some spices that are universally popular, used in every cuisine known to man or woman. And there are some that are closely identified with one particular type of food or one particular geographic region.

In this regard, cardamom is something of an anomaly. It is not by any means one of the universal spices; indeed, it's a safe bet that many fine cooks have never used it at all. So is it one that is identified with a specific area? No—*two* areas, quite different from each other.

Through the ages, those who have traveled to Arab lands have returned home telling of the cardamom-flavored coffee that is so popular there, and of the elaborate ritual with which it is served to visitors. And in Scandinavian countries, especially Sweden, cardamom is used so extensively in fancy breads and other baked goods that in that part of the world you cannot think "cardamom" without thinking of bread.

The hot, arid deserts of Saudi Arabia and the frosty lands of Scandinavia—we can hardly imagine two more different climates. How could one spice have become so snugly settled into these two lands? We may never know; one of the fascinating things about spices is the way they catch the fancy of some cultures and not others.

One of the most logical explanations—that the spice is most closely identified with the area where the plant grows naturally—doesn't help at all. For cardamom is native not to Arab desert or Swedish mountains, but to tropical rain forests of India, Sri Lanka, and China.

Is cardamom used in the foods of these Asian lands? Of course. But mostly in combination with other spices, especially in the many curries that are the heart and soul of Indian cuisine.

Cardamom is the third most expensive spice in the world, after saffron and vanilla. The reason: the individual pods must be harvested from the flower stalks by hand. And since any flower stalk at any point has some flowers, some barely formed fruits, and some pods ready to be picked, the harvesters must examine each one carefully.

Botanically, cardamom is in the same family as ginger, and there is a certain resemblance between the two plants in overall appearance. But that's where the similarity ends. With ginger, it is the underground stems (often called roots) that we use as the spice; with cardamom, the seeds inside the small fruit. And you would never mistake the taste of one for the other.

The cardamom plant has long, strappy leaves on stalks that may reach as much as fifteen feet high. The American food plant it most resembles is corn, except that cardamom doesn't die at the end of a season, and it's a tropical plant that won't grow in your backyard, unless you happen to live in Hawaii.

Several times a year, each cardamom plant sends out long flower stalks from its base; as the flowers fade, they produce small green fruits. The seeds inside these fruits are our spice. Each fruit has about fifteen to twenty of these hard, black, sticky seeds.

The fruits (called pods) are light green, about the size of a bean, and have three approximately flat sides. They are harvested when they are almost but not quite ripe, still green and firm. These pods are then spread out to dry, either in the sun (sometimes on village rooftops) or in special drying rooms. Those dried indoors retain more of their green color than the sun-dried ones. Pods that are noticeably white have actually been bleached; some people believe this cosmetic treatment makes the pods more appealing, but the flavor of the seeds inside is unchanged.

In addition to the areas of the Far East where it is native, cardamom is grown commercially in Guatemala and other Central American countries, in Vietnam, and in Tanzania. In fact, it grows lustily anywhere it's planted in the tropics. However, most of the world's supply of the commercial spice is still produced in India, from whence it was first introduced to the West some two thousand years ago.

History and Legend

Cardamom was known to the Greeks and Romans since before the birth of Christ. In the fourth century B.C., Greek traders brought it in from the

The coffee ritual in Arab cultures has for many years fascinated visitors to those regions. Let us step back in time a bit and observe the coffee ceremony in a Bedouin camp, where the ritual is most pronounced.

First the green coffee beans are roasted and then ground by hand in a brass mortar and pestle. The rhythmic clinking sound that permeates Bedouin camps, noted by many European visitors, is from this grinding. Then cardamom pods are broken apart and the seeds dropped into a pot of hot water. If there is a distinguished visitor in camp, only the most perfect cardamom pods are used, and they are first displayed to the visitor before being broken into the pot.

Into the same pot go some sugar, a pinch of ground saffron or cloves, and the pulverized coffee beans. This mixture is boiled for two to three minutes, then strained and poured into small cups. Again, if an honored guest is present, the pouring takes on greater significance. A ceremonial brass pot with a long curving spout is used; in the spout are stuffed several cardamom pods so that the coffee passing through them takes on additional flavor. The host pours for all the guests, starting with those of highest status.

To signify their appreciation of the fine brew, guests accept several refills and drink each one noisily.

The amount of cardamom used would probably seem overwhelming to most of us. One visitor, noting that the air was always heavily scented with cardamom, recorded that two teaspoons of seeds went into the pot for every cup of coffee, and the cups were small.

East; they gave us the name by which we know this spice, *kardamomum*.

It was hugely popular in ancient Rome, as much for perfume as for flavoring, and by the first century A.D. was being imported from India on a grand scale. It is, by the way, still used in the perfume industry today.

About one thousand years ago, the Vikings came upon cardamom in the trading area at Constantinople, and so introduced it into Scandinavia, where, as we know, it remains popular to this day.

Medicinal and Other Uses

Chewing cardamom seeds is an old trick for sweetening the breath. Asians used it two thousand years ago just before being brought into the presence of their leaders. In central Europe, even now, some people use it to disguise the smell of alcohol on their breath after a hard night of drinking.

Apicius, the great gastronome of first-century Rome, who never met a fancy dish he didn't like, suggests chewing cardamom to help settle the stomach after overindulging.

He was right. Cardamom is another spice with carminative properties, meaning that it helps break up intestinal gas. However, other, more common household spices provide the same service and do it better (dill, caraway, fennel, anise), and so more often you might find cardamom as part of a home-remedy mixture. Such a mixture (or even cardamom alone) will soothe colic in babies and promote digestion in people of all ages.

In many parts of the Middle East, the greatest value of cardamom is its purported aphrodisiacal effects. This belief is very ancient (cardamom is mentioned several times in *The Arabian Nights* in this context) and very modern: Many people still put great faith in the power of cardamom.

That is one reason behind the old saying that a poor man in an Arab country would rather surrender his rice than his cardamom. Another

---

Here is an old recipe for an all-purpose tonic from medieval England:

> Take four ounces of hartshorne, one ounce of cardamom, one ounce of cinnamon, one ounce of saffron, two handfulls of red sage, as much balm; steep these for twenty-four hours in two quarts of sack, or as much good brandy which you please. Distill it in a cold still as quick as you can, and let it drop on four ounces of sugar candy. Drink of this when low-spirited.

Should you feel inspired to try this, you may encounter some difficulty with the first ingredient. I'm not sure where one would find hartshorne (ground-up deer antlers) these days, now that Sherwood Forest is closed to hunting. And the cost of an ounce of saffron in today's market would make you sicker than you were to begin with.

On the other hand, two quarts of sack, which is a kind of wine, or good brandy, thus nicely sweetened and spiced, would go a long way toward improving anyone's spirits. And then you won't care that you had to omit the horne of a hart.

reason may be more practical: Cardamom does have a cooling effect on the body, a quality much to be cherished in lands where summertime temperatures can top one hundred twenty degrees.

Craft Projects

There was a time (before synthetic this and that were commonplace) when homemakers relied on natural products for household necessities. One such item that has become popular again is a small bag of spices and aromatic herbs, known as a "sweet bag" or, more commonly today, a sachet.

Spice bags were slipped into closets and cupboards, to protect the family's clothing and bed linens from mice, moths, and other troublemakers, and also to make them smell fresh and sweet. Today they perform the same service in dressers, lingerie chests, and linen closets, although since the invention of mothballs the modern focus is likely to be on fragrance alone.

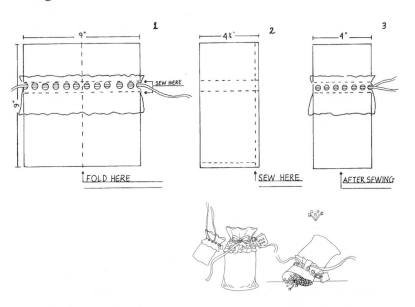

Spice bag for closets. Choose a pretty fabric with a fairly tight weave and cut a square; 9 inches is suggested here, but any size will work. Hem the top, and sew on a piece of lace or trim. Thread a length of narrow ribbon, in complementary color, through the holes (Step 1).

Fold in half, right sides together, and stitch bottom and long side (Step 2). Turn right side out (Step 3).

Fill with spices, pull the top closed, and tie with ribbon. Add a label describing the ingredients, if you wish.

Modern sachets, intended just for fragrance, are often filled with a potpourri mixture (see page 126). If you make your own potpourri, you could use it to fill small bags following the directions here. And they don't have to be hidden in a drawer or the closet, either. You might enjoy setting a sachet bag out on the dresser or tying it to the bedpost; squeeze it as you pass by, to release the aroma into the room.

Make your spice bag in any size (see page 66 for instructions), and fill it with any of the sweet spices (cinnamon, cloves, allspice, anise or fennel seed) or a mixture. Cardamom is especially nice.

Cooking with Cardamom

Cardamom, even more than most spices, loses its punch once exposed to air. You will have the freshest, strongest taste if you buy whole pods and strip out the seeds yourself as you need them. The pods crush easily with your fingers, or spread them out on a cutting board and run a rolling pin over them. (The pods themselves don't have much taste.) Next best is the whole seeds, removed from the pod (this is called "decorticated cardamom"); you may use them as is or grind into powder just before using. Preground cardamom may seem convenient, but it is inferior in taste.

In cooking, the two most common uses of cardamom are those we have already met: The baked goods of Scandinavia and the scented coffee of the Middle East. We owe it to ourselves to become acquainted with this spice in both of these traditional ways and others as well.

Use Cardamom with:
- Beef and veal stews
- Chicken or turkey pot pie
- Hamburgers and meatloaf
- Fruit soups
- Fruit salads, and dressings for such salads
- Split pea soup
- Sweet potatoes
- Winter squash
- Carrots and parsnips
- Apple pie, pumpkin pie, baked apples

Cooks in Sweden and Norway use cardamom far more than we do, and not only in their wonderful breads. Ground seeds are added to hamburgers and meatloaf, and in fact cardamom is what gives the distinctive flavor to the celebrated Swedish meatballs. Cardamom adds a mysterious and very pleasing note to many meat dishes—pork, chicken, beef, or veal.

When I was working on this chapter I made a batch of scones for

> Mix ¹/₂ teaspoon of ground cardamom into 1 cup sugar. Store in tightly covered jar. This is an interesting and delicious variation for cinnamon sugar. Use it in coffee, on toast, on baked or fried apples . . . anywhere you would normally use cinnamon sugar.

breakfast, and decided to add some cardamom to the batter. The taste was thoroughly wonderful, but the brown powder definitely affected the color; it looked like I had used whole wheat flour, which I had not. In this case the color didn't bother me, but if it should ever be important to you, first steep whole seeds in warm milk for a while, then strain them out and use the cardamom-flavored milk in the recipe.

Cardamom is also an important part of the spice mixture for curries in the Far East, where all self-respecting cooks keep supplies of the individual spices and assemble a blend for each dish.

⋅≺ Fresh Fruit with Cardamom Sauce ≻⋅

Use any fresh fruit that is in season.

¹/₂ cup water
¹/₂ cup orange blossom honey
¹/₄ teaspoon powdered cardamom
6 large fresh mint leaves, chopped
¹/₄ teaspoon salt
¹/₂ cup good port wine
¹/₈ cup Benedictine

In saucepan, mix water, honey, cardamom, mint, and salt; simmer for 2 minutes, to blend flavors. Remove from heat and cool to room temperature. Stir in wine and Benedictine, mixing thoroughly.

Peel and slice fruit, enough for 8 servings:

- Melon, all kinds
- Avocado
- Apple
- Oranges

Arrange fruit attractively on salad plates lined with red lettuce leaves; drizzle sauce over fruit.

Garnish plates with parsley and pitted black cherries or red seedless grapes.

⋆⟨ Cardamom Buns ⟩⋆

These lightly sweet buns are perfect for brunch or teatime.

1¹/₂ cups milk
¹/₂ cup sugar
1 teaspoon salt
1 teaspoon orange peel
¹/₂ cup butter, cut into small pieces
2 packages yeast
4 cups sifted all-purpose flour
1 teaspoon ground cardamom
1 egg, beaten
sugar
1 cup finely chopped nuts (almonds, walnuts, or pecans)

Heat milk to simmering. In mixing bowl combine sugar, salt, orange peel, and butter. Pour hot milk over mixture, stirring until butter melts. Cool to lukewarm. Sprinkle yeast over warm mixture; stir until yeast is dissolved. Add 1 cup flour; beat until smooth. Sift remaining flour with cardamom; gradually add to dough, beating thoroughly after each addition.

Let rise in warm place (80°) until doubled. Turn out on floured board and knead until smooth. Roll about ¹/₂-inch thick; with a sharp knife, cut into strips ¹/₂-inch wide. Twist two strips together, and then cut the twists into 2-inch lengths. Place on greased baking sheet, cover with clean dishtowel.

Let rise again until doubled. Brush with beaten egg; sprinkle lightly with sugar and nuts. Bake in 400° oven for 10 minutes, or until done and brown. Serve warm.

Makes 2 dozen buns.

Variation: The dough can be formed into many different shapes, including simple rounds. Another nice shape is a coiled bun. Divide the dough into 10 equal pieces, and roll each piece into a very thin rope. Coil the rope into a circle, smoothing the end underneath.

Serve with Honey-Orange Butter

Mix ¹/₂ cup softened butter with 2 tablespoons undiluted orange juice concentrate and 2 tablespoons honey.

⚡ Squash and Apple Bake ⚡

2 pounds butternut squash
2 apples, peeled, cored, and sliced
1/3 cup brown sugar
3 tablespoons melted margarine or butter
1 tablespoon flour
1 teaspoon salt
1/2 teaspoon cardamom

Cut squash in half, remove seeds, peel and cut in 1/2-inch slices. Arrange in square baking dish and cover with apple slices. Combine other ingredients and sprinkle over top. Cover and bake at 350° for 50 to 60 minutes, or until a fork easily pierces the squash.

⚡ Indian Rice ⚡

This colorful rice is particularly nice with chicken or pork.

1/2 cup butter, divided
1 cup rice
1/4 cup finely chopped onion
4 whole cardamom pods
1 bay leaf
1/4 teaspoon saffron
dash cinnamon
1/4 teaspoon coarsely ground black pepper
1/4 cup currants or raisins
1/4 cup slivered almonds
2 cups chicken stock

Melt half the butter in large saucepan; add rice and onion and sauté until golden. Pinch the cardamom pods open and scrape out the black seeds, discarding the outer pod; crush the seeds. Crumble the saffron. Add the spices, raisins, and almonds to rice along with remaining butter and cook for 1 minute. Heat chicken stock in microwave or small saucepan and add to other ingredients when very hot. Cover and cook over low heat 25 to 30 minutes. Remove bay leaf before serving.
   Serves 4 to 6.

❧ Swedish Meatballs ❧

These tender meatballs take a bit more time than ordinary ones, but the taste is extraordinary.

2 ounces pork sausage
3 whole eggs
³/₄ cup finely chopped onion
3 cloves garlic, finely minced
³/₈ teaspoon nutmeg
³/₈ teaspoon fresh ground pepper
¹/₈ teaspoon powdered cardamom
¹/₂ tablespoon salt
2 slices white bread
³/₈ cup milk or half-and-half
2¹/₂ pounds ground beef
1 to 2 tablespoons vegetable or olive oil
¹/₂ cup Burgundy wine, divided
¹/₂ cup water
2 tablespoons chopped parsley
³/₄ cup sour cream
1 beef bouillon cube
¹/₂ cup water mixed with 1¹/₂ tablespoons flour
¹/₄ teaspoon Kitchen Bouquet (can be found in most supermarkets)
minced parsley

In large mixing bowl, mix together the pork sausage, eggs, onion, garlic, nutmeg, pepper, cardamom, and salt. Toast the bread and crumble it. In small bowl, mix crumbs with milk. Add the crumbs and the ground beef to the sausage mixture; use your hands to blend very well.

Form meat mixture into small balls, about 1 inch in diameter. Heat oil in large saucepan or Dutch oven, and brown meatballs on all sides. Drain off any excess oil, and add ³/₈ cup of wine, water, and parsley to the pan. Simmer on low heat for 30 minutes.

Drain cooking liquid into another pot, and add to it the sour cream, bouillon, remainder of wine, water/flour mixture, and Kitchen Bouquet. Simmer this sauce over low heat until thick and smooth, stirring well to avoid curdling sour cream. Pour the sauce onto meatballs and simmer very gently for about 20 minutes. Do not boil.

Serve with broad noodles; garnish with additional minced parsley.
Serves 6.

❧ Cardamom Butter Cookies ❧

1 cup butter
1¼ cups sugar
2 eggs
1 teaspoon vanilla extract
3 cups sifted all-purpose flour
1 teaspoon baking powder
½ teaspoon salt
1 teaspoon cardamom
½ teaspoon cinnamon
¼ teaspoon allspice

Cream butter and sugar together until the mixture is light and fluffy. Add eggs and vanilla and beat thoroughly. Sift all dry ingredients together. Stir into butter mixture and mix well. Chill dough at least one hour. Roll out and cut with cookie cutters. You can also form dough into two rolls, chill, and cut crosswise into thin slices. Bake in 350° oven 8 to 10 minutes, depending on thickness of slice.
Makes 8 dozen thin cookies.

❧ Cardamom Coffee ❧

12 cups of freshly brewed coffee
5 cardamom pods
1-inch section of cinnamon stick
sugar to taste
1 whole nutmeg

Brew the coffee and pour into a large saucepan. Break the cardamom pods apart with your fingers (or run a rolling pin over them) and strip out the seeds. Place the seeds and cinnamon stick in with the coffee, along with sugar if you like your coffee sweetened, and simmer for ten minutes (don't let it boil). Strain and pour into individual mugs. Grate a bit of fresh nutmeg on top of each serving.
Makes 12 cups.

⁌ Cardamom Honey ⁌

Delicious on toast, scones, or waffles.

2 cups honey
1 teaspoon ground cardamom (freshly ground is best)

Soften honey at room temperature or in microwave. Stir in cardamom, mix thoroughly, and let sit at room temperature an hour or so for flavors to blend. Store in covered container in refrigerator; keeps indefinitely.

For Other Recipes Featuring Cardamom, See:

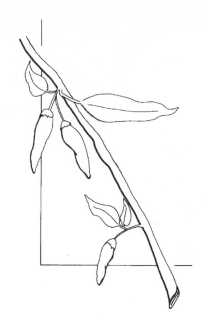

Cayenne

Botanical name: **Capsicum annuum**
Part used as spice: **Fruit**
Available as: **Powder**

In another part of this book, the chapter on chili peppers, you will find a description of an entire group of plants known as Capsicum. Cayenne is one part of the overall Capsicum story, and so is paprika, but since those two are so familiar to us as spices in their own right, both have their own chapter.

Cayenne, as a spice, is always in powdered form. What makes cayenne cayenne and not, say, paprika is that cayenne is *hot*. It is not made from any specific variety of Capsicum, but could be from any one (or several) types—as long as they are hot enough. The official specifications of the Department of Agriculture define cayenne as the dried, ripe fruit of any red species of Capsicum that has between 30,000 and 50,000 Scoville heat units. (The Scoville system is a way of measuring how hot various types of chili peppers are; the very mild Banana pepper has 0; the Habañero, which will take the top of your head off, has 300,000. For comparison, the Jalapeño, which you have probably tasted at some point, has 2,500 to 5,000.)

Now, just to keep things interesting, you will find in some top-quality garden catalogs the seeds for a variety of peppers named "Cayenne." If you buy the seeds, grow the plants, pick the peppers, dry and grind them, you will definitely have cayenne. But the commercial spice that you buy at the supermarket does not necessarily come from that specific plant. Hot red peppers, dried and then ground up into a fine powder—that's cayenne.

All the Capsicum plants are natives of the New World—Mexico, Central America, South America. They were used for thousands of years before being "discovered" by Columbus and other voyagers and brought back to Europe.

One such "discovery" was in the northeastern part of South America, the territory we now know as French Guiana. There, in a town named

Cayenne, which lies on the Cayenne River, Spanish explorers found native people eating these strange peppers. When the fiery hot peppers began to be cultivated in Europe, they were called Ginnie peppers (sometimes spelled Ginny), a corruption of "Guiana." Somewhere along the line (we don't know exactly where) the name Cayenne began to be used for these hot peppers, and today it is applied only to the powdered form of the spice.

Cooking with Cayenne

The main point to remember about cayenne is that it is hot. Follow recipes carefully. You can always add more, if your Scoville tolerance is high, but you can't take it out.

We usually encounter cayenne in ethnic dishes such as Mexican chili, Chinese hot and sour soup, or Indian curries. Although Americans tend to assume these dishes are HOT, they are not preordained to be so. All these dishes, and their cousins, can be made in a spectrum of hotness, a factor determined largely by the relative degree of cayenne.

Even for those who do not enjoy having a hole burned in their tongue, a small pinch of cayenne adds a bit of intrigue to many foods: hamburgers, meatloaf, ground beef casseroles, cornbread, appetizer dips and spreads. And there is a wickedly delicious cheese cracker that gets its indispensable tang from cayenne (see page 77).

✢⚮ Spiced Walnuts ⚮✢

4 teaspoons butter or margarine
1 cup walnuts, halves or large pieces
¹/₄ teaspoon salt
dash cayenne pepper
¹/₄ teaspoon ground cumin
¹/₄ teaspoon ground coriander

Melt butter in a medium skillet. Add walnuts to pan and sauté, stirring until golden brown, about 3 minutes.

Combine salt, cayenne, cumin, and coriander. Sprinkle over nuts. Mix well and serve.

Makes 1 cup.

—Spice Islands

⋖ Senegalese Soup ⋗

4 cups chicken stock
4 egg yolks
2 cups cream
1 teaspoon curry powder
1/4 teaspoon cayenne
1/4 teaspoon salt
1 cup cooked, minced chicken
grated rind of 1 lemon

In the top of a double boiler, heat chicken stock to scalding. Using a whisk, thoroughly mix egg yolks, cream, curry, cayenne, and salt in a separate bowl. Stir 1/2 cup hot chicken stock into egg mixture, then add this mixture to remaining stock in double boiler. Cook until thickened, stirring constantly. Just before serving, stir in chicken and grated lemon rind.

Variations: This soup is also good cold. Remove thick stock from heat and chill in refrigerator. Add chicken and lemon just before serving.

This recipe can be used as a base for other soups. Instead of chicken, add chopped spinach, broccoli, artichokes, or avocados.

⋖ Chili Cheese Cornbread Muffins ⋗

2 cups yellow cornmeal
1/2 cup all-purpose flour
1 teaspoon baking powder
1 teaspoon sugar
1 1/4 teaspoons salt
2 eggs
2 1/2 cups milk
2 teaspoons oil or melted shortening
1/4 teaspoon cumin
1/8 teaspoon cayenne
1 cup shredded cheddar cheese
1/4 cup minced onion
1 cup fresh or frozen corn
1 4-ounce can green chili peppers, rinsed, seeded, and chopped
1/4 cup chopped red bell pepper

Prepare muffin tin for baking: Cover inside of cups with a thin coating of butter, sprinkle flour over butter, shake off excess. Or use paper baking cups.

In large mixing bowl, combine cornmeal, flour, baking powder, sugar and salt. In separate bowl, beat eggs, then add milk, oil, and spices; stir thoroughly. Fold in cheese, onion, corn, green chilies, and red peppers. Add cheese mixture to dry ingredients, mixing lightly.

Spoon about 1/3 cup batter into prepared muffin cups. Bake at 375° for 25 to 30 minutes.

Makes 15 muffins.

⋅≼ Cheese Biscuits ≽⋅

These spicy-hot treats, so good with beer and cocktails, have been the ultimate Southern appetizer for decades.

1/2 pound butter
1/2 pound sharp cheddar cheese
2 1/2 cups flour
1 teaspoon salt
1/2 teaspoon cayenne pepper
 pecan halves

Cream butter and grated cheese. Add flour, salt, and pepper. Shape into long rolls. Wrap in wax paper and refrigerate overnight. Slice into rounds and press a pecan half into each round. Bake at 400° for 12 minutes.

Makes 2 to 3 dozen, depending on size.

⋅≼ Corn Pudding ≽⋅

Even though it's called pudding and has the texture of a custard, this is not dessert but a flavorful side dish. Try it with barbecued chicken or hamburgers.

2 cups fresh or frozen corn
2 tablespoons flour
1 teaspoon salt
1 tablespoon sugar
2 eggs
1 cup milk (warm)
3 tablespoons butter, melted
1/4 teaspoon cumin
1/8 teaspoon cayenne
1/4 teaspoon chili powder

In mixing bowl, combine corn, flour, salt, and sugar. In separate bowl beat eggs with milk, melted butter, and spices. Fold egg mixture into corn. Pour into greased baking dish and bake 30 minutes at 350°. Dish is done when a toothpick comes out clean.

Serves 6.

⚜ Turkey Picadillo ⚜

1 pound ground turkey
1 teaspoon ground cumin
3/4 teaspoon salt
1/2 teaspoon black pepper
1/4 teaspoon cayenne
1/4 teaspoon ground allspice
1/4 cup finely chopped onion
1 tablespoon minced garlic
1 tablespoon olive oil
1 can (8 ounces) tomato sauce
1/4 cup sliced pimento-stuffed green olives
1/4 cup golden or dark seedless raisins
12 large Boston or iceberg lettuce leaves

In a medium bowl combine turkey, cumin, salt, pepper, cayenne, and allspice. Mix well; set aside.

In a large nonstick skillet heat olive oil until hot; sauté onions and garlic until soft. Add turkey mixture; cook, stirring, until turkey is no longer pink. Stir in tomato sauce, olives, and raisins; cook, stirring occasionally, until most of the liquid has evaporated, 3 to 4 minutes.

To serve: In each lettuce leaf place about 1/4 cup turkey mixture; roll up lettuce, folding in sides to enclose filling.

Serve with rice, if desired.

Makes 4 servings (12 rolls).

—Adapted from American Spice Trade Association

⚜ Hot Texas Red Chili ⚜

The assertiveness of the cayenne in this version of chili earns it a place in this chapter.

1/4 cup olive oil
3 pounds coarsely ground lean beef
1 quart water
3 teaspoons salt

1 tablespoon sugar
10 cloves garlic, chopped or pressed
6 tablespoons chili powder
1 teaspoon cumin
1 teaspoon oregano
1 teaspoon cayenne pepper
3 tablespoons paprika
3 tablespoons flour
6 tablespoons yellow cornmeal
1/2 cup water

In large pan, heat olive oil until it is quite hot. Add meat and sear over high heat, stirring constantly until meat is no longer red. Add water and simmer about 1¹/₂ hours. Add salt, sugar, and spices, and cook 30 minutes more. Blend flour and cornmeal into ¹/₂ cup water and add to mixture. Cook till thickened, about 5 minutes.

Serves 6.

⚜ Pork Vindaloo ⚜

1¹/₂ pounds lean pork
¹/₂ cup vinegar
2 onions, chopped
1 teaspoon minced garlic
1¹/₂ teaspoons powdered ginger (or 1 teaspoon minced fresh ginger)
1 tablespoon mustard seed
1 teaspoon ground turmeric
¹/₂ teaspoon cayenne
¹/₈ cup vegetable or olive oil
1 can chicken broth
6 medium potatoes, peeled and quartered

Trim all visible fat from meat and cut meat into 1-inch cubes. In large bowl mix the vinegar, onions, garlic, and spices; add meat to this and mix to coat meat well. Marinate in refrigerator for at least 2 hours.

When ready to cook, heat oil in a Dutch oven or large saucepan. Lift the meat from the marinade and brown lightly. Add chicken broth and marinade and cook over medium heat for 20 minutes. Add potatoes and cook over low heat, covered, for about 45 minutes or until potatoes are tender.

Makes 4 servings.

For Other Recipes Featuring Cayenne, See:
Spicy Black Bean Dip, p. 147
Caribbean Black Bean Soup, p. 148

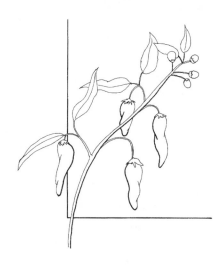

Chili Peppers

Botanical name: **Capsicum annuum; C. frutescens**

Part used as spice: **Fruit**

Available as: **Fresh peppers, green and red; whole dried red peppers; dried pepper flakes**

> Peter Piper picked a peck of pickled peppers;
> A peck of pickled peppers Peter Piper picked.
> If Peter Piper picked a peck of pickled peppers,
> What kind of pickled peppers did Peter Piper pick?

Yes, I know that's not how it goes. But here we are less concerned with where the heck the peck is, and more concerned with what kind of peppers they are. Because Peter is going to help us appreciate the mystery of plant relationships.

Take a look back at the section in the Introduction that talks about Latin nomenclature; refresh your memory about genus and species. All peppers belong to the genus *Capsicum*; the word loosely translates to "I'll bite you." One species, *Capsicum frutescens*, gives us the Tabasco pepper. Another species, *C. chinense*, is the hot-as-Hades Habañero. But almost all other peppers that we are likely to encounter belong to just one species: *C. annuum*.

And here's the really amazing part: Even sweet peppers, which most of us call bell peppers, belong to that same species, along with the many hot peppers that make our eyes water and our noses run.

To distinguish among the many types of chilies we would have to move down to the next level of names: varieties (such as Jalapeño, Serrano, Anaheim, etc.). Do you really need to pay attention to the different varieties? Yes, if you (1) live where fresh chilies are sold or (2) are interested in growing your own. In either case, it's a good idea to know

To put out the fire if you underestimate the hotness of chilies, drink some milk, eat yogurt or ice cream, or grab a banana.

Don't bother drinking water. The part of the chili that is burning a hole in your mouth is an oil, so water won't have any effect on it. Drink beer instead. Really. The alcohol dissolves the oils.

what you're getting. But if you purchase a hot pepper product from a commercial spice manufacturer you won't be able to tell which variety of pepper it came from (except for paprika).

In a nutshell, all the following "pepper" spices are part of the same group:

- Cayenne (which is very, very hot)
- Paprika (which is not hot at all)
- Hot pepper flakes (which is what you find in shakers at your favorite pizza joint, so you probably know how hot they are)
- Dried whole chilies (which range from medium to very hot)

History and Legends

Chilies are indigenous to the subtropical areas of the Western Hemisphere: Mexico and Central and South America. We know from remains uncovered in archaeological sites in Mexico and South America that hot peppers were known and used as many as nine thousand years ago. Peppers played several important roles in Mayan and Aztec cultures—in foods, in medicine, in religious rituals—for many thousands of years before Europeans came calling.

Christopher Columbus is responsible for the rest of the world learning about chilies. On his second voyage through the West Indies, which lasted from 1493 to 1496, he was accompanied by a Spanish physician named Diego Alvarez Chanca, who is remembered today for the detailed letter he sent to Seville describing the flora and fauna of the area. Noting the custom of spicing cooked yams with chili (which the natives called *aji*), Chanca wrote: "Also there is much axi, which is their pepper, and it is stronger than pepper, and the people won't eat without it, for they find it so very wholesome."

Here we see the initial confusion between chilies and pepper; because black pepper was all the Europeans knew up to that point, they gave the name "pepper" to the chili plants, assuming they were somehow related. It's also worth noting that this European physician picked up on the locals' belief in the beneficial characteristics of this plant;

long before his time, and for long after, chili peppers have been a staple of folk medicine.

Another observer on that second voyage wrote this account of the strange new plant:

> In those islands there are also bushes like gorse bushes [a small European shrub] which make fruit as long as cinnamon full of small grains as biting as pepper; those Caribs and the Indians eat that fruit like we eat apples.

So, among the many wondrous things that Columbus and his men brought back home was this amazing plant. It quickly caught on in southern Europe, where the climate is warm enough to permit a crop to grow and mature. Less than one hundred years after Columbus's return, chili peppers were being cultivated throughout Spain and Portugal.

Then, in the seventeenth century, Portuguese traders sailing to the ports of India and the East Indies introduced the peppers to the people of those regions. Here, in the land of spices, these spicy peppers were an instant hit. So, among those ironic twists we find in the story of spices, here is one more: Columbus went out to find a new sea route to the Spice Islands, and instead found a new land with, among other wonders, a spice so intriguing that a few hundred years later it was adopted by the residents of the islands he had sought.

The plants grow easily in any tropical area, and today much of the world's crop of chili peppers comes from India.

In the days when India was under the control of Great Britain, many British army personnel stationed there acquired a liking for the hot spicy curries of that area. The more they grew to enjoy the local cuisine, the more they found the regular food served in the army mess too insipid. So a new condiment was born: Hot chilies were steeped in some form of alcohol (sherry was a favorite) until the chili essence was extracted; then the chilies were strained out, producing a liquid so overpoweringly hot that no discernible sherry flavor remained. A few drops could bring a bland soup up to acceptable levels of fierceness.

Medicinal and Other Uses

In centuries past, hot peppers in their many forms—dried, crushed, powdered, juiced, or extracted essences—have been ascribed many healing qualities.

In classical Indian medicine, it was considered effective treatment for constipation. The Mayans and Aztecs of Central America, who of course had never heard of Vitamin C, nonetheless believed eating peppers would cure diarrhea and made a chili gargle for sore throats.

Many years later, as chili peppers became familiar to Europeans, they were also incorporated into European medicine. The well-known English herbalist Nicholas Culpeper (1653) recorded the recipe for a popular remedy for indigestion and other ills: Bake chilies, flour, and yeast into a dry cake, crush it to a powder, and add the powder to foods. Thus consumed, Culpeper wrote, it gives "great relief" to stomach problems and "helps digestion, gives an appetite, and provoketh the urine."

He was right. Or at least mostly right. We know now that red pepper stimulates both saliva and the gastric fluids that cause the contractions commonly known as hunger pangs. So much for the appetite. The same properties act on the bladder and the urinary tract, "provoking" more frequent urination.

This urinary stimulation, incidentally, is sometimes mistaken for sexual arousal. And that explains why, for centuries, people have considered red pepper an aphrodisiac. Spanish priests in service to Mexico warned that pepper "inciteth to lust" and pleaded with the Indians to avoid it; history does not record that they paid any attention.

And what of the old suggestion to use peppers for digestive distress? Chemically, at least, the ingredients in hot peppers do have a positive effect on the digestive system. However, the heat in capsaicin (the primary chemical constituent in hot peppers) can also be very irritating to the stomach lining, and so today we are encouraged to use other, safer spices as digestive aids (anise, caraway, fennel, cumin, and dill).

Not too long ago, some people still suggested a poultice of crushed hot peppers to ease the pain of sore muscles and stiff joints, as from

Along with their curative properties, the fiery power of these peppers was duly noted by European scientists. The famous herbalist John Gerard (1597) wrote, "It hath in it a malicious quality, whereby it is an enemy to the liver and other of the entrails." Indeed.

arthritis. A poultice is a home remedy made from some part of a plant (chopped or crushed), blended with enough water to make a thick paste and laid directly on the skin or on a piece of fine cloth that is in turn laid on the skin.

Now it is true that hot peppers cause blood vessels to dilate, which brings an increased supply of blood to the area and gives it a sensation of being warm. So you can see why poultices, liniments, and salves made from chilies were once thought to be a good idea. But in fact they can actually burn the skin enough to raise blisters. Chili poultices are no longer recommended.

Earlier in this century, chilies were suggested as treatment for dropsy, quinsy, gout, malaria, and even toothache, as well as for "ulcerated sore throat." We don't see too much dropsy these days, and as for ulcerated sore throat, common sense tells us that putting very powerful irritants in contact with open sores will be extremely painful.

Which brings us to an important point. Much of what was used as folk medicine in generations past has now been scientifically validated. And some of it is utter nonsense. Just because a remedy is written up in older texts about "natural" medicinal treatments doesn't mean you should do it.

As an extreme example, I have read that in some societies men made a juice of hot peppers and dropped it into their eyes to improve their eyesight as they went off on fishing expeditions. Surely everyone realizes that putting hot peppers in your eyes will not make you see better.

Are we clear about this? **Do not put any part of a hot pepper into your eyes.**

So far we have mostly seen that old remedies using hot peppers are now discouraged. Are there any accepted beneficial uses? Yes.

For one, chili peppers act as an irritant on the lining of your nose and mouth, which has the effect of loosening up nasal congestion. (Think back to the last time you ate hot salsa; didn't you need extra hankies?) So next time you have a cold, add lots of hot pepper to your homemade chicken soup.

Also, very spicy foods increase your level of perspiration, which is nature's air conditioning: As perspiration evaporates, it cools your skin. That is one reason hot foods are so popular in hot climates.

All peppers (both sweet and hot) are nutritionally rich. They are good sources of iron, calcium, and potassium and excellent sources of vitamin A, vitamin C, vitamin E, and other antioxidants. Peppers, in fact, have more vitamin C than any other vegetable; unfortunately, the process of drying eliminates most of it, so look for vitamin C primarily from fresh peppers.

Crafts

A chili pepper is a handsome thing, especially when it has reached its full color. As it dries, the color becomes deeper and less fluorescent but is still attractive. Whole peppers, dried or fresh, form the visual and textual heart of several craft items.

One of the most engaging qualities of human nature is the urge to make beautiful the things of daily life. Wherever chilies grow, they are harvested when ripe and dried for use later in the year. They could just as easily be spread out to dry and then dumped into a basket any which way, but instead they are usually arranged into graceful hangings of various shapes.

In small towns throughout Mexico and the American Southwest, practically every home is covered with long strings of peppers (called *ristras*) hanging in the sun to dry. Nowadays, with the recent popularity of Southwestern themes in home decor, you can find *ristras* for sale in trendy shops (at trendy prices). Or you can make your own.

Project: Chili *Ristra*

The simplest *ristra* is merely fresh whole chilies threaded together. Using fine-gauge wire, or a needle with a large eye and strong thread or twine, pierce through the base of the peppers near the stem; keep going until all the chilies are used. Twist the top end of the wire into a loop for hanging.

To make the *ristra* more decorative and to disguise the wire hanger at the top, you may want to add short strips of raffia at the top. Raffia is a natural product: Dried fibers from a large-leaved palm, separated into long thin strips that can be used like ribbon. It is sold in most craft stores, in bundles rather like knitting yarn.

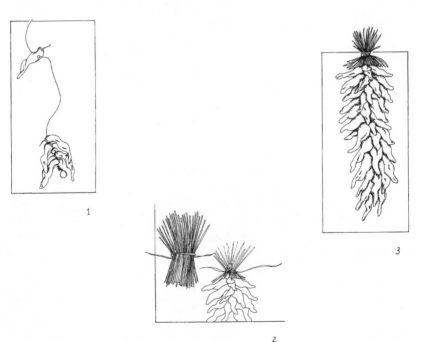

Chili ristra. Thread fresh chilies onto twine or thin wire, attached to a wire hanger (Step 1).

Make a bundle of short strips of raffia and tie them onto the top, to hide the wire hanger from view (Step 2).

Hang the finished *ristra* in the sun to dry (Step 3).

The luscious colors of whole chilies add a strong accent to wreaths made of natural materials. Here are two versions.

Project: Chili-Grapevine Wreath

The simplest style uses as a base a grapevine wreath (sold in craft shops and variety stores, available in many sizes). To it you will add clusters of chilies, as few or as many as you wish, and finish with a decorative bow.

Simple chili wreath. At the craft shop, buy a grapevine wreath in whatever size you prefer. Using thread or very fine wire, tie together fresh chilies in clusters of three. Tie the clusters to the wreath, overlapping them to hide the stems. Add a bow of ribbon or raffia to cover the last section of stems.

Project: Chili Wreath

A very handsome, dramatic wreath can be made from just chilies, packed tightly together. To maintain a good shape, purchase a wire wreath base from a craft shop, in whatever size works for the amount of chilies you have. Try to use chilies of the same size and color, for the most attractive wreath.

Using very thin-gauge wire, thread the chilies into a long strip. Attach that strip to the outer circle of the wire form. Then make a second strip, a bit shorter, and wire it to the inner circle. That's all there is to it. Hang it in your kitchen where you can snip off chilies as needed (if you can bear to part with them), or give to a friend on a special occasion.

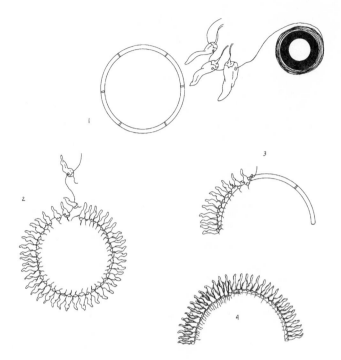

Chili wreath. Thread whole chilies into a long strip, using fine wire (wire on a spool is easy to work with) (Steps 1 and 2).

When strip is long enough, wire it to the outside circle of a wreath form made of heavy wire (Step 3).

Make a second strip and wire it to the inside circle, overlapping the chilies (Step 4).

Growing Your Own

Making these craft items is more cost-effective if you have access to large quantities of fresh chilies. The easiest way to accomplish that—well, maybe not the easiest but certainly the most satisfying—is to grow your own. Unless you live in an extremely cold climate, this is definitely doable.

In this book, I won't be able to show you how to grow your own peppers, but excellent advice and encouragement are readily available. You might want to look into:

- Public libraries and bookstores, for the many wonderful books on gardening techniques.
- Your local County Extension Office, for the useful, inexpensive gardening publications.
- Local gardening organizations such as garden clubs, plant societies, Master Gardener groups; for workshops open to the public, or for contact with knowledgeable individuals.

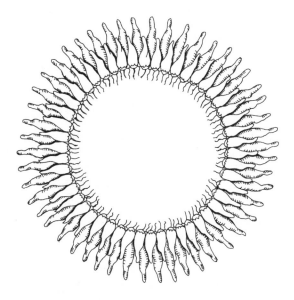

The finished wreath is particularly handsome if you are able to use chilies of all the same size.

- Mail-order seed companies, whose catalogs (often free) are usually filled with valuable information; check the Appendix at the back of this book.

One thing to keep in mind: If you start with fresh chilies for any of these craft projects, remember that they will shrink somewhat as they dry. So use more than you think you need to fill in an area; once they shrink and shrivel, the finished look will be just right.

Cooking with Hot Peppers

By now you know that two spices that we know by specific name are members of the Capsicum group: cayenne and paprika. And the commercial spice called chili powder is actually a blend of ground chilies and other spices. All three of these have their own chapter in this book. In this chapter we concentrate on hot red peppers in three forms: fresh, dried whole, and dried flakes.

But which peppers should you use for what? As a practical matter, the choice for cooks comes down to this:

- If you want hot taste in powder form so that it easily mixes in with other dry ingredients, choose *cayenne*.

This is a book about spices, and so we concentrate on products you would find in the spice section of an average supermarket. But hot peppers, which are part of so many cuisines, are marketed in many different forms.

Perhaps you became acquainted with the first two listed here in those little pots on the table in Asian restaurants; they are also available for sale in Asian markets or in the "ethnic foods" section of your supermarket. Both are excruciatingly hot.

- *Chili paste* is dried chili pods coarsely ground with a little vinegar; it has the texture of thick mustard. Think Thai.
- *Chili oil* is vegetable oil in which large quantities of hot chilies have been steeped until the essential oils are extracted. Think Szechuan.
- *Hot sauce* (Tabasco and other generically named hot-pepper sauces) is made from dried red peppers and vinegar; it is fire in liquid form. Think Cajun.
- *Chili sauce*, with a texture like catsup and bottled like it, is a much milder American product. Think wimp.

- If you want pieces of the pepper to show up in the finished dish (or if you run a pizza parlor), choose *hot pepper flakes*.
- If you want intact peppers (for visual impact), choose *whole dried peppers*; or, if you know how to tell which variety is which, fresh whole chilies.
- *Paprika* has its own unique and mild taste; you cannot use it interchangeably with hot peppers. If you make Chicken Paprika with cayenne, for example, you'll be extremely sorry.
- *Chili powder* (the one that is a blend of several spices) also has its own taste. You can substitute it for cayenne or other forms of hot pepper but you'll get the familiar "chili con carne" taste instead of just plain fire.

Cooking with Fresh Chilies

If you want to experiment with fresh chilies rather than the dried products in the spice section, here are a few things you should know.

1. You can't tell by size or shape which chilies are hot and which are mild. Often the smallest are the hottest. You just have to learn to recognize each type. Color isn't much of a clue either. All peppers are green when they first appear on the plant, and only turn red as they mature. Even at the green stage, hot peppers are hot.

2. The heat in the chili is a chemical called capsaicin. It is so incredibly powerful that dissolved in a ratio of one to one million, you can still taste it.
3. Capsaicin is in the seeds and, even more, in the white ribs that the seeds are attached to. Just picking up a hot chili will not burn your fingers, but once you cut into it, you are exposing your fingers and your eyes to this chemical.
4. When cooking with fresh chilies, wear gloves, especially if you have any small cuts on your fingers, and don't rub your eyes. You can't compensate for not wearing gloves by washing your hands afterward; capsaicin is not water soluble. Wiping your fingers in vinegar, however, will help.

⅋ Chicken Quesadillas ⅋

This recipe is easy to double for a party.

¹/₂ pound boneless, skinless chicken breast, cut into thin strips
2 tablespoons chopped onion
³/₄ teaspoon ground cumin
¹/₄ teaspoon hot red pepper flakes (see note)
¹/₂ teaspoon dried oregano
¹/₂ teaspoon garlic powder
1 cup chopped tomatoes
2 flour tortillas
¹/₄ cup shredded cheddar cheese

Preheat oven to 450°.

Coat a nonstick skillet with cooking spray; sauté chicken over medium-high heat for 3 minutes. Add onion, spices, and tomatoes; sauté 2 minutes. Remove from heat.

Spray cooking spray lightly over a baking sheet. Place tortillas on baking sheet and cover each with half the chicken mixture. Sprinkle cheese evenly over chicken.

Bake about 8 minutes. Cut each into 6 wedges.

Note: This makes a somewhat mild sauce; pass a shaker or bowl of additional hot pepper for those who like it hot.
Makes 6 servings.

—McCormick/Schilling

⅍ Chili Cashews ⅀

1 tablespoon olive oil
10 dried hot chili peppers
¹/₄ teaspoon garlic powder
1 can (12 ounces) salted cashews, peanuts, or mixed nuts
¹/₄ teaspoon chili powder

Heat olive oil in heavy frying pan. Crush chili peppers and add to oil along with garlic powder; mix well. Add nuts and cook over medium heat for 7 to 8 minutes, stirring constantly. Mix seasonings and nuts together thoroughly. When nuts are toasted, remove from pan and drain on paper towels. Sprinkle chili powder over hot nuts; pour into bowl and stir so that chili powder is well mixed with nuts.
Makes about 2 cups.

⅍ Cucumbers with Tomato Relish ⅀

This appetizer comes from Burma; use cucumber slices as scoops for the cool relish.

2 to 4 small dried whole hot red chilies
2 tablespoons water
1 large onion, cut into chunks
4 cloves garlic, halved
2 teaspoons chopped fresh ginger
2 tablespoons salad oil
¹/₄ teaspoon turmeric
1 large can (28 ounces) tomatoes
salt

Use kitchen gloves to protect your hands while you slice open the chilies and remove the seeds. In a blender or food processor, whirl chilies, water, onion, garlic, and ginger until well minced. Heat salad oil in a large, deep frying pan over medium heat; add onion mixture and turmeric. Cook, stirring, until liquid has evaporated (about 5 minutes). Remove from heat.

Drain the liquid from tomatoes and discard. Whirl the tomatoes in blender until smooth. Add to onion mixture; season to taste with salt. Cook over medium heat, stirring, until reduced to about 2 cups. Serve at room temperature.

Cucumber slices

Peel 2 large cucumbers. Slice on the diagonal into long, thin ovals. Arrange on serving platter, with bowl of relish in center.
Makes about 10 servings.

⋅≷ Seafood Firepot ≷⋅

Like many Thai dishes, this soup features the tangy, refreshing taste of lemon grass. If you can't find it, substitute grated lemon peel. And don't forget to wear gloves for slicing the peppers.

3 quarts chicken broth
3 cups water
1 stalk fresh lemon grass or 1/4 cup sliced dry lemon grass
1 or 2 small hot chilies, thinly sliced
Peel from 1 lime
18 small live hard-shell clams, scrubbed
1 1/2 pounds large shrimp, shelled and deveined
About 2 pounds cooked whole crab, cleaned and cracked
2/3 cup lime juice
1/2 cup fresh coriander (cilantro) sprigs
3 green onions (including tops), sliced
Lime wedges

In a large stockpot or kettle, combine broth and water. Remove tough outer leaves from lemon grass and slice remainder into short lengths. Loosely tie lemon grass, chilies, and lime peel in a cheesecloth bag and add to pot. Bring to a boil over high heat; cover, reduce heat, and simmer for 45 minutes. Discard seasonings.

Add seafood to kettle. Cover and simmer until clams open and shrimp turn pink (about 7 minutes). Stir in lime juice.

Pour seafood and broth into a large serving bowl. Garnish with cilantro and sliced onions. Serve with lime wedges.
Makes 4 to 6 servings.

⋅≷ Pak Choi Kimchee ≷⋅

Kimchee is a fiery hot pickled cabbage that is served with Korean foods as regularly as catsup is with American foods.

1 pound pak choi or Chinese cabbage
2 cloves garlic, minced
3 small slices fresh ginger root
¹/₂ teaspoon hot chili flakes
1 scallion, cut into 2-inch lengths
1 tablespoon soy sauce
1 teaspoon rice vinegar
1 teaspoon salt
2 teaspoons sugar

Cut enough pak choi (also spelled bok choy) to make 3 cups into 1-inch lengths, using mostly the stalks.

Combine garlic with ginger, chili flakes, scallion, soy sauce, and vinegar. Add the pak choi and mix well with your hands. Add salt and sugar, mixing again until well combined. Let stand for 1 to 2 hours at room temperature as it will make its own juice, then refrigerate until ready to serve. Refrigerated, this will keep a couple of days.

Makes 1 pint.

—Renée Shepherd

⤳ Dilly Beans ⤳

When you see how attractive these jars of pickled beans are, the whole red peppers contrasting with the green beans, you'll be glad you took the time to pack them neatly.

5 cups vinegar
5 cups water
¹/₂ cup salt
4 pounds green beans, whole (about 4 quarts)
32 dried hot red peppers
4 teaspoons mustard seed
4 teaspoons dill seed
8 cloves garlic

In a saucepan combine vinegar, water, and salt; heat to boiling, then reduce heat to simmer while you prepare the jars.

Wash beans thoroughly; drain and cut into lengths that fit pint jars, minus ¹/₂-inch head space. Wash 8 pint jars and keep them hot while you fill one jar at a time. Into each jar, place ¹/₂ teaspoon mustard seed, ¹/₂ teaspoon dill seed, and 1 clove garlic. Pack beans tightly into jar, taking care to line them up in neat vertical formation. Fit four hot peppers down between the beans, spacing them evenly.

Pour boiling liquid over beans, filling to ¹/₂ inch from top of jar. Seal

and process in boiling water for 5 minutes (see p. 165 for canning instructions).
Makes 7 to 8 pints.

⊰ Kung Pao Chicken ⊱

The famous Szechuan dish from your favorite Chinese restaurant, ready for you to make at home.

1 tablespoon cornstarch
1 tablespoon sherry
1/2 teaspoon salt
1/8 teaspoon white pepper
1 1/2 pounds boneless chicken breasts, cut into bite-size pieces
4 tablespoons salad oil, divided
Cooking sauce (see below)
4 to 6 small dried whole hot red chilies
1/2 cup salted peanuts
1 teaspoon minced garlic
1 teaspoon grated fresh ginger
2 green onions (including green ends), cut into 1-inch lengths

In a medium bowl, combine cornstarch, sherry, salt, and pepper. Add chicken and stir to coat, then stir in 1 tablespoon of the oil and set aside for 15 minutes.

Meanwhile, prepare cooking sauce and set aside.

Heat 1 tablespoon of the oil in a wok or wide frying pan. Test heat by dropping in one drop of water; if it sizzles, pan is ready. Add chilies and cook until they just begin to turn dark; watch carefully, don't let them burn. Remove chilies and set aside.

Add remaining oil to wok and increase heat to high. When oil begins to smoke, add garlic and ginger. Stir once, then add chicken and marinade that clings to it. Stir 2 or 3 minutes, just until chicken is opaque. Add peanuts, chilies, and onions.

Stir cooking sauce and pour into wok; cook until sauce thickens, about 2 minutes.

Cooking Sauce
Combine 2 tablespoons soy sauce, 1 tablespoon white wine vinegar, 1 tablespoon dry sherry, 3 tablespoons chicken broth or water, 2 tablespoons cornstarch, and 2 tablespoons sugar.
Makes 4 servings.

Asian Hot-Sweet Chicken with Broccoli

¹/₄ cup packed brown sugar
3 tablespoons soy sauce
1 teaspoon ground ginger
1 teaspoon hot red pepper flakes (see note)
1 pound boneless, skinless chicken breast halves, cubed (about 3–4 breasts)
2 tablespoons peanut or vegetable oil, divided
1 pound broccoli, trimmed and cut into bite-size pieces
¹/₂ cup chicken broth, divided
1 tablespoon cornstarch
2 tablespoons sesame seeds, toasted

In nonmetal pan or zip-top bag, combine brown sugar, soy sauce, ginger and pepper. Add chicken, turn to coat all sides with marinade. Cover; marinate in refrigerator for 2 hours or overnight.

In large skillet or wok, stir-fry broccoli in 1 tablespoon hot oil over medium-high heat for 1 minute. Add ¹/₄ cup broth; cover and steam for 1 minute. Remove broccoli from skillet; reserve. In skillet, stir-fry chicken in 1 tablespoon hot oil until chicken is cooked, about 3 to 5 minutes. Add cooked broccoli. Combine cornstarch and remaining ¹/₄ cup broth; stir into chicken mixture. Stir-fry just until hot and sauce is thickened and glossy. Sprinkle with sesame seeds.

Makes 4 servings.

Note: This is medium-hot for most tastes. For milder heat level, use ¹/₄ to ¹/₂ teaspoon red pepper flakes.

—Spice Islands

For Other Recipes Featuring Chili Peppers, See:
Chili Cheese Cornbread Muffins, p. 76
East Indian Potatoes, p. 231
Garden Chicken Paprika, p. 249

Chili Powder

Available as: Ground spice blend

Chili peppers, as you have seen in the chapter that describes them, are available in a thousand different forms: whole fresh chilies, whole dried chilies, dried flakes, and dried powder (which is either cayenne or paprika, depending on the variety of pepper used).

The spice called "chili powder" is none of these. Chili powder is actually a blend of several spices. The usual ingredients and their approximate proportions are:

- Dried, ground chili pepper—85%
- Dried, ground cumin—10%
- Dried, ground oregano—4%
- Dried, powdered garlic—1%

Different brands of chili powder can taste slightly different from one another; they may contain different types of chilies or different proportions, or both. The differences are subtle, however; to use the name "chili powder," manufacturers are required to meet guidelines as to degree of hotness. The important thing to remember is that chili powder is not fiery hot, not like cayenne; and that the other seasonings give it a more rounded flavor than chilies alone.

The most familiar use of chili powder is as the key flavoring ingredient in the meat-bean dish we call chili con carne, or just plain chili. In many parts of the country, but especially the Southwest, people take their chili very seriously. Chili cooks have been known to guard their

What we call chili powder is an American invention. It was originally created by an Englishman living in Texas in the mid-1800s, who was trying to re-create the complex flavors of curries he had learned to enjoy while serving in the British army in India. Or so the story goes.

If the story is true, this gentleman was following in the culinary footsteps of other good cooks a few hundred years before him. The Aztecs, who had developed an advanced civilization long before Europeans ever set foot in Mexico, used spice blends based on the chili peppers that grew in the fields around them.

recipes with their lives—or to flaunt them proudly in competitions known as chili cookoffs. Most of these recipes call for additional spices, but chili powder is still the core of the flavor.

There are other uses, too, primarily in Mexican dishes such as tamales, enchiladas, and tacos.

Use Chili Powder in:
- Sauces for Mexican dishes: huevos rancheros, tamales, enchiladas, tacos, etc.
- Salad dressing (especially for taco salad)
- Beef and pork stews
- Scrambled eggs
- Cocktail sauce for seafood
- Steamed or baked vegetables, especially cauliflower, carrots, and corn
- Spanish rice
- Marinades for steak
- Shellfish (add to cooking water)
- Cream soups (tomato, pea, potato)
- And, of course, chili

⤐ Guacamole ⤏

Here's a way to make guacamole ahead of time—and prevent discoloration.

1 large ripe avocado
1/2 ripe tomato, peeled and finely chopped
1/2 green pepper, seeded and finely chopped
1 teaspoon onion salt
1/2 teaspoon chili powder
1/2 teaspoon salt
1/4 teaspoon black pepper
1/2 teaspoon olive oil
1 teaspoon lime juice
1/2 cup mayonnaise

Peel avocado and mash with a fork; you can leave lumps, if you like that texture, or blend to a smooth paste. Stir in chopped vegetables, spices, olive oil, and lime juice. Spread mayonnaise over top; cover the mixture completely, so that no air reaches it; this will keep it from darkening.

When ready to serve, blend in mayonnaise. Serve with corn chips.
Makes 2 cups.

⋅⋞ Sauce for Baked Squash ⋟⋅

Spoon this sauce into the hollow of a baked winter squash.

1/2 cup butter, melted
1/2 cup honey
3 tablespoons sweet chowchow or other pickle relish
1 tablespoon chili powder
1 clove garlic, crushed
1 teaspoon salt
1/8 teaspoon pepper
1/8 teaspoon nutmeg

Mix all ingredients; serve warm.
Makes 1 cup.

⋅⋞ Chili Rarebit ⋟⋅

1 tablespoon butter
1/2 pound American cheese, cut into small pieces
1/4 teaspoon salt
1 teaspoon chili powder
3/4 cup beer

Melt butter in a double boiler over hot water or in a crockpot. Add cheese, salt, and chili powder. Cook over low heat until cheese melts, stirring occasionally. When cheese is melted, add beer slowly; stir until smooth.
Serve on plain toast.
Makes 3 or 4 servings.

⋅⋞ Cincinnati Chili ⋟⋅

2 pounds ground beef
1 cup chopped onion
1/2 cup chopped celery
1 can (15 ounce) tomato sauce
1 can (6 ounce) tomato paste
4 cups water
1 tablespoon lemon juice

Spice Blend
  2 tablespoons chili powder
  1 1/2 teaspoons ground cinnamon
  1 teaspoon garlic powder
  1/2 teaspoon black pepper
  1/2 teaspoon ground allspice
  2 tablespoons sugar
  1/2 teaspoon salt
  2 bay leaves

Additions
  Cooked spaghetti
  1 can (15 ounce) kidney beans, drained and rinsed
  shredded cheddar cheese
  chopped onion

Cook ground beef, onion, and celery in Dutch oven or large pot over medium-high heat until beef is no longer pink, stirring often. Drain. Combine spice blend and stir into beef mixture. Add tomato sauce, tomato paste, water, and lemon juice. Bring to a boil, reduce heat and simmer 1 to 1 1/2 hours, stirring occasionally.

Remove bay leaves with slotted spoon; discard. Serve chili over spaghetti and beans; top with cheese and onion.

Makes 6–8 servings.

—McCormick/Schilling

⋖ Spicy Pot Roast ⋗

Long, slow cooking develops the flavors of the spicy sauce and makes the meat very tender. For a Southern-style barbecue sandwich, pull the meat into fine shreds and pile on buns.

  2 green peppers, chopped
  4 medium onions, chopped
  1 teaspoon salt
  1 teaspoon black pepper
  1 clove garlic
  2 bottles catsup (20 ounces each)
  1/2 cup sugar
  1 teaspoon chili powder
  1 teaspoon powdered ginger
  10 cloves

1 teaspoon dry mustard
1 teaspoon cinnamon
1 teaspoon allspice
2 bay leaves
2 tablespoons Worcestershire sauce
1 cup cider vinegar
1 6–7 pound chuck roast

Preheat oven to 250°.

Mix all ingredients into a sauce and pour over roast; cover. Bake 6 to 6½ hours. When done, the meat can be sliced or shredded with two forks and served as a sandwich, or with rice or noodles.

Serves 12 to 15.

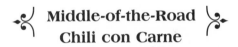

Middle-of-the-Road Chili con Carne

This beef-and-bean chili is flavorful but not fiery hot—sort of middle of the road.

1 pound ground beef
½ cup chopped onion
1 teaspoon minced garlic
1 teaspoon salt
3 tablespoons chili powder
1 8-ounce can tomato sauce
1 can (15 ounces) red kidney beans
2 tablespoons vinegar

Spray a large pan with cooking spray or use 1 teaspoon of olive oil to coat pan; crumble the beef into the pan and cook until it is no longer pink. Add onions and garlic and sauté till translucent. Drain excess fat from pan. Stir in remaining ingredients; mix well. Cover and simmer 45 minutes, stirring occasionally.

Serves 4 to 6.

❦ Peach Chutney ❧

A delicious, unusual condiment for baked ham, pork, or chicken; mix it with mayonnaise for out-of-this-world turkey sandwiches.

1 medium onion
1 small garlic clove
1 cup seedless raisins
1 cup crystallized ginger, chopped
5–6 pounds peaches
2 tablespoons mustard seed
2 tablespoons chili powder
1 teaspoon salt
1 quart vinegar
2¹/₄ cups brown sugar

Put onion, garlic, raisins, and ginger through food grinder using fine blade; or mince in food processor using steel blade. Peel peaches, dice and measure: You should have 3 quarts. Mix peaches with remaining ingredients. Add the raisin mixture and mix well. Simmer an hour, or until deep brown and rather thick. Pack into hot sterilized jars and seal. Process 10 minutes in boiling water bath. (See page 165 for complete canning instructions.)
   Yield: 4 to 6 pints.

For Other Recipes Featuring Chili Powder, See:
   Corn Pudding, p. 77
   Hot Texas Red Chili, p. 78
   Chili Cashews, p. 92
   Spicy Black Bean Dip, p. 147
   Ginger Beef Strips, p. 198

Cinnamon

Botanical name: **Cinnamomum zeylanicum; C. cassia**
Part used as spice: **Dried bark**
Available as: **Whole sticks, ground powder**

The spice we call cinnamon is taken from the inner bark of an evergreen tree that grows in tropical areas of the Orient.

Actually, there are several different trees, all close cousins to each other; the two main ones are *Cinnamomum zeylanicum* and *Cinnamomum cassia*. *C. zeylanicum* is native to the island of Sri Lanka (formerly known as Ceylon, hence the species name *zeylanicum*); the spice produced from its bark is light brown or tan in color, with a delicate cinnamony taste. This is what most of the world considers "true cinnamon."

C. cassia, which grows in southern China, Indonesia, and several countries in Southeast Asia, produces a darker, reddish brown spice with a stronger, more pungent flavor. Most of what is commercially available in American markets is cassia, or a cassia/cinnamon mixture, although in the United States the name "cinnamon" is used for everything.

In both cases, the way of harvesting the spice is the same. In commercial plantations, the tops of trees are lopped off when the trees are about eight feet tall; this forces many side branches to grow. When they are about three years old, these branches are large enough to harvest.

The branches are cut from the tree, workers make two vertical cuts down the entire length of the branch, and the bark is peeled off in two half-sections. One is slipped inside the other, and they are left to dry for a few days until the outer bark begins to separate from the inner bark, which is where the flavor resides. Then the outer bark is scraped off, and the sections of the inner bark are slipped back together and left to dry.

Cinnamon and Cold-War Politics

In addition to powdered and stick cinnamon, there is a third form: cassia buds, picked from the tree before the flowers open and dried for commercial use. They look a lot like cloves, and have a recognizable cinnamony taste. They work well where you would not want to use the powdered form, when making pickles, for instance.

However, you'll have a hard time finding them. Commercial cassia buds are mostly produced in China and, like many products from what we used to call Communist China, were for many years considered "enemy products" and not allowed into the United States. Even though trade with the People's Republic of China is no longer forbidden, an American market for cassia buds has never really developed.

As they dry, the pieces curl inward, producing what is called a "quill"; as a last step the quills are cut into three-inch lengths, the familiar short logs we call cinnamon sticks. Powdered cinnamon is simply these dried quills, broken into pieces and ground to a fine powder.

In the introduction to this book, the suggestion is made that you buy whole spices wherever possible and grind them as needed, since in whole form they retain their flavor longer. This is also true of cinnamon, but if powdered cinnamon is what you want you'll have to buy it in that form; there is no easy way to grind stick cinnamon down in your home kitchen.

History and Legends

Cinnamon is one of the oldest known spices in recorded history. In the Bible (Exodus 30), God instructed Moses to prepare a holy anointing oil containing two hundred fifty shekels of sweet cinnamon, five hundred shekels of cassia, along with myrrh, calamus, and olive oil. It is also mentioned in the description of markets in Ezekiel, and in Proverbs as a body perfume. Ointments made fragrant with cinnamon and cassia leaves were common in ancient Greece and Rome.

Even before biblical times, cinnamon was known and used in Asia, where it was often burned as incense in temple ceremonies. Cinnamon holds a special place in ancient Chinese religion. At the mouth of the Yellow River, according to religious belief, was a beautiful garden named Paradise and in this garden was the Tree of Life, the fruit from which would give everlasting life and happiness to any who ate it. The Tree of Life was a cassia tree.

In Indonesia, part of the ritual for weddings was a ceremonial drink

> **The Ancient Law of Supply and Demand**
> Pliny, a historian and naturalist in ancient Rome, once wrote, "There is a tale of cinnamon growing under the protection of a terrible kind of bats . . . invented by the natives to raise the price."

for the bride and groom made from wine in which were steeped two cassia buds that originally grew side by side on the same branch. This symbol of harmony and togetherness is still honored in modern Indonesia.

Nero, emperor of Rome in the first century A.D., burned a year's supply of cinnamon on his wife's funeral pyre. The spice was then, as for many centuries to come, worth more than gold, and this extravagant gesture was meant to signify the depth of his loss.

In all these ancient civilizations, cinnamon had to be imported, at great expense, from the land where it grows naturally: the island of Ceylon, just off the pointy tip of India. Later, when entrepreneurism and adventure combined to produce Europe's great Age of Discovery, cinnamon was the number-one goal of the explorers and their sponsors.

When the Europeans discovered and took over the Spice Islands, first the Portuguese, then the Dutch, and then the British controlled the cinnamon trade with an iron hand. Under Portuguese and Dutch rule, anyone caught stealing and privately selling even one quill of cinnamon was put to death.

Today, commercial plantations of cinnamon and cassia trees are found in China, India, Sumatra, Malaysia, Indonesia, Vietnam, and other areas of Southeast Asia; but the very finest "true cinnamon" still comes from the ancient land of Ceylon.

Medicinal and Other Uses

Leaves of the cinnamon and cassia trees, once used medicinally in Europe, are still common in Eastern medicine as a treatment for diarrhea. In modern pharmacology, the distilled essential oil of cinnamon is used in antidiarrhetic formulas and as a sweetener in cough syrups.

One of the natural ingredients of cinnamon and cassia is a type of phenol that slows down the growth of the bacteria that causes meat to spoil. So its use as a flavoring spice for meat dishes, especially in warm climates, is logical. Also logical, though somewhat less appetizing: It was used as embalming powder in ancient Egypt, more than three thousand years ago.

Crafts Using Cinnamon Sticks

Cinnamon sticks, because of their size and sturdiness, lend themselves to several kinds of craft projects where other spices just wouldn't work.

Project: Cinnamon Trivet

To protect your table from hot casserole dishes, you first put down this cinnamon-stick trivet. Then, when you place the hot dish on it, the heat warms the cinnamon sticks and soon the sweet fragrance is released.

Scientists tell us that most of what we think of as taste is actually smell; certainly our appreciation of good food is enhanced by its aroma. So using this trivet will actually make the food taste better, especially when the dish being served contains cinnamon.

Start with a circle of wood, approximately seven inches in diameter. If you want the finished trivet to have a painted or stained top, do that step now.

Using wood glue, fasten four short lengths of wood (such as molding strips or screen door lath) to the bottom, to serve as "feet." If you elect not to add the feet (and it is optional), finish the bottom in some way, so it won't scratch your tabletop. Either sand it well, or cover with a piece of felt.

On the top surface, glue cinnamon sticks in a radiating pattern, and add one perfect pod of star anise in the center.

You can also make a square version of this trivet. Cut a piece of wood 6 × 6 inches, lay the cinnamon sticks side by side to completely cover the wood, gluing them on as you align each.

Cinnamon trivet. Cut a 7-inch circle from 3/8-inch (or thicker) plywood. (Or purchase a small round wooden cutting board.) Paint, varnish, or stain one surface, if desired. Glue short strips of wood to the bottom (optional). Arrange cinnamon sticks in a sunburst pattern and attach with heatproof glue. Glue a star anise pod in the center.

Project: Potpourri Fixative

In another section of this book (see page 126) you will find general instructions on making sweet-smelling potpourri. You may be surprised to learn that the primary fragrance of most modern potpourri comes from essential oils, added to the mixture of dried flowers and other botanicals. These oils, distilled from aromatic plants of all kinds, are highly concentrated forms of the original fragrances.

Unfortunately, they tend to evaporate rather quickly, and so potpourri mixtures include some substance that acts like a blotter, to absorb the oil and release it slowly and gradually. As a group, these are called "fixatives." Common fixatives are chopped dried roots of certain plants, dried moss, gum resins, even ground-up corncobs. And a very special fixative for holiday potpourri is stick cinnamon.

The porous quality of the cinnamon sticks absorbs the oils easily, and of course the cinnamon itself adds a light aroma. To use cinnamon as fixative, place drops of the essential oil of your choice directly onto the cinnamon stick, keep in a tightly closed jar for a few days to allow the oil to be fully absorbed, and then add the sticks to your potpourri mixture. For a double-rich effect, drop cinnamon oil onto cinnamon sticks.

Because we so readily associate the aroma of cinnamon with holiday baking, these cinnamon sticks are especially appropriate for potpourris you make up for the Thanksgiving or Christmas season. Make a large batch, and use some for gifts.

⚜ Christmastime Potpourri ⚜

10 drops cinnamon oil
10 drops pine or balsam fir oil
4 cinnamon sticks
¼ cup whole cloves
10 pods of star anise (optional but pretty)
1 quart of mixed botanicals: small cones, dried seed heads, bay leaves,
  dried rosemary needles, etc.

Using an eyedropper, drop the oils directly onto the cinnamon sticks. Place cinnamon sticks, cloves, and star anise into a lidded jar, close tightly, and store in a dark cupboard for 2 days. Using a large bowl and an easy touch, stir your botanicals together with the spices and put the whole batch into a large container with a lid. Keep in a cupboard for at least 3 weeks. During this time, the oils that are trapped in the cinnamon will slowly release and will be absorbed by the potpourri mixture. After 3 or 4 weeks of this "curing," the potpourri is ready. Place some in your prettiest glass bowl and make up gift packages with the rest.

Simmering Potpourri

Put about two cups of water in a small saucepan on the stovetop, and add several cinnamon sticks plus your choice of these spices and fragrant things: orange peel, lemon peel, whole cloves, whole nutmeg (cracked), star anise, whole allspice, gingerroot. Bring to a simmer. Refill water as needed.

This will make your whole house smell wonderful; it's especially nice during the winter holidays.

Project: Christmas Ornaments

Make a stiff dough by combining 1 cup of ground cinnamon with 3/4 cup smooth applesauce; add more applesauce if needed. Roll out dough as if you were making cookies and cut into holiday shapes with cookie cutters. Use skewer or icepick to make a hole near the top. Lay ornaments on a cake rack, and set aside to dry for 2 to 3 days. Tie on a pretty ribbon, and hang in your kitchen or on the Christmas tree; or add to a package as a fragrant decoration.

Project: Other Cinnamon Gifts

- Make up bags of potpourri following the recipe on page 107. Package in closable plastic bags (so the fragrance doesn't dissipate) and then wrap as usual.
- To make your potpourri gift even more special, search antique stores, thrift stores, and yard sales for pretty containers: small baskets, old sugar dishes, small glass pitchers, inexpensive brass bowls. Package the potpourri separately in airtight bags, then put the bag inside the container, and wrap it all together.
- Experiment with simmering potpourri (above) until you get a blend you think is fabulous, then make up a large batch of it. Put 1 cupful in closable plastic bags, then wrap in pretty paper or gingham squares. Add a tag explaining how to use it.
- Add cinnamon sticks as a special "garnish" to your gift by tying several sticks into the final bow (see page 294). This is especially pretty with solid-color paper, in green, red, or gold.

Cooking with Cinnamon

Cinnamon is one of our most popular "sweet" spices, familiar in many kinds of pies, cakes, sweet rolls, and fruit concoctions. In Central and South America and the Middle East cinnamon is often added to meat dishes; it doesn't make them taste sweet, just richer. And cinnamon sticks are a nice addition to many hot drinks.

Quick Cinnamon Tips

- *Keep a shaker handy.* Fill a large kitchen screwtop shaker with a cinnamon-sugar mixture, and keep it in your handiest spot, ready to add whenever inspiration hits you. Start with 1 cup sugar and 1 tablespoon powdered cinnamon; taste, and add more cinnamon if you like it spicier.
- *Cinnamon shortcake biscuits.* Use a baking mix and follow the instructions on the package, using the amount that will make about 10 biscuits. Add about 2 tablespoons of sugar and 1/2 teaspoon cinnamon to the dry ingredients, then just before baking dust the tops with a cinnamon-sugar mixture.
- *Sunday morning French toast.* Whisk in a pinch or two of cinnamon to the egg-milk mixture for French toast. To make the toast extra special, use raisin bread.
- *Apple pie chimneys.* When you make a two-crust pie, make slits in the top crust as usual, then stand a cinnamon stick upright in each one. These work like chimneys, venting the steam away, and at the same time adding a cinnamon taste.

Cinnamon-flavored Beverages

Cinnamon adds a wonderful undertone to many hot beverages, but since it doesn't always dissolve thoroughly by the time you'd want to drink your drink, powdered cinnamon is not the best choice. Stick cinnamon works much better; use it as a stir stick in hot drinks and it will impart a hint of flavor without any chalky residue.

Add a Stick of Cinnamon to:
- Hot chocolate (use it to stir in the melting marshmallows)
- Hot coffee and espresso drinks
- Hot apple cider
- Mulled wine
- Hot tea, especially herbal blends

Cinnamon and Comfort

All of us have special foods from childhood that we associate with tender loving care from parents, when we were sick, sad, or otherwise out of sorts. Even as adults, those special treats can still help us cope with a difficult world. For many (me included) that treat is cinnamon toast.

Part of the deal with these comfort foods is they have to be *just exactly* like what you remember from childhood. Everyone has a certain way of making cinnamon toast, but here is the way my mama used to make it.

Turn the broiler unit on in the oven. Take a piece of bread and butter it generously. Sprinkle on sugar and cinnamon—first one, then the other. Slide the whole thing under the broiler until the bread is toasted. The sugar and cinnamon caramelize and the top gets a sweet crunchy crust.

You can, of course, make ordinary toast in the toaster and then sprinkle on sugar and cinnamon, but believe me it's not the same.

◦⟨ Fried Apple Rings ⟩◦

Serve with sausage and pancakes for breakfast; with pork chops or ham for dinner.

1/2 cup sugar
1 teaspoon cinnamon
2 tablespoons butter
4 cooking apples

Mix sugar and cinnamon in small bowl (or use your cinnamon shaker, if you have one). Melt butter in saucepan. Core apples but do not peel; slice fairly thickly, 1/2 inch or more. When butter is foaming, add apple rings and cook on one side till brown. Turn over, sprinkle cinnamon mixture on the top, and cook till bottom is also brown, adding more butter if needed. Serve hot.
Makes 6 servings.

◦⟨ One-Rise Cinnamon Rolls ⟩◦

Topping
1 cup heavy whipping cream (do not substitute)
1 cup brown sugar

Filling

1/2 cup sugar
2 teaspoons cinnamon
1/2 cup butter, softened

Rolls

3 to 31/2 cups flour, divided
1 package yeast
1/4 cup sugar
1 teaspoon salt
1 cup hot tap water
2 tablespoons butter, softened
1 egg

Mix cream and brown sugar and pour into an ungreased 9 × 13 inch pan. Mix ingredients for filling and set aside.

In a large bowl blend 11/2 cup flour and next six ingredients. Beat three minutes with electric mixer at medium speed. Stir in remaining 11/2 to 2 cups flour. Knead on floured surface for one minute.

Press or roll dough into a 15 × 7 inch rectangle. Spread filling over dough. Starting at long side, roll tightly; seal edge. Slice crosswise into 16 rolls. Place cut side down on top of cream mixture. Cover and let rise until doubled in bulk, 35 to 45 minutes. Bake at 400° for 20 to 25 minutes. Cool 10 to 15 minutes before turning out on tray.

Makes 16 rolls.

Use extra-long sticks of cinnamon as stir sticks in hot cider, hot chocolate, even coffee.

⚮ Jasmine Tea Bread ⚮

Jasmine tea, from the Orient, is lightly scented with the fragrance of flowers; there is just a hint of floral flavor in this sweet bread, perfect for teatime. These baked loaves freeze well.

1/2 cup butter or margarine
2 cups sugar
2 eggs
1/2 teaspoon vanilla extract
grated rind of two oranges
grated rind of one lemon
grated rind of one lime
6 cups flour
2 teaspoons baking powder
2 teaspoons baking soda
1 teaspoon salt
1/2 teaspoon cinnamon
1/4 teaspoon mace
1 1/2 cups orange juice
1 cup brewed jasmine tea
1 cup chopped nuts

Preheat oven to 350°. Butter the baking pans, either four 7 × 3 × 2 loaf pans or two 9 × 5 × 3 pans.

In a large mixing bowl beat the butter until it is fluffy, then beat in the sugar; cream the two together until very light. Add eggs one at a time, beating after each addition. Mix in vanilla and fruit rinds.

Into a separate bowl, sift together the flour, baking powder, baking soda, salt, cinnamon, and mace. In another bowl or pitcher, combine the orange juice and the tea.

Add the flour mixture to the butter mixture alternately with the tea mixture, beating well after each addition. Fold in the nuts and mix well. Turn into buttered baking pans and bake until skewer comes out clean, about one hour for the larger pans and 40 minutes for the smaller ones. Cool loaves in the pans for 10 minutes, then turn out on wire racks.

Makes 4 small loaves or 2 medium loaves.

❧ Super Carrot-Raisin Salad ❧

This makes enough for a large gathering, but any leftovers will keep in the refrigerator for up to a week.

7 or 8 large carrots
1 cup raisins
1¼ cups mayonnaise
3 tablespoons honey
3 teaspoons vinegar
1 teaspoon cinnamon

Peel or scrape carrots and grate coarsely. Add raisins. Mix mayonnaise, honey, and vinegar. Sprinkle cinnamon over the dressing and fold it in thoroughly. Toss carrots with dressing. Marinate in refrigerator at least 2 hours before serving, 4 hours if possible.

Variation: For a lower-calorie version, substitute plain yogurt for 1 cup of the mayonnaise. Blend the yogurt with ¼ cup mayonnaise, then mix in the honey and vinegar.
Makes about 2 quarts.

❧ Cinnamon Glazed Carrots ❧

2 tablespoons butter
1½ pounds carrots, trimmed, scrubbed and left whole if small,
    quartered if mature
½ teaspoon salt
2 teaspoons sugar
water
½ teaspoon ground cinnamon

In a saucepan, melt the butter. Then add carrots, salt, and sugar, and enough water to barely cover the carrots. Cover and cook just until the carrots are tender, 5 to 10 minutes. (Time will vary depending on age and size of carrots.) Remove the lid. Bring to a boil and cook until the water has completely evaporated, leaving the carrots coated with a sticky, buttery glaze. Sprinkle with the cinnamon, mix, and serve immediately.
Serves 4 to 6.

—Renée Shepherd

Spiced Onions and Beets

Serve this colorful relish with meat or cheese entrees. It will keep for weeks in the refrigerator, and the flavor improves as it ages.

2 cups sliced mild onions such as Walla Walla or Vidalia (2 medium-large onions)
2 cups sliced beets, fresh or canned (15-ounce can)
1/2 cup white vinegar
3/4 cup water or beet juice
1 cinnamon stick
4 cloves
1/4 cup sugar
1/2 teaspoon salt
pepper to taste
dash of garlic salt

If using fresh beets, cook, peel, and slice. Place cinnamon and cloves into cheesecloth bag or infuser. Combine all ingredients in saucepan and bring to boil. Simmer gently for 10 minutes. Remove spice bag. Serve cold or hot.

Makes 6–8 servings.

Apple Baked Beans

2 cans of baked beans (2 pounds total)
2 cups diced apples
1 cup pecan pieces
1/2 cup brown sugar
1/4 cup maple syrup
1/4 cup catsup
1/4 cup butter
1 teaspoon cinnamon
1/8 teaspoon nutmeg

Preheat oven to 375°.

Spread nuts in an ungreased pie pan and toast in oven for 5 minutes. Cool and chop coarsely. In a large mixing bowl, combine all ingredients. Mix well. Pour into casserole dish and bake 1 hour.

Makes 8 servings.

❧ Chicken in Orange Juice ❧

Serve with lots of plain rice, to soak up the delicious sauce.

¹/₂ cup flour
1 tablespoon salt
¹/₂ teaspoon lemon pepper
1¹/₂–2 pounds chicken, cut in pieces
¹/₄ cup salad oil
6-ounce can frozen orange juice concentrate
1 8¹/₂ ounce can crushed pineapple
³/₄ cup dry sherry or any white wine
¹/₂ cup raisins, preferably golden
¹/₂ cup sliced almonds
¹/₄ teaspoon ground cinnamon
¹/₈ teaspoon ground cloves
2 tablespoons sugar, optional

Preheat oven to 325°.

Mix flour, salt, and lemon pepper, and dredge chicken pieces in mixture. Brown chicken pieces in hot oil, then arrange them in a shallow baking dish. Mix together the juice, pineapple, sherry, raisins, almonds, cinnamon, and cloves. Taste sauce and add sugar if desired. Pour the mixture over the chicken pieces.

Bake chicken for 30 minutes, basting several times. Increase temperature to 350° and bake 15 minutes longer; check frequently to avoid over-browning.

Serves 4 to 6.

❧ Chocolate Cinnamon Biscotti ❧

1¹/₄ cups flour
³/₄ cup plus 1 teaspoon sugar, divided
¹/₄ cup cocoa
1 tablespoon ground cinnamon
³/₄ teaspoon baking powder
¹/₄ teaspoon ground nutmeg
¹/₈ teaspoon salt
¹/₄ cup butter or margarine, softened
3 egg whites, divided
¹/₂ teaspoon almond extract
¹/₄ cup sliced almonds, toasted
¹/₄ cup dried cranberries

Preheat oven to 350°. Grease a large baking sheet; set aside.

In a large mixing bowl combine flour, 3/4 cup sugar, cocoa, cinnamon, baking powder, nutmeg, and salt. Using an electric mixer on medium speed, beat in butter until mixture resembles coarse crumbs. Add 2 egg whites and almond extract; beat until a soft dough forms, about 1 minute. Stir in almonds and cranberries.

On a lightly floured board shape dough into a 15 × 2-inch log; place on prepared baking sheet. In a small bowl lightly beat remaining egg white; brush over log; sprinkle with remaining 1 teaspoon sugar. Bake until log is firm but slightly pliable, 30 to 35 minutes.

Using two spatulas, remove to a wire rack; set baking sheet aside. Cool until log can be handled, about 10 minutes. Reduce oven temperature to 325°. Transfer log to a cutting board; using a serrated knife cut into 1/2-inch thick diagonal slices. Place cut-side down on baking sheet; bake until crisp, about 15 minutes.

Remove from baking sheet to wire rack. Cool completely before storing in a tightly covered container.

Makes 1 1/2 dozen.

—American Spice Trade Association

Poached Pears

2 cinnamon sticks, broken in half
1/2 cup sugar
1 cup water
1 cup red wine
4 ripe pears

Make a poaching liquid by simmering the cinnamon and sugar together with the water and wine until the sugar is dissolved.

To prepare pears, peel all around but leave the stem in place. Cut a thin slice from the bottom to make a flat base. Stand the pears in a saucepan, pour in the simmering liquid, and cover; cook until pears are just tender, about 10 minutes. Remove pears, increase heat to medium, and cook until liquid is reduced by half. To serve, place one pear upright in shallow dessert dish, pour sauce over. Serve warm or at room temperature.

Serves 4.

Shortcut: Use canned pear halves. Drain, saving liquid. Cook the liquid with 2 cinnamon sticks until reduced to half. Add an equal amount of red wine. Add pears to liquid, heat through.

❧ Cinnamon Clouds ☙

2 egg whites
¹/₈ teaspoon salt
¹/₂ teaspoon ground cinnamon
¹/₂ cup firmly packed light brown sugar
¹/₄ cup coarsely chopped pecans
¹/₄ cup mini semisweet chocolate chips

Preheat oven to 275°. Line 1 large or 2 small baking sheets with aluminum foil; set aside.

In the large bowl of an electric mixer place egg whites and salt. Beat until soft peaks form, about 2 minutes. Add cinnamon; gradually add brown sugar; beat on high speed until stiff peaks form, about 5 minutes. Fold in pecans and chocolate chips.

With heaping teaspoonfuls, form mounds about 1¹/₄ inches wide, about 1 inch apart on baking sheet. Bake until dry on the outside but moist in the center, about 40 minutes. (If using 2 baking sheets, place on 2 different oven racks; switch sheets halfway through baking.)

Turn off oven; let pan remain in oven until cookies are dry, about 1 hour. Remove cookies, peel off any foil. Store in a tightly covered container for up to 3 weeks (or freeze, in damp or humid climates).

Makes 2³/₄ dozen.

—American Spice Trade Association

❧ Spiced Iced Tea ☙

Make a strong batch of your favorite tea. Add in stick cinnamon (broken in pieces) and whole cloves while it is steeping; strain before adding to pitcher with ice. Other tasty additions: lemon peel, orange peel, bits of candied ginger. Strain; serve over ice with a mint leaf for garnish.

Another way to add extra flavor: Save the liquid drained from canned fruit, add to tea.

Hot Buttered Rum

¹/₄ cup rum
1 stick cinnamon
1 teaspoon sugar
1 teaspoon butter

Place ingredients in large mug, fill with boiling water. Stir with cinnamon stick until butter and sugar are melted. For fancy occasions, drench a sugar cube in rum, light it with a match in the bowl of a spoon, and gently place it in the mug.

Iced Spiced Coffee

6 cinnamon sticks
8 cloves
1 tablespoon grated orange peel
1 pot extra-strong coffee or espresso
half-and-half (optional)
brown sugar (optional)

Brew enough coffee for 6 servings. While it is still very hot, transfer coffee to saucepan and add cinnamon, cloves, and orange peel; cover and let steep for 1 hour. Strain out and discard spices and peel. Chill. To serve, fill glasses with cracked ice, pour in coffee, top off with half-and-half, and sprinkle brown sugar on top.
Yield: 6 portions.

Instant Russian Tea Mix

My mother says she has made tons of this in her lifetime; my brother swears it got him through college.

¹/₂ cup instant tea powder, unsweetened
2 cups powdered orange drink (such as Tang)
1¹/₃ cups sugar
1 teaspoon cinnamon
¹/₂ teaspoon ground cloves
1 teaspoon grated lemon rind

Mix well; store in tightly covered container. For individual cup of tea, add 2 teaspoons mix to 1 cup of boiling water.

❦ Honey Spice Dressing ❧

This is delicious on fruit salads.

¹/₂ cup bottled French dressing
1 tablespoon honey
¹/₂ teaspoon cinnamon
¹/₄ teaspoon ground cloves
¹/₈ teaspoon powdered ginger

Combine all ingredients and mix well. Store in covered container in refrigerator.
Makes about ¹/₂ cup.

For Other Recipes Featuring Cinnamon, See:

Swedish Fruit Soup, p. 38
Beet Surprise Salad, p. 39
Island Chicken Salad with Citrus Rum Dressing, p. 40
Baked Spiced Pork Chops, p. 42
Mulled Cider, p. 43
Indian Rice, p. 70
Cardamom Butter Cookies, p. 72
Cincinnati Chili, p. 99
Spicy Pot Roast, p. 100
Pickled Peaches, p. 131
Spicy Pumpkin Pie, p. 133
Bishop, p. 134
Mincemeat Refrigerator Cookies, p. 142
Sloppy Josés, p. 150
Walnut Pastries, p. 178
Malaysian Chicken and Sweet Potato Kurma, p. 196
Gingerbread, p. 198
Ginger Peach Freeze, p. 199
Gingerbread Gypsies, p. 200
Ginger Tea, p. 201
Spicy Carrot Pickles, p. 215
Apple Cider Squash, p. 217
Deep Dish Apple Pie, p. 244
Pfeffernusse, p. 262
Malaysian Spiced Rice, p. 299
Spiced Chicken Livers, p. 300
Spicy Banana Nut Bread, p. 317
Gingered Peach Snap, p. 318
Cinnamon-Vanilla Milk Shake, p. 319

Cloves

Botanical name: Syzygium aromaticum (also known as Eugenia caryophyllata)

Part used as spice: Dried flower buds

Available as: Whole or ground cloves

Cloves are one of what the spice world calls "The Big Four"—along with cinnamon, nutmeg, and pepper—and share with them the amazing romantic, bloody, greedy, tragic, adventurous history that swirls around all the spices from the Orient. More on that history in a moment; first, let's meet the spice.

Cloves come from a beautiful evergreen tree that is native to certain islands of the East Indies, the fabled Spice Islands. It is said that the trees are so fragrant that you can smell them from the sea long before you are in sight of the island where they grow. All parts of the tree have the characteristic clove aroma, but it is the flower buds, before they open, that have the most.

Timing is critical. When the flower buds first form, they are pale green and not especially aromatic. As they move toward maturity, they turn from green to yellow, then to pink, and finally bright red just before they open up into small red flowers. By the time they flower, it's too late for the spice crop; it's even too late when they are still in bud form but bright red.

The time to pick is just when the buds turn red at the base, and so in areas where the trees are grown commercially, plantation supervisors keep a sharp eye on the buds. Temporary workers are brought in to harvest the buds, in the time-honored way. Women and girls pick the flower clusters from the lower branches, men and older boys use ladders made of bamboo to reach the upper limbs.

On the ground, workers separate the buds from the stems by brushing the flower clusters against the palm of their hand. They must get the amount of pressure just right; too much, and the top knob of the bud breaks away from its base; too little, and nothing happens, so the motion has to be repeated—a costly mistake for people paid by the pound.

The buds are spread out in the sun to dry, where they eventually turn very dark brown and shrink to one third their original size. And that's a clove.

The name comes from its shape, which resembles a small nail or tack: The French *clou* and the Spanish *clavo* both mean "nail," and we can see the derivation of "clove" in both words.

History and Legend

Like the other Oriental spices, cloves have a rich tradition throughout Asia. From Chinese literature dated the third century B.C. we learn that visitors who were granted an interview with the emperor were required to take a clove from a dish held by a servant and chew it before reaching the royal room, so that their breath would not offend the emperor. The Chinese name for cloves means "chicken-tongue spice," perhaps because chewing a whole clove this way would numb the tongue slightly.

As a caravan import, cloves were well known to the Romans; they were listed on the customs records at the port of Alexandria, among the spices brought in from India. In the first century A.D. the Roman naturalist Pliny described them in his writing, but said they were only good for fragrance. Three hundred years later, they were well known in Europe as a culinary spice, and by the eighth century, they were an important commodity in European commerce.

Matters continued in this way—Arabians bringing spices to Mediterranean ports, for trade with European merchants—for some time. Eventually, rulers of European nations, increasingly determined to take control of this market away from the Arab traders, sent explorers in search of a sea route to the Spice Islands.

Under the sponsorship of Portugal's King Emmanuel, Ferdinand Magellan, perhaps the greatest navigator of all time, sailed from Lisbon in 1505, and discovered a route around Cape Horn at the tip of South America. Eventually he found his way to the Spice Islands, and claimed them for his king. The Portuguese controlled the Spice Islands trade throughout the 1500s, until they were defeated and expelled in 1605 by the Dutch.

What were they fighting over? Cloves.

One of the Spice Islands was the small island of Amboina, thirty miles long and fifteen miles wide. Scientists believe that this is the first natural habitat of the clove tree, and that it quickly spread to other nearby islands. Certainly by the time the Europeans arrived, this valuable commodity was growing wild throughout the Spice Islands.

The Dutch, astute businessmen, decided to manipulate the world price of cloves by controlling the supply. They designated only two islands—Amboina and nearby Ternate—for clove production. The island of Amboina was divided into four thousand lots, each of which was decreed to be planted with one hundred twenty-five trees. Any clove trees growing anywhere else were to be dug up and burned; it was strictly forbidden to plant any new trees except on the government plantations.

The Dutch accomplished this tight monopoly through a combination of bribes and brutality: To secure their cooperation, kings on the islands where the trees were destroyed were paid tributes in cash; any islanders who planted a tree, or tried to sell cloves on their own, were executed.

It is a sad story of the colonialist mentality, fueled by greed, crushing the local culture. The residents of these islands considered the clove trees magical. By long tradition, they planted a clove tree each time a child was born; the tree was the child's special guardian. If the tree grew straight and strong, so would the child. If something happened to the tree, the child was in grave danger. Imagine their heartbreak when the Dutch ordered the trees destroyed.

Ironically, destroying the trees also changed the climate of the islands, for the worse. Dutch soldiers stationed there became ill so frequently that they were rotated out after only six months. Since the Dutch records of those times are one-sided, we do not know how the native people fared; it gives some comfort to imagine that they were less affected by the change than the Europeans.

The Dutch regularly checked on the islands where the trees had been destroyed, to be sure no random seedlings had sprouted, not even from a bird dropping. Then, to solidify their position, the Dutch engineered a rebellion of natives that enabled them to retaliate with great force; thousands of islanders were killed in the fighting. All told, throughout the European struggles for control of the Spice Islands, an estimated sixty thousand native people were slaughtered in the name of trade.

But history has a way of evening the score. After nearly one hundred and fifty years of harsh measures enacted to keep an iron grip on the clove industry, the Dutch were blindsided by a French missionary-turned-adventurer with a most auspicious name: Pierre Poivre (Peter Pepper).

Somehow he managed to steal a few clove seedlings and took them to a French-held island off the east coast of Africa, Isle de France (now called Mauritius), where he was scheduled to be installed as governor and where the climate and mountainous terrain offered the perfect conditions for cloves. When those seedlings survived, he decided to go for broke. French sailors on two small, fast ships from Isle de France slipped into a harbor at one of the smaller Spice Islands, persuaded a local official to sell sixty small trees, and managed to get away before Dutch harbor police could catch them.

Imagine Pierre's pride at being able, in 1775, to present France's King Louis XVI with the first cloves grown in French territory. From this one plantation, clove trees were shipped to other French islands, such as Bourbon (now called Reunion), near Madagascar, and Martinique in the Caribbean.

Over the next few centuries, the islands in the Indian Ocean east of Africa gradually became the leading producers of cloves. Zanzibar and Pemba, two islands just off the coast of what is now Tanzania, and later the larger island of Madagascar were intensively planted with clove trees, which thrived in this ideal climate. In Zanzibar as recently as 1972, there was still a law on the books calling for the death penalty for smuggling cloves.

Today most cloves sold in the United States come from either Madagascar or Brazil. Zanzibar cloves no longer dominate the market, as they once did, and today much of what they produce goes to Indonesia. The islands of Indonesia, the original Spice Islands, also have large plantations of clove trees, but the Indonesians consume all that they produce, plus some imports, primarily in the form of clove cigarettes.

Medicinal and Other Uses

The main chemical in cloves—eugenol—has several properties:

- It is a mild local anesthetic.
- It is a rubefacient (causes the blood vessels near the skin to dilate and bring more blood to the surface, thus making you feel warm).
- It is a carminative (breaks up and helps get rid of intestinal gas).

No wonder physicians through the ages have found cloves very useful. They have been prescribed for all manner of illnesses: fevers, paralysis, neuralgia, rheumatism, dyspepsia, and assorted problems of the brain, stomach, kidney, and spleen.

Probably the best-known medicinal use of cloves is in the dentist's chair. Because oil of cloves is antiseptic as well as a local anesthetic, dentists for centuries have used it to relieve the pain of toothache and to prepare the patient's mouth for dental work.

In addition to these purely medicinal applications, cloves are surrounded by a wealth of superstition and folklore.

- Women in the East Indies once distilled an alcoholic beverage from the immature buds, and drank it to heal a broken heart.
- In ancient times, Greeks, Romans, and Persians included it in love potions; the shape of a clove clearly suggested special powers for men.

- In Indonesia, cloves were woven into special necklaces for children, to protect them from illness and any temptation to mischief.
- Some adults stuffed their nostrils with cloves, so that evil spirits could not get into their brain via that route.
- In Germany in the sixteenth century, a prominent physician suggested that people with cold feet should sprinkle ground cloves on top of their head, which would warm their whole body. Actually, there may be something to this: We know that cloves have the effect of bringing blood to the surface of the skin, creating a warming sensation.
- The taste of cloves is often described as "hot," and the spice itself is given similar qualities, as we see in two old superstitions: that the trees are so hot nothing will grow under them; and that a jug of water, put in a cupboard where cloves are stored, will evaporate in two days.

Cloves are used in other ways, too.

- Clove cigarettes, made of two parts tobacco to one part crushed cloves, are very popular in Indonesia. Nearly forty billion cigarettes are manufactured a year, using almost half of the world's annual supply of cloves.
- Oil of cloves adds a sweet fragrance to many perfumes, lotions, and other cosmetics; it is also added to medicines, mouthwash, and toothpaste, both as a flavoring agent and for its antiseptic action. Dentists still use it to relieve the pain of toothache, as they did so long ago.
- Eugenol, the active ingredient in oil of cloves, is also found in cinnamon and allspice. When isolated out, it has been used to make artificial vanilla; this use has declined in recent years, however, for a cheaper substitute has been found.

Crafts and Household Items

Whole cloves are used to make two very popular craft items: potpourri mixtures and pomanders. Both are simple, although one of them (the potpourri) takes time and some ingredients you might not ordinarily have on hand.

Project: Making a Pomander
I'm willing to bet that at some point in your childhood you made one of these as a class project, perhaps for Christmas or Mother's Day. But that doesn't mean that it's only for children to do. In fact, pomanders have a long history in medicine and hygiene.

During the height of the great plagues in Europe, people tried to avoid going outside and exposing themselves to this highly infectious disease. When they had no choice but to venture out, they wore around their neck a carved metal ball that was stuffed with herbs and spices believed to keep the plague away; as they walked along, they would bring the ball to their nose and inhale through the carved openings. (They didn't know it, but they were partly right; many herbs have antiseptic properties.) This ball, about the size of an apple, was called a *pomme d'ambre,* meaning "apple of ambergris" (one of the ingredients), and that is the origin of the modern word "pomander."

Even after the worst of the plague terror had abated, household managers continued to make pomanders and hang them where the family's clothes and linens were stored, as a convenient and attractive way to keep out damaging insects.

Today we make pomanders for sweet-smelling holiday decorations and sometimes for closet deodorizers. But we should never forget that time in history when our ancestors in their terror tried everything they could think of to avoid the devastating infection they called the Black Death.

The simplest form of pomander involves nothing more than an orange (or a lemon, but oranges are traditional) and some whole cloves. Oranges with thin skin work best, if you can find them, but this is not critical. In any case you'll find it much, much easier to insert the cloves if you predrill the holes with a nail, an icepick, a knitting needle, or something similar. Then stick one clove in each hole, and you're done. In a few weeks, the orange peel will dry and shrink. The flesh of the orange inside dries also, but because the cloves act as a preservative, they don't rot—not usually, anyway. Some people report keeping their pomanders for years.

To increase their longevity, you can take one extra step: Just after you have inserted all the cloves, roll the orange in a bowl of powdered cinnamon. This acts as a fixative and additional preservative, and provides further insurance that your orange will not rot. (If you doubt cinnamon's ability as a preservative, check the chapter on cinnamon and read how the Egyptians used it.) If you do other floral crafts that call for powdered fixatives such as orris root, and have some on hand, you can use these instead.

A basket or clear glass bowl full of clove-studded oranges is a very pretty table decoration at Christmastime, and makes the whole house smell wonderful. If you want to go one step further and hang the pomanders, you'll find this much easier to do if you plan ahead. The drawings on pages 126 and 127 show you how.

Before you do anything else, put two pieces of masking tape on the orange, one crossways and one lengthwise. This will leave a clean "track" for ribbon at the end.

Then make your holes for the cloves. Use a lot, particularly if you

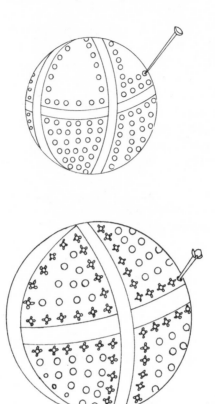

Orange pomander. If you wish to hang the finished pomander, the first step is to place two intersecting pieces of masking tape around the orange; this keeps spaces clear for ribbon. Then use a nail or a skewer to make small holes in the orange, and insert a clove in each hole.

hope to keep this pomander for a long time. But remember that the orange will shrink quite a bit overall, so leave some room between the clove heads. Your best bet for long-lasting pomanders: Completely cover the surface of the orange (except for the ribbon tracks) in a checkerboard way. Stagger empty spaces the size of a clove head between the cloves. When it has shrunk as much as it is going to, this orange will be fully covered with cloves very tight up against one another.

After all the cloves are in place, strip off the tape and tie a pretty ribbon both ways around; where they meet, make a loop and add a longer piece of ribbon so you can hang the pomander.

Project: Making Potpourri

You can buy the wonderful fragrant mixtures of flower petals, herbs, and spices known as potpourri in many gift shops, or you can make

When all the cloves are in place, remove the masking tape and tie a pretty ribbon in the two tracks. Make a loop on top, with long ends for a hanger.

your own. It is not a complicated process, but it does take time. Also, for your first project you will need some ingredients you probably do not have on hand, so you will need to plan ahead.

Potpourri has four categories of ingredients:

1. *The botanicals:* The dried flower petals, whole flowers, herb leaves, seed pods, etc.—all the parts of plants that were once alive. Collect and dry your own, or purchase from craft shops or floral craft supply houses (see Appendix).
2. *The oils:* Most of the time, your botanicals will not retain all the fragrance that you would want, and so fragrance is added, in the form of essential oils or fragrance oils. Available at craft shops, gift shops, some natural food stores, and by mail order (see Appendix), these oils come in an astonishing array of fragrances.
3. *The fixative:* Over time, these fragrance oils evaporate; to slow down that process, they are first combined with substances that absorb them and "fix" them in place for gradual release. Several substances act as fixatives: orris root, oak moss, gum benzoin, and others; they are available from the same sources as the oils.
4. *The spices:* Here is where we come in: To the mixture of botanicals, which are primarily for their beauty, potpourri makers add spices, for the depth they add to the fragrance. Whole spices work best.

I'm going to give you very abbreviated instructions for making potpourri, and just one recipe; if you get hooked on making this lovely product, and it's easy to do, there are a number of wonderful books in your local library or your favorite bookstore that can give you more information.

Here are the steps.

1. First, begin collecting (or ordering) the botanicals, and spread them out in a warm, dry spot to dry. (If you order or purchase botanicals, they will already be dry.)
2. In a container with a tight lid, mix the fixative and the whole spices with the required amount of oils. Leave it for a few days, to blend.
3. In a large bowl, very gently fold the fixative/spice mixture together with the botanicals.
4. Store the mixture in a tightly closed container for several weeks; during this time the fragrance is absorbed by all the botanicals.
5. Display in pretty bowls, lined baskets, pitchers, whatever looks right to you. Or, to make the fragrance last, keep your mixture in a covered jar and remove the lid when you have company.

Autumn Meadow Potpourri

2 cups dried flowers in the yellow/orange range: calendula, santolina, zinnia, strawflowers, etc.
1 cup dried herbs: rosemary, marjoram, basil, or a combination
1 handful attractive seed heads, such as love-in-a-mist or dried hops
1 tablespoon whole cloves
1 tablespoon whole allspice
2 tablespoons orris root
3 drops bergamot oil
2 drops spearmint oil

Mix spices, orris root, and oils; store in covered jar for 1 week. Carefully fold into the botanicals; store in tightly closed container for 3 weeks, occasionally stirring gently.

Potpourri. A colorful and fragrant mixture of spices and dried flowers adds visual beauty and scent to indoor spaces. Stored in a clear glass jar with a removable top, it will keep its fragrance for a long time.

Cooking with Cloves

Take a whole ham, use a knife to score a grid of diamond shapes, then insert a whole clove in the center of each diamond, and there you have it: The main course for Easter dinner. You've seen it a million times. For some people, it may be the first and only use of whole cloves they have ever encountered. And that's a pity, for cloves are much more versatile than we give them credit for.

The flavor of cloves is strong and piercing; it can easily overwhelm everything else. In small amounts, cloves add an intriguing wisp of taste. Just one clove in a beef stew, for instance, gives richness to the overall flavor without a specific clove taste.

If your recipe calls for both cloves and onions, here's a way to get incredibly rich flavor. Pierce a few holes in an unpeeled onion and insert whole cloves. Roast the onion in a 350° oven for 1 hour, then add the whole onion to the cooking pot. If the cloves seem loose, first wrap the entire onion in a piece of cheesecloth to keep cloves from floating free.

Whole cloves, as is true of many other spices, have more flavor than ground spice that has been sitting on the shelf for a while. But you don't

Bouquet garni. One or two layers of cheesecloth, tied with natural (undyed) string or kitchen twine, is a simple way to get the flavors of spices and herbs into your foods.

want them floating loose in the finished dish, especially if it is something like a stew where they might be overlooked, because they could cause someone to choke. One good solution is to put the cloves in some kind of infuser (container with holes; see illustration on page 10). The infuser goes down into the dish as it cooks, and is easily retrieved at serving time.

Another way to go is to wrap the cloves and other whole spices and herbs in a simple cheesecloth bag tied with string; this is known as a "bouquet garni."

Use Whole Cloves in:
- Pork roasts (insert into skin as with ham)
- Fruit pickles
- Sweet cucumber pickles
- Stews, pot roast
- Mulled wine, cider, or tea (use cheesecloth bag or infuser)

Use Powdered Cloves in:
- Baked goods: cakes, cookies, sweet breads
- Chocolate desserts
- Vegetables: beets, sweet potatoes, boiled onions, winter squash
- Beet, potato, tomato, and pea soups
- Baked fruit dishes
- Fruit syrups
- Mincemeat
- Fruit preserves and chutneys
- Cranberry and other fruit juices

⤙ Pickled Peaches ⤚

8 pounds small or medium-sized peaches (about 5¹/₂ quarts prepared
   peaches)
2 tablespoons whole cloves
4 sticks cinnamon
4¹/₂ cups sugar
4 cups vinegar
2 cups water

Put cloves and cinnamon loosely in clean, thin white cloth or cheese-cloth and tie top tightly. Cook spices, sugar, vinegar, and water for 10 minutes. Meanwhile, wash and peel peaches; leave whole. Add peaches to syrup; cook slowly until tender, but not broken. Let sit overnight.

In the morning remove spices. Drain syrup from peaches; boil syrup rapidly until thickened. Pack peaches in hot sterilized jars. Pour hot syrup over peaches, filling jars to top. Seal. Process 20 minutes in boiling water bath. (See page 165 for canning instructions.)

Yield: 7 to 8 pints.

⤙ Harvard Beets ⤚

1 large can (15 ounces) sliced or whole beets
¹/₄ cup cider vinegar
¹/₄ cup sugar
1 tablespoon cornstarch
1 teaspoon grated orange peel
¹/₈ teaspoon ground cloves
1 tablespoon butter

Drain beets, reserving the juice. Combine beet juice, vinegar, sugar, cornstarch, orange peel, and cloves in small saucepan. Cook over medium heat, stirring constantly, until sauce thickens. Stir in beets and butter; simmer until beets are thoroughly heated, about 5 minutes.

Serves 4.

⚜ Sweet-Sour Red Cabbage ⚜

¹/₂ cup butter
¹/₄ cup diced onions
¹/₄ cup brown sugar
1 teaspoon salt
¹/₂ teaspoon black pepper
1 teaspoon ground allspice
¹/₄ teaspoon ground cloves
2 pounds red cabbage, finely shredded
¹/₂ cup boiling water
¹/₂ cup wine vinegar

In large skillet or saucepan, melt butter and sauté onions until golden. Stir in sugar, seasonings, and shredded cabbage. Add water, cover, and simmer 15 minutes. Add vinegar, simmer 10 minutes longer.
Serves 8.

⚜ Consommé Royale ⚜

2 10¹/₂ ounce cans beef consommé
2 bay leaves
6 whole cloves
4 peppercorns
3 whole allspice
¹/₂ teaspoon grated lemon peel
¹/₄ cup thin slices of fresh mushrooms (garnish)
1 scallion (garnish)

In medium saucepan combine consommé, spices, and lemon peel. Heat just to the boiling point; cover and let steep 10 minutes.

Meanwhile, prepare the garnishes: Clean and slice 1 large mushroom very thinly. Slice the white part of one scallion very thinly. Slice the green tops into 2-inch lengths and then slice them lengthwise into very thin strips; the strips will curl gently.

Strain out the spices from the consommé, bring back to boil, and pour into serving bowls.

Garnish each serving with several thin slices of fresh mushrooms, a few slices of the white part of the scallion, and 2 or 3 green scallion curls.
Serves 4 to 6.

·≷ Apple Pot Roast ≷·

4 pounds chuck roast
2 tablespoons vegetable shortening or olive oil
1¹/₂ teaspoons salt
³/₄ teaspoon ground ginger
5 whole cloves
1 bay leaf
¹/₄ teaspoon black pepper
1 cup apple juice
¹/₂ cup dry red wine
2 large onions
4 medium red Delicious apples

Heat oil in Dutch oven or roaster pan and brown roast on all sides. Mix spices into apple juice with wine; pour over meat. Bring to boil, then reduce heat, cover, and simmer 2 hours.

Meanwhile, slice onions and core and slice apples (leave skin on, if you like that texture); to prevent darkening, keep apple slices in bowl of lightly salted water until time to add to meat.

When meat is tender, add apple and onion slices. Cover and simmer 30 minutes more.

To serve, remove meat to heated platter and surround with apples and onions. Serve with rice, roasted potatoes, or broad noodles.

Serves 6.

·≷ Spicy Pumpkin Pie ≷·

1¹/₂ cups canned pumpkin
³/₄ cup sugar
¹/₂ teaspoon salt
1¹/₄ teaspoon cinnamon
1 teaspoon ginger
¹/₂ teaspoon nutmeg
¹/₂ teaspoon ground cloves
2 slightly beaten eggs
1 13-oz. can evaporated milk
1 9-inch unbaked pastry shell
whipped cream (optional)

Preheat oven to 400°.

In mixing bowl combine pumpkin, sugar, salt, and spices. Beat in eggs and milk. Lift edges of pastry and crimp so they are taller than usual, as the filling is generous. Pour filling into pastry shell. Bake for 50 minutes or until knife comes out clean.

If you wish, make a small batch of whipped cream to which you have added a pinch of ground cloves; pipe whipped cream around the perimeter of the pie just before serving.

⋅❊ Molasses Clove Cookies ❊⋅

These keep well in a tightly covered container, especially if equipped with a lock.

3 cups sifted all-purpose flour
2 teaspoons baking powder
1 teaspoon salt
1 teaspoon ground cloves
1 teaspoon ground ginger
2 cups sugar
1¹/₂ cups melted butter
2 eggs
¹/₂ cup molasses
1¹/₂ cups quick-cooking rolled oats

Preheat oven to 375°.

In large mixing bowl, sift together flour, baking powder, salt, cloves, ginger, and sugar. Beat eggs, and add to flour along with melted butter and molasses. Using electric mixer, blend until smooth. With a large spoon, stir in rolled oats.

Drop by teaspoonfuls 1 inch apart onto ungreased cookie sheet. Bake 10 minutes.

Makes 3 dozen cookies.

⋅❊ Bishop ❊⋅

This hot wine punch is a very, very old recipe from England; it was popular in the 1700s. Roasting the oranges first really brings out the flavor.

4 oranges
4 tablespoons whole cloves
2 cinnamon sticks
2 tablespoons whole allspice
3 slices fresh ginger

1 gallon water
10 teabags
1 bottle port or red wine
sugar

Preheat oven to 350°.

Stick 1 tablespoon of whole cloves into the skin of each orange; make a small hole first with a skewer or knitting needle so the clove doesn't break. Roast oranges in ungreased baking pan for 1 hour.

Meanwhile, simmer spices in water in large kettle or stockpot for 10 minutes. Strain out spices and add teabags to the hot water; steep 5 minutes. Remove teabags.

Add oranges and wine to the kettle, and add sugar to taste. Simmer till sugar is dissolved and flavors are mixed. Serve hot.

Makes about 20 cups.

Variation: A similar idea uses apples and cider instead of oranges and tea. Insert whole cloves into unpeeled apples; heat with cider in saucepan or crockpot.

For Other Recipes Featuring Cloves, See:
Beet Surprise Salad, p. 39
Mulled Cider, p. 43
Spicy Pot Roast, p. 100
Spiced Onions and Beets, p. 114
Chicken in Orange Juice, p. 115
Iced Spiced Coffee, p. 118
Instant Russian Tea Mix, p. 118
Honey Spice Dressing, p. 119
Mincemeat Refrigerator Cookies, p. 142
Sloppy Josés, p. 150
Malaysian Chicken and Sweet Potato Kurma, p. 196
Ginger Tea, p. 201
Old-Fashioned Baked Beans, p. 207
Tomato Juice Cocktail, p. 207
Spicy Carrot Pickles, p. 215
Spiced Raisin Sauce, p. 229
Deep Dish Apple Pie, p. 244
Pfeffernusse, p. 262
Arroz Con Pollo, p. 281
Malaysian Spiced Rice, p. 299

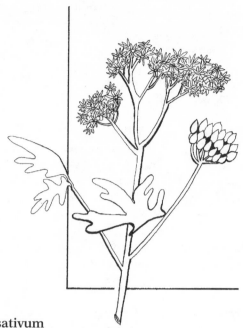

Coriander

Botanical name: **Coriandrum sativum**

Part used as spice: **Seeds**

Available as: **Whole or ground seeds**

There is one plant from which we get two spices—mace and nutmeg—and another from which we get one spice and one herb: coriander and cilantro. The leaves are the herb cilantro, popular in Mexican and Asian cooking, and the seeds are what we know as coriander.

Just like hemlines and hairdos, styles in food come and go. Today cilantro is chic; not too long ago, it was considered inedible. From the beginning, people have commented on its strong aroma. In fact, its very name (from the Greek word *koris*, meaning "bug") suggests something nasty. Even now, people either love it or hate it.

Coriander, the spice, tastes very different from the leaves. The flavor is somehow sweet and tart at the same time; some have described it as a mixture of lemon peel and sage, others as a blend of orange, anise, and cumin.

The plant that produces coriander is one of the Umbelliferae family; several of its cousins have a place in this book—anise, caraway, cumin, dill, and fennel—and so you may have already encountered some of the characteristics that these cousins have in common. (All these umbellifers, purely by coincidence, cluster in the early part of the alphabet, so if you happen to read this book straight through, you will find some repetition in the descriptions; my apologies.)

Like the other umbellifers, coriander is native to the area around the Mediterranean but quickly spread throughout Europe, the Middle East, and southern Asia. At one time or another, it has been grown commercially in India, several countries in the Middle East, eastern Europe, and Central and South America. In the United States it is cultivated commercially in Kentucky, where it is used by distillers. Most of what is on our spice shelves today comes from Morocco, in northern Africa, or Romania in central Europe.

Coriander can grow anywhere in the temperate zone—even, should you care to, in your garden. All the umbellifers are easy to grow, but with this one you must make a decision: Do you want coriander or cilantro? You cannot have a full crop of both from the same plant. If you want cilantro, you'll have to keep cutting off the flower stalks as soon as they form; once the plant has flowered and set seed, the leaves are too harsh tasting. If you want coriander, you'll have to let the flowers form, which means the leaves no longer taste right. Of course you could plant a whole bed and use some plants for cilantro and let others go to seed for coriander.

Immature seeds don't have the coriander flavor, so you have to wait till the seeds are starting to turn brown before you harvest them. At that point, be ready to act fast because once they're ripe, the seeds start falling from the plant. Early in the morning, when the plants are covered with dew (so that the seed coatings are somewhat pliable and less likely to be knocked off by motion), cut off the seed head or pull up the entire plant. (If you do this when the plant is dry, the seeds will fall off when you touch the plant.) Shake the seed head into a paper bag, and use a kitchen sieve to separate the seeds from the chaff.

During World War II, when a shortage of raw materials forced the confection industry to be resourceful, coriander seeds were used as the basis for the small candies known in Europe as *confits* ("confections"). The seeds were covered with a hard candy shell made from colored sugar. They were part of the scene for every carnival, festival, and circus; clowns riding on the carnival wagons in the preshow parade would toss these small candies to the crowd. Later these confections were replaced with small bits of paper, and this is the source of our word "confetti."

History and Legends

Because this plant is native to the countries around the Mediterranean, it is natural that its use developed there first. It was used as medicine by the Egyptians as far back as 4000 B.C., and is one of the plants listed in the Egyptian medical record known as the Ebers Papyrus (1550 B.C.). Apparently Egypt remained the coriander capital for many centuries, for the Roman scholar we know as Pliny the Elder (first century), whose records of the natural world served as the foundation of botany for many centuries, wrote that the very best coriander came from Egypt.

Coriander was part of the Hanging Gardens of Babylon, and was well known in Palestine, for it is mentioned several times in the Old Testament.

The Greeks considered it primarily a medicinal plant; Hippocrates (400 B.C.) recommended it as a general tonic. But the Romans changed it into a cooking spice, starting with the statesman and orator Cato the Elder in the third century B.C., who eloquently expressed his fondness for the taste. Roman soldiers, as they moved across Europe, brought the seeds with them and thus spread the plant throughout the continent and England.

Since at least the fourth century, coriander has been grown and used in China, and there is an old Chinese belief that if someone under the grip of a spiritual trance were to eat coriander seeds, that person would live forever.

Once considered an aphrodisiac, coriander plays that role in several of the stories of *The Thousand and One Nights*. In rural areas, where replacement of livestock was essential, it was fed to animals during the mating season, to make sure romantic encounters happened in a timely fashion.

Medicinal and Other Uses

As we have seen, the great Greek physician Hippocrates prescribed coriander for general well-being, and it was once used to treat migraines. Today, however, coriander has little medicinal importance except as a flavoring for medications that would otherwise taste so awful no one would take them.

Like the other umbellifers, coriander has a carminative effect (helps with intestinal gas), although it is milder in this respect than some of the others. It's still a good home remedy for indigestion or a queasy stomach; make a tea by steeping seeds in boiling water.

As far back as 1574, chemists in Europe were distilling the essential oil of coriander. Today it is used in perfumes, candy, and alcoholic beverages, especially gin.

Cooking with Coriander

It's probably fair to say that American cooks are not very familiar with coriander—at least, not that they're aware of. The whole seeds are a common ingredient in mixed pickling spice, and the powdered spice is the primary constituent (by volume) of most commercial curry powders.

Beyond those two products, the most common use of coriander is in the manufacture of sausage. If you've ever had a hot dog, you've tasted coriander, for that is the spice that gives them their distinctive taste; in fact, coriander is often called the "hot dog spice."

But coriander deserves to be more widely known. It is an unusual taste—definitely spicy but with a flowery, fruity undertone—and complements a wide range of foods.

Use Coriander with:
- Baked apples or pears
- Applesauce
- Ham or pork roast; rub onto surface of meat before baking
- Cream soups, especially pea
- Cooked beets
- Stuffing for turkey, chicken, or Cornish hen
- Sweet breads, cakes, cookies

> For a very continental touch, crush one coriander seed and drop it into the bottom of the cup before pouring in coffee or hot chocolate.

⋖ Melon Appetizer ⋗

1 medium-sized Crenshaw melon
1 medium-sized Persian melon
2 tablespoons lime juice
2 tablespoons honey
1/4 teaspoon ground coriander
1/4 teaspoon ground nutmeg
mint leaves
lime slices

Halve melons and remove seeds. Using melon baller or metal measuring spoon, cut fruit into balls. In small bowl, mix lime juice, honey, and spices. Pour dressing over fruit in large bowl and fold in gently. Cover and chill.

Serve in clear glass bowl; garnish with fresh mint leaves and lime slices.

Makes 8 to 10 servings.

Grilled Vegetable Salad with Warm Orange Vinaigrette

2 medium zucchini, cut in 1/2-inch thick lengthwise slices
2 medium green bell peppers, halved and seeded
1 medium eggplant, cut in 1/2-inch thick crosswise slices
1 large red onion, cut in 1/2-inch thick slices
2 tablespoons olive oil, divided
Warm Orange Vinaigrette (recipe follows)

Heat an outdoor grill or preheat oven broiler. On the grill or rack of a large broiling pan arrange vegetables in a single layer (if using broiler, you may need to broil vegetables in two batches). Lightly brush vegetables with 1 tablespoon of the oil. Grill 4 to 5 inches from heat until vegetables are tender, about 10 minutes, turning and brushing with remaining 1 tablespoon oil after 5 minutes.

Place vegetables on a cutting board; cool slightly. Cut into bite-size pieces; place in a serving bowl and toss with Warm Orange Vinaigrette.
Makes 6 cups (4 servings).

Warm Orange Vinaigrette
2 tablespoons olive oil
2 teaspoons ground cumin
1 teaspoon ground coriander
2 tablespoons orange juice
1 tablespoon cider vinegar
1/2 teaspoon salt

In a small saucepan over medium-low heat, heat oil, cumin, and coriander, stirring occasionally until fragrant, about 1 minute. Remove from heat; stir in orange juice, vinegar, and salt.
Makes about 1/3 cup.

—American Spice Trade Association

 Roasted Coriander Corn

6 ears of corn, in husks
1/2 cup softened butter
1 teaspoon salt
5 coriander seeds, crushed
1 teaspoon dill weed
dash nutmeg

Pull husks down to expose the corn but do not tear off; remove silk. Soak corn plus husks in cold water 30 minutes or longer. When ready to roast, drain well. Combine butter with spices and spread over corn. Pull husks back around corn, then wrap in aluminum foil. Place on grill about 5 inches from coals; cook 25 minutes, turning several times. Remove foil and husks.

Serves 6.

Variation: Use 1 teaspoon seasoned salt and a dash dry mustard in place of salt and spices.

⤌ Persian Lamb ⤏

2 pounds lean boneless lamb
1/4 cup butter
1/4 cup minced onions
1/2 teaspoon turmeric
2 teaspoons ground coriander
1/2 teaspoon ground cumin
1/4 teaspoon ground ginger
1/2 teaspoon paprika
2 teaspoons salt
3 medium-size tomatoes, peeled, seeded, diced
1/2 cup plain yogurt

Trim away any excess fat and cut lamb into 2-inch cubes. Melt butter in heavy saucepan or Dutch oven and sauté onions until golden. Add lamb, turmeric, coriander, cumin, and ginger, and cook until meat is browned, about 15 minutes.

Add paprika, salt, and tomatoes. Cover and simmer gently for about 1 1/2 hours or until meat is tender; check occasionally and add water if sauce begins to stick. Stir a bit of the hot sauce into the yogurt, and then add it back to the pan. Serve hot with steamed rice.

Makes 6 servings.

⊰ Caribbean Pork and Bean Stew ⊱

1 pound dry beans (white or red)
1¹/₂ quarts water, divided
1¹/₂ pounds lean pork roast
¹/₄ cup diced onion
¹/₄ cup diced green bell pepper
¹/₂ teaspoon ground coriander
¹/₄ teaspoon garlic powder
¹/₄ teaspoon black pepper
¹/₄ teaspoon oregano
2 teaspoons salt, divided
1 medium-size tomato
1 medium-size potato
1 cup cubed yellow winter squash or pumpkin

Wash beans; cover with 1 quart water. Bring to a boil and boil for 5 minutes. Turn off heat; cover and let beans soak for 1 hour. (Alternatively, cook beans the day before.)

Meanwhile, trim fat from pork roast and cut meat into 6 pieces. Add meat and remaining water to beans. Stir in onion, bell pepper, seasonings, and 1 teaspoon salt. Simmer until beans are almost tender. Add the remaining 1 teaspoon salt.

Peel tomato and potato; cut into cubes and add to stew along with cubed squash or pumpkin. Continue simmering for 30 to 40 minutes, or until vegetables and meat are tender.

Serve in bowls with hot rolls or cornbread.
Makes 6 servings.

⊰ Mincemeat Refrigerator Cookies ⊱

³/₄ cup shortening
1 cup sugar
1 egg
1 teaspoon grated lemon peel
¹/₄ teaspoon crushed coriander seed
¹/₂ teaspoon pure vanilla extract
2¹/₂ cups all-purpose flour
¹/₂ teaspoon baking soda
¹/₂ teaspoon salt
1 teaspoon cinnamon
dash nutmeg
¹/₄ teaspoon ground cloves

¹/₄ teaspoon ground ginger
¹/₂ cup mincemeat
¹/₂ cup chopped nuts

Cream shortening and sugar together until fluffy. Add egg; beat well. Stir in lemon peel, coriander, and vanilla. Sift flour, measure and sift again with soda and spices. Add dry ingredients to creamed mixture, beating thoroughly. Stir in mincemeat and nuts. Roll dough into logs 1¹/₂ inches in diameter and wrap in waxed paper. Chill. When ready to bake, preheat oven to 375° while you cut dough into thin slices and place on baking sheet. Bake 9 to 10 minutes.
Makes 8 to 9 dozen.

For Other Recipes Featuring Coriander, See:

Spiced Walnuts, p. 75
Seafood Firepot, p. 93
Roasted Spice Gazpacho, p. 150
Bengali Beef Stew, p. 152
Mt. Olympus Chicken, p. 184
Malaysian Spiced Rice, p. 299
Egyptian Eggplant, p. 308

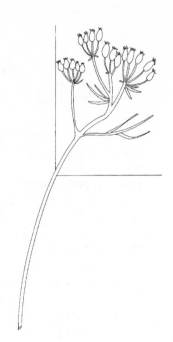

Cumin

Botanical name: **Cumimum cyminum**
Part used as spice: **Seeds**
Available as: **Whole or ground seeds**

You can't have curry without it, or chili con carne either.

Think about that for a minute. Curry is an East Indian dish; chili is Mexican. Isn't it amazing that two countries so far apart in geography and culture should share such a fondness for the same spice? To my way of thinking, that is the real magic about spices: the delicate connecting thread that they weave.

Cumin belongs to the Umbelliferae family, that large group so richly represented in the spice/herb world (see anise, caraway, coriander, dill, and fennel in this book). It is the baby of the family: a smaller plant than the others, with undistinguished flowers and foliage.

It is thought to be indigenous to the Nile Valley, but spread throughout northern Africa into all countries of the Mediterranean, and then to Asia on the eastward leg of the spice trade. From northern Africa the Moors introduced it to Spain, and from there the Spanish conquistadors took cumin to New Spain (Mexico), where, as we will see, it was warmly adapted into the cuisine.

Cumin is another of those trouble-free plants that grow anywhere in the temperate region; today we import it from Sicily, Iran, and India, but it could—and does—grow throughout the world.

How do you pronounce it? The American Spice Trade Association says the "official" pronunciation is "cum-in." That is, like "come into my parlor," not "cue-men" as in "cue the music" or "coo-men" as in babytalk.

History and Legend

Cumin is one of the spices of antiquity. The Egyptians included it in the mix of spices they used to mummify kings and queens. It is mentioned in several places in the Bible. Two great Greek physicians—Hippocrates and Dioscorides—wrote about cumin, which tells us that it was used medicinally as far back as the fourth century B.C.

Pliny, the Roman naturalist of the first century A.D., described a kind of cosmetic made from cumin. It was a common practice in his day for people to drink a tea made from cumin to give themselves a pale complexion, a mark of beauty. Then, he reports, some clever young students started drinking the same tea to make themselves pale—as if they had stayed inside studying for weeks at a time.

A man who enjoyed a good meal, Pliny also thought cumin was the very best appetizer spice of all. The Romans used it as a substitute for pepper, which was very expensive then; they also made a cumin paste and spread it on bread.

A Fable About Cumin

From ancient Saxony comes this tale: It seems that a peasant family was graced by the presence of a fairy in the woods near their home, who brought good fortune to the family. The wife, worried that the fairy might one day depart, baked a special loaf of bread loaded with cumin (which everyone knew had the power to keep people from leaving) and left it out for the fairy. When she ate the bread, the fairy immediately tasted the cumin and became very angry at this sign of distrust. So she moved on, and many bad things befell the family.

This spice is the source of some intriguing superstitions, many of them built around its reputed ability to hold things in place:

- To keep evil spirits from stealing a family's bread, bakers added cumin to the dough.
- And if someone did grab a loaf of bread with intent to steal, the cumin would hold the thief in place.
- Young men and women gave their sweethearts a potion containing cumin, to keep them and their affections from wandering.
- Put cumin in feed for chickens and ducks, and they will not stray from the yard.
- Bride and groom carried some seeds in their pockets during the wedding ceremony, guaranteeing that both would remain faithful all their days.

- Also, Greeks considered cumin a symbol of meanness and miserliness. To describe someone who was very tight with money, they would say, "He must have eaten too much cumin today."
- The Romans, too, used this spice as a symbol of greed; Marcus Aurelius, emperor of Rome in the second century A.D., well known in his own time for his avarice, was nicknamed Cumin.
- To be sure of having a very successful crop of cumin, curse the seeds fiercely while you sow them.

Medicinal Uses

Since the days of Hippocrates, cumin has been used in healing various ailments, including:

- Jaundice
- Indigestion
- Headaches
- Pleurisy

Like the other umbellifers, cumin is carminative (meaning it will break up and dispel intestinal gas). In fact, many of the herbalists in past centuries said it was more effective at this than either caraway or fennel, but those two were used more often because people preferred their taste.

Today its primary medicinal application is in veterinary medicine; cumin is often used to treat diseased pigeons.

Cooking with Cumin

Traditionally, cumin has been compared with, equated with, and even confused with caraway. This is partly because the seeds look quite similar. Furthering the confusion is a common mistranslation into English from recipes of India, where cumin is often used but caraway rarely so. Some people think their taste is similar, too; indeed, they are more like each other than either one is like, say, cloves, but they are not interchangeable.

The taste of cumin is very definite, very assertive; it doesn't blend in with other flavors like caraway does. A little goes a long way; enough soup to serve six people would need only 1/4 teaspoon of cumin.

This spice is found in cuisines of the Middle East, North Africa, Europe, India, Mexico, and the American Southwest. In Spain it goes into meat stews along with cinnamon and saffron. In Turkey, it goes with vegetables and meat mixtures. Cooks in Germany add it to sauerkraut and roast pork. In the Netherlands it goes into a special kind of

Edam cheese. In the Middle East it is baked into bread and cake, and is a traditional flavoring for couscous. And it is an essential ingredient in chili powder and in spice mixes for curry.

The flavor of cumin is very popular in Mexican and Tex-Mex dishes. In fact it may be the second most distinctive taste in those cuisines (after chili peppers). Texans use chili powder (which contains cumin) to make chili con carne and then add more cumin, to get the taste just right.

Cumin was quite popular in England up until the seventeenth century, when it was mostly replaced by caraway. In the United States today, when so many are intrigued with expanding our palates to include the foods of other regions, it has become popular again. In 1900 the United States imported 150,000 pounds; in 1968, 4 million pounds; and in 1992, 11.5 million pounds.

Use Cumin in:
- Meatloaf
- Cheese casserole
- Marinade for chicken
- Vegetable salad
- Soups and stews
- Cabbage dishes and sauerkraut
- Rice (add to the cooking water)
- Deviled eggs

⁌ Spicy Black Bean Dip ⁍

1 can (15 ounce) black beans
1 teaspoon ground cumin
1 teaspoon chili powder
1/4 teaspoon dried oregano
1/4 teaspoon garlic salt (or 1/4 teaspoon minced fresh garlic plus 1/8
*   teaspoon salt)*
1/8–1/4 teaspoon cayenne
1 cup chopped tomatoes

Drain beans, reserving 2 tablespoons liquid. Rinse beans and drain again. Combine beans, reserved liquid, and spices in blender or food processor. Cover and process until beans are coarsely chopped.

Transfer mixture to a small saucepan; cook over medium-low heat 5 minutes, stirring occasionally. Add tomatoes and cook 5 more minutes, still stirring occasionally.

Serve with pita, bagel, or tortilla chips.
Makes 1 1/2 cups.

—McCormick/Schilling

⋅⅋ Cumin Seed Wafers ⅋⋅

Serve warm from the oven with homemade tomato soup, or with green salad as a first course.

>*3/4 cup butter, softened*
>*1 cup shredded sharp cheddar cheese*
>*2 cups sifted all-purpose flour*
>*1/2 teaspoon onion salt*
>*1 1/2 teaspoons ground cumin*

Cream butter and cheese together, mixing thoroughly. Sift flour with onion salt; mix in cumin. Gradually add flour to the cheese mixture; knead a few times to blend well. Form dough into rolls about 1 1/2 inches thick. Wrap in waxed paper or foil and chill several hours or overnight.

When ready to bake, preheat oven to 400°. Slice dough into thin rounds (1/4 inch) and bake on a lightly greased cookie sheet until lightly brown, about 10 minutes. Carefully lift off with spatula. Serve hot or cold.

Makes 3 dozen.

⋅⅋ Caribbean Black Bean Soup ⅋⋅

A wonderful soup with lively rich flavor and smooth, hearty texture.

>*1 pound (about 2 1/2 cups) dried black beans*
>*2 to 3 tablespoons olive oil*
>*2 large onions, chopped*
>*3 cloves garlic, chopped*
>*3 stalks celery, with leaves, chopped*
>*1 1/2 to 2 pounds ham hocks or ham shank*
>*10 cups chicken stock*
>*1/2 teaspoon cayenne pepper*
>*1 1/2 teaspoons cumin*
>*2 tablespoons balsamic vinegar*
>*1/4 cup dry sherry*
>*salt and freshly ground pepper to taste*

Garnishes:
Low-fat sour cream, chopped hard-boiled eggs, chopped scallions, and cilantro.

Cover the beans with water and soak overnight. The following day, heat oil in a large soup pot and sauté vegetables until soft. Rinse soaked beans and add them to the pot along with the ham hocks and chicken stock. Bring to a boil, reduce heat, add cayenne and cumin. Cover and simmer over low heat for 2½ to 3 hours, or until beans are soft, stirring occasionally.

Remove ham hocks and refrigerate to cool. Skim excess fat from soup, then puree soup in batches in a food processor or blender. Return bean puree to soup pot. Cut ham meat from bones in small pieces and add to soup.

Bring soup to a simmer over low heat. Just before serving, add vinegar, sherry, and salt and pepper to taste. Serve hot with a dollop of sour cream surrounded by chopped egg, scallions, and cilantro.

Serves 10.

—Renée Shepherd

⁘ Cumin-Scented Basmati Rice ⁘

Cook rice according to directions on package.

For each quart of cooked rice, sauté ⅛ cup of cumin seeds in ¼ cup oil until seeds are toasted and brown. Remove seeds from heat and stir into hot cooked rice.

⁘ Pork Tenderloin with Cumin and Orange ⁘

1½ pounds pork tenderloins
⅓ cup orange juice
2 teaspoons ground cumin
1 teaspoon garlic powder
¼ teaspoon pepper
¼ teaspoon cayenne

With a fork pierce pork on all sides. In a large reclosable bag combine orange juice, cumin, garlic powder, pepper, and cayenne. Add pork; seal, turning bag to coat meat well. Marinate at room temperature for 10 minutes, turning bag occasionally.

Preheat broiler. Place tenderloins on a broiling pan sprayed with nonstick cooking spray. Broil 3 to 4 inches from heat, basting frequently with marinade until tender, 8 to 9 minutes per side. Slice pork crosswise into thin rounds.

In a small saucepan bring any remaining marinade to a boil; serve with meat, if desired.

Makes 6 servings.

—American Spice Trade Association

⋅⋉ Roasted Spice Gazpacho ⋊⋅

Roasting the vegetables before adding them to the soup immeasurably enhances their flavor; this extra step is well worth it.

    3 tablespoons olive oil, divided
    1 medium zucchini, sliced lengthwise
    1 medium onion, in thick slices
    1 medium green bell pepper, halved and seeded
    3 large tomatoes, halved and cored
    1¹/₂ teaspoons ground cumin
    1¹/₂ teaspoons ground coriander
    1 teaspoon garlic powder (or minced fresh garlic)
    2 cups tomato juice
    ¹/₂ teaspoon salt

Garnish: Plain yogurt, lime wedges

Heat an outdoor grill or preheat your oven's broiler. On the grill or rack of a broiler pan arrange zucchini, onion, and bell pepper in a single layer; brush with 1 tablespoon of olive oil. Grill 4 to 5 inches from heat until tender, about 5 minutes; turn and brush other side with oil; grill for another 3 minutes. Add tomatoes, cut side up; brush top with oil and grill 2 minutes. Place vegetables on a cutting board; cool slightly.

Meanwhile, in a small saucepan over medium-low heat, heat 1 table-spoon oil; add cumin, coriander, and garlic; cook, stirring occasionally, until fragrant, 1 to 2 minutes. Coarsely chop vegetables; place in a large bowl; stir in tomato juice and salt. Cover and refrigerate until chilled, about 4 hours.

Serve with a spoonful of plain yogurt or sour cream, if desired. Pass lime wedges to be squeezed into soup.

Serve with hot crusty bread.

Makes 6 cups.

—Adapted from American Spice Trade Association

⋅⋉ Sloppy Josés ⋊⋅

Your children may prefer to call them Sloppy Joes, but the extra spices give this a definite Latino flavor. Serve over hot rice.

    2 teaspoons vegetable or olive oil
    1 cup chopped onion
    1 teaspoon bottled minced garlic (or 1 clove, minced)

1¹/₄ pounds extra-lean ground beef
¹/₂ teaspoon ground cumin
¹/₂ teaspoon black pepper
¹/₈ teaspoon ground cloves
¹/₈ teaspoon ground cinnamon
1 14¹/₂-ounce can stewed tomatoes
¹/₄ cup sliced, pimiento-stuffed green olives, drained
¹/₄ cup raisins
¹/₄ cup white wine, optional

Heat oil in a large skillet over medium heat; sauté onion and garlic until limp, about 30 seconds. Add meat to same skillet, and brown, stirring often. As meat cooks, stir in spices.

When meat is no longer pink, add in tomatoes, olives, raisins, and wine. Simmer and stir for about 5 minutes, until most of the liquid has evaporated. The meat mixture should be moist but not soupy.

Makes 4 servings.

⋰ Mexican Egg Salad ⋱

6 hard-cooked eggs
¹/₄ cup finely chopped celery
¹/₄ cup finely chopped sweet pickle
¹/₄ cup mayonnaise
1 teaspoon vinegar
¹/₄ teaspoon dry mustard
1 teaspoon seasoning salt
¹/₈ teaspoon white pepper
¹/₈ teaspoon crushed cumin seed

Chop eggs; add celery and pickle. In a separate bowl, combine remaining ingredients, mixing well. Carefully fold into eggs. Use as a filling for sandwiches; especially good on dark rye or pumpernickel bread.

Or, use to make a meatless main-course salad for lunch. Line 2 serving plates with red-leaf lettuce, pile 1 cup egg salad in center, and surround it with garnishes: 3 black olives, 1 cherry tomato sliced in half, fresh parsley. Top with a round slice of green bell pepper.

Makes 2 cups.

⟜ Bengali Beef Stew ⟝

The spices give a definite East Indian character to this stew.

1 tablespoon vegetable oil
1 medium onion, chopped
1 pound boneless beef for stew
1/2 cup yellow split peas
1 teaspoon salt
1/4 teaspoon paprika
1/4 teaspoon hot red pepper flakes
1/2 teaspoon ground cumin
1/2 teaspoon ground coriander
1 cup water
2 carrots, thickly sliced (optional)
1/2 pound fresh green beans, cut into short pieces (optional)

In large skillet, heat oil to smoking point. Add chopped onion and beef; cook until meat loses its red color. Add split peas, spices, and water.

Cover and simmer until split peas and meat are done, about 30 minutes; or cook 15 minutes in pressure cooker. If you wish to include the vegetables, add them during the last 10 minutes of cooking.

Serve over plain, steamed white rice.

Serves 4 to 6.

For Other Recipes Featuring Cumin, See:

Spiced Walnuts, p. 75
Chili Cheese Cornbread Muffins, p. 76
Corn Pudding, p. 77
Turkey Picadillo, p. 78
Hot Texas Red Chili, p. 78
Chicken Quesadillas, p. 91
Warm Orange Vinaigrette, p. 140
Persian Lamb, p. 141
Malaysian Spiced Rice, p. 299

Curry Powder

Available as: Ground spice blend

In India, where the concept originated, the word "curry" refers to a cooked dish containing several ingredients and an assortment of spices, which will vary according to the principal ingredients of the dish. There may be, for example, vegetable curries with sweet, aromatic spices; meat curries with hot, pungent spices; seafood curries with mild, faintly tangy spices.

Indian cooks prepare a spice blend for each curry from individual spices, roasting them separately and then grinding them together. Thus the spice mixture will be different depending on the type of dish, the region of the country, and the mood of the cook. Many Indian cupboards contain a spice blend known as garam masala (either homemade or purchased in the market), which also has many variations, and which is in any case only the starting point for flavoring the dish. But most Indians have never heard of curry powder—or if they have, they don't believe in it.

If you were to give an Indian cook an American spice jar labeled "curry powder," that cook would probably return it with a gentle smile. What we call curry powder is a Western invention, an attempt to replicate the flavor of Indian curries. But, since there is no one "curry" taste, what we really have is a modern spice product with a distinct flavor of its own.

Commercial curry powders contain at least a dozen separate spices, often as many as twenty. The exact formulations used by the major manufacturers are secret, but in general the primary ingredients and their approximate proportions are:

- Coriander, 35%
- Turmeric, 18% (provides the yellow color)
- Fenugreek, 10%
- Cinnamon, 8%
- Cumin, 6%
- Cardamom, 6%
- Ginger, 5%
- Pepper, 5%

- Cloves, 3%
- Cayenne, 1%
- Allspice, 1%
- Mustard seed, 1%

Curry or Not?

There are two plants named "curry," and they have nothing to do with the spice named curry powder. One is a small herb known as "curry plant," whose leaves do smell like curry powder but which turn unpleasantly bitter when cooked. The other is a small Asian tree called "curry leaf." Its leaves, fresh, taste like curry and are occasionally added to cooked dishes in India; when dry, they lose their flavor.

A few spice companies offer both hot and mild versions of curry powder (for example, see Frontier Herbs in the Appendix), and some of the smaller mail-order companies listed in the Appendix of this book specialize in custom blends closer to the Indian originals.

Cooking with Curry Powder

Of course you need curry powder if you intend to make a curry (we're talking American curries here), and you need enough of it to make a recognizable difference. But curry powder, just a pinch, also works as a special spice that adds a light, fragrant, spicy taste to many foods; it's not identifiably curry, just a pleasant, faintly mysterious flavor.

You will find both kinds of recipes in this section. In addition, here are some other ideas for using curry powder.

Use Curry Powder in:
- Rice (add to the cooking water)
- Deviled eggs (mix in with the yolk mixture)
- Potato salad (add to the mayonnaise, or sprinkle on top)
- Split pea soup
- Clam chowder
- French dressing (use instead of dry mustard)
- Mayonnaise-based dressing for fruit salad
- Lentil soup, baked lentils

Store curry powder in a dark cupboard; turmeric, one of its primary components, loses flavor when exposed to sunlight.

Your First Curry Dinner

Here's a simplified plan, using the most basic kind of curry sauce. This is a dinner for four; it allows you to do most of the work ahead of time.

1. Cook, cut into bite-size pieces, and chill: chicken breast, lamb, shrimp, or veal, enough for 4 generous servings.
2. Cook a huge pot of plain white rice.
3. Make curry sauce: Melt 2 tablespoons butter in saucepan; add 2 teaspoons curry powder, stir it around for a few seconds; add 2 tablespoons flour, stir for a few seconds; whisk in 2 cups milk (or half milk and half chicken stock), stirring until very smooth; let simmer a few minutes until it is thick. Taste the sauce; if it seems too wimpy, stir in more curry powder. Take off stove and chill.
4. Set out small bowls of garnishes (see list below). Only the chutney and the coconut are truly essential, but the more of these little bowls of add-ons you have, the more special everything looks.
5. Just before the guests arrive, assemble the curry: Place the sauce in a large saucepan over low heat, fold in the cooked meat, stir till heated through; keep warm. Reheat the rice.
6. To serve, pile the rice on a platter. Pour the curry on top, leaving a wide border of plain rice, to accentuate the color contrast. Garnish the curry with a few chopped scallions. Set the platter in the middle of the table, surrounded by the small bowls of garnishes. Pause briefly for the ooohs and aaahs.
7. Serve each guest some of the rice and curry. Pass around the garnishes; people help themselves to spoonfuls of whatever garnishes are appealing, and mix them into the curry on their plate.
8. Beverage of choice: ice-cold beer.

A full-fledged dinner featuring a curry has a certain degree of ritual. The traditional approach calls for the curried dish to be accompanied by a variety of relishes and garnishes, which are passed to all diners and added into the curry according to their preferences:

mango chutney
shredded coconut
tamarind sauce
raisins

chopped roasted peanuts
sweet pickles, chopped fine
red bell peppers, chopped
hard-cooked eggs, whites and yolks chopped separately
cooked crumbled bacon
fresh pineapple, chopped
sliced olives
whole seedless grapes

It is a very nice way to entertain; the eating process encourages interaction and conversation. To host a dinner party featuring curry, you can select one of the main-course dishes in the recipe section in this chapter. Or, for an extremely simple curry dish, follow the step-by-step plan on page 155.

◦≼ Mulligatawny ≽◦

The famous soup from India.

1/4 cup butter
1 3-pound chicken, cut in pieces
1/4 cup chopped onion
1/4 cup chopped green pepper
3 quarts chicken stock
1 tablespoon curry powder
1 teaspoon turmeric
1/8 teaspoon mace
1 tablespoon chopped fresh parsley
1/4 teaspoon black pepper
6 tablespoons flour

Melt butter in large saucepan or Dutch oven. Add chicken pieces, onion, and green pepper; cover and cook over low heat 20 minutes. Stir in seasonings and simmer 30 to 40 minutes.

When chicken is tender, remove it from pan and cool in refrigerator. Strain stock. (At this point, you can refrigerate stock overnight; remove congealed fat when fully chilled.)

Return stock to saucepan. Cut meat from chicken bones and add to stock. Simmer 15 minutes. Make a thin, smooth paste by mixing together the flour with an equal amount of water. Then stir into the soup; continue cooking until thickened.

Makes 3 quarts.

❊ Chilled Tomato Soup ❊

1 medium cucumber
1 teaspoon Worcestershire sauce
¹/₂ teaspoon curry powder
1 can (10¹/₂-oz) condensed cream of tomato soup
2 cups buttermilk
cracked black pepper

Chop unpeeled cucumber into small bits; scrape out and discard seeds if they are large. In blender or food processor, mix Worcestershire sauce and curry powder, and then blend in the undiluted tomato soup. Add buttermilk slowly and blend completely. Stir in cucumber pieces but do not liquify. Chill thoroughly.

Sprinkle cracked black pepper on top of each serving.
Makes 6 to 8 servings.

❊ Madras Spinach Salad ❊

¹/₄ cup white wine vinegar
¹/₄ cup salad oil
2 tablespoons chutney, chopped
2 tablespoons sugar
¹/₂ teaspoon salt
1¹/₂ teaspoons curry powder
1 teaspoon dry mustard
¹/₂ cup peanuts
2 medium apples
8 cups (10 ounces) fresh spinach, torn into bite-size pieces
¹/₂ cup yellow raisins
2 tablespoons sliced green onion

Shake together in a jar: vinegar, oil, chutney, sugar, salt, curry powder and mustard.

Spread peanuts in shallow pan and toast in 350° oven for 5 minutes. Core apples but do not peel; chop finely.

Place torn spinach in large salad bowl; top with apple, raisins, peanuts, and green onion. Shake dressing well; pour over salad and toss.
Makes 6 to 8 servings.

ᛤ Yogurt Curried Cauliflower ᛢ

The creamy cauliflower combines perfectly with the smooth yogurt and curry sauce.

> *1 large head cauliflower*
> *1 tablespoon butter*
> *1 cup fresh plain yogurt*
> *1/2 teaspoon curry powder*
> *2 teaspoons seasoned bread crumbs*

Steam the cauliflower whole for 10 to 15 minutes, just until tender; do not overcook. (To give a bright whiteness to the cauliflower, add a few drops of vinegar to the steaming water.)

Remove the cauliflower carefully to serving plate and dot with butter. Combine the yogurt and curry powder and spread over the cauliflower. Sprinkle with bread crumbs and serve promptly.

Serves 4 to 6.

—Renée Shepherd

ᛤ Chutney Rice ᛢ

> *1 cup chopped onion*
> *1 cup sliced celery*
> *4 tablespoons butter*
> *3 cups cooked rice*
> *1/2 cup flaked coconut*
> *1/4 cup mango chutney*
> *1/2 teaspoon ground ginger*
> *1 teaspoon curry powder*

Sauté onion and celery in butter. Add remaining ingredients and mix well; heat over low flame or in microwave. Serve hot.

Serves 6 to 8.

ᛤ Country Captain ᛢ

This is a perfect party dish, for much of it can be made the day ahead. Country Captain is often considered the state dish of Georgia.

12 skinless, boneless chicken breasts
flour
salt
2 tablespoons vegetable oil
1 tablespoon butter
2 onions, finely sliced
2 green peppers, seeded and sliced
2 cloves garlic, minced
2 1-pound cans of tomatoes
1/2 teaspoon white pepper
1 teaspoon thyme
2 teaspoons curry powder
3 cups raw rice
1/4 pound slivered almonds
1/4 cup dried currants
1/4 cup red wine or water
1 tablespoon chopped fresh parsley

Preheat oven to 350°.

Coat chicken with flour and a little salt. Heat oil in large skillet and brown chicken on all sides; sauté chicken in several batches, if necessary. Remove chicken from skillet and arrange in very large casserole dish; keep warm.

Melt the butter in same skillet; add onion, green pepper, and garlic and cook until wilted. Add the tomatoes with their liquid, white pepper, thyme, and curry, and mix well. Pour the tomato sauce over the chicken. Cover tightly and bake until the chicken is very tender, about 30 minutes.

Meanwhile, cook the rice and prepare the garnishes. Place the almonds in an ungreased shallow baking pan and toast in the oven until browned, about 10 minutes. Plump the currants in 1/4 cup wine or warm water.

To serve, remove chicken breasts from sauce and arrange them in the center of a large warmed platter. Surround the chicken with a ring of rice. Stir the currants into the tomato sauce, and pour sauce over chicken. Scatter almonds over the rice, and sprinkle parsley over the chicken.

Curries are much better if made a day ahead. Just refrigerate the chicken and sauce overnight and reheat when ready to serve. Cook the rice ahead too, if you wish, and reheat in the microwave or oven.

Makes 12 servings.

⚬⟨ Quick Lamb Curry ⟩⚬

3 tablespoons all-purpose flour
1 teaspoon salt
1¹/₂ pounds lamb, cut in 1-inch cubes
2 tablespoons olive oil, divided
1¹/₂ tablespoons curry powder
2 onions, coarsely chopped
1 clove garlic, minced
3 carrots, sliced
1 can (13³/₄ ounces) beef broth
1 tablespoon tomato paste
¹/₂ cup plain yogurt
cooked rice

Combine flour and salt; then dredge lamb pieces in this mixture. Heat 1 tablespoon olive oil in large nonstick skillet over medium-high heat. Brown lamb, working in batches if necessary. Remove lamb to plate. Mix curry powder into remaining flour mixture; reserve.

Reduce heat to medium. Add remaining oil and cook onion, garlic, and carrot until onion is soft. Sprinkle reserved flour over vegetables in skillet. Cook 1 minute, stirring constantly.

Stir in beef broth and tomato paste, blending thoroughly. Add lamb to skillet, scraping in any juices that collected on the plate. Simmer 15 minutes. Transfer to serving bowl; fold in yogurt.

Serve with rice.

Makes 6 servings.

⚬⟨ Curried Fruit Medley ⟩⚬

An uncommonly good, light dessert.

2 cups fresh or canned pear halves
2 cups fresh or canned peach halves
2 cups fresh or canned pineapple slices
¹/₄ cup butter or margarine
¹/₂ cup brown sugar
1 tablespoon curry powder
¹/₄ teaspoon salt
low-fat sour cream (optional)

Preheat oven to 350°.

If using canned fruit, drain well; save juices for another use. Arrange fruit in a 2-quart baking dish.

In a small saucepan, melt butter; add sugar, curry powder and salt. Heat until sugar is dissolved. Pour over fruit. Bake 25 to 30 minutes. Serve hot, topped with a dollop of sour cream, if you wish.

Serves 8 to 10.

For Other Recipes Featuring Curry Powder, See:

Senegalese Soup, p. 76

Malaysian Chicken and Sweet Potato Kurma, p. 196

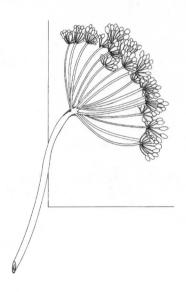

Dill Seed

Botanical name: **Anethum graveolens**
Part used as spice: **Seeds**
Available as: **Whole or ground seeds**

Dill is another member of the fabulous family of Umbelliferae, along with several others in this book—anise, caraway, coriander, cumin, and fennel. They all have that distinctive upside-down-parasol flower shape, similar natural chemicals, and a long history as garden plants grown for food, magic, and medicine.

Like the others, dill is native to the Mediterranean region and southern Russia, but soon spread throughout the temperate regions of the world, where it grows easily. Commercially, it is grown in India (most of our seeds are imported from there), Russia, Scandinavia, Turkey, and California (producer of much of the commercial dill weed).

The very pretty, wispy leaves also have the dill taste, but milder than the seeds; the foliage is harvested, dried, and sold commercially as "dill weed." If you grow it in your garden (and it is not hard to do), you can enjoy the fresh foliage as garnishes.

History and Legend

Dill is one of the plants that were known by, and grown by, people in the most ancient civilizations. The Babylonians and Assyrians, two great kingdoms in the area we now call the Middle East, cultivated it for its medicinal value and for its magical properties.

It is as easy to grow as a weed, and in some areas people think it *is* a weed. In ancient Palestine, so the story goes, a group of angry citizens decided to get back at the local ruler by paying their taxes in dill seed.

Since the plant was as common then as Queen Anne's lace (another umbellifer) is in the United States today, this was a clear insult. It was the equivalent of saying, "Here's what we think of you, buster: A handful of weed seeds."

It's a wonder their joke didn't backfire, however, for in those days, and for long after, dill was considered one very powerful plant:

- Because it was thought to have magical properties, dill was part of the formula for love potions and aphrodisiacs.
- Newborn calves were rubbed with dill mixed with salt, to protect them from the Evil Eye.
- Roman gladiators were given a strong tea made from dill as a stimulant.
- In the Middle Ages physicians advised their patients with epilepsy to hold a piece of dill in their left hand to prevent attacks.
- About the same time, people troubled with insomnia put a sprig of dill under the pillow to help them sleep better.
- In Germany, brides carried dill as a token of good fortune to the marriage.
- In early America, it was one of the "meeting house seeds"; on their way to church, people stashed a few seeds in their pockets, to allay their hunger during long sermons.

Medicinal Uses

For close to 4,000 years, dill has been used by medical practitioners to treat:

- Hiccups
- Stomachache
- Indigestion
- Insomnia
- Bad breath

In medieval Europe, dill seeds were burned to make a powder that was used on bleeding wounds.

For centuries, nursing mothers have drunk dill tea as a way to increase milk flow.

But perhaps the best-known medicinal application has to do with intestinal disorders. Archaeologists have found evidence in the Egyptian tombs that Egyptians used dill seeds to help promote digestion. They were right. Dill is a carminative, a substance that breaks up and helps dispel intestinal gas.

Dill is especially helpful with digestive upset in babies, because it also contains a mild sedative. In fact, the very name "dill" comes from the

Here's a safe home remedy for gas: Brew a cup of dill tea (1 teaspoon seeds steeped in 1 cup boiling water), sweeten to taste. This works as well today as it did in ancient Egypt.

Norse word *dilla*, meaning "to lull." Through the centuries mothers have given dill tea to colicky babies, both to calm them and to relieve their abdominal distress. In colonial America mothers made a dense cake with dill, for teething babies to chew on.

Its carminative property is the reason dill was first put in the pickling solution for cucumbers. Cucumbers were notorious for giving people gas; everyone knew that dill would get rid of it; finally someone figured out that putting the two together in the first place would prevent the problem. Nowadays plant breeders have developed "burpless" cucumbers to eliminate the problem, but we are so accustomed to the taste of dill in our pickles that they wouldn't taste right without it.

Cooking with Dill Seed

Dill goes with pickles like peanut butter goes with jelly, like cranberries go with turkey, like . . . you know. But peanut butter goes with other things as well, and so do cranberries, and so does dill. It's time to expand our horizons.

Dill seeds are very similar in taste to caraway seeds, except milder, and can be used in many of the same ways. As always, the choice of whether to use whole seeds or the ground powder is primarily a question of texture: Do you want crunchy bits in the finished dishes, or not?

Use Dill Seeds with:
- Strong vegetables such as carrots, turnips, cauliflower, and cabbage (add to the cooking water)
- Lamb chops and steak (mix ground seed with salt and pepper and rub into the meat before broiling)
- Meat stews (use either whole or ground seeds)
- Potato salad, egg salad, cole slaw (toast seeds first, fold in at last minute)
- Sauces based on sour cream
- Mayonnaise-based salad dressings
- Fish or shellfish (put whole seeds in the poaching water)
- Sauces for fish (dill is a classic with salmon)
- Crumb topping for vegetable casseroles
- Bean soups
- Tomato juice, vegetable juice
- Fruit soup

- Apple pie (add whole seeds to the sliced apple mixture)
- Chicken à la king and similar dishes (add to the cream sauce)

As you might guess, the largest single use for dill is in making pickles. This combination is not a new idea. The English herbalist John Parkinson, writing in 1629, said: "[Dill] is put upon pickled cucumber where it doth very well agree, giving to the cold fruit a pretty spicie taste."

If you do decide to try a hand at the dill pickle recipe that follows, here is an important description of proper canning technique:

Basic Canning Instructions

1. Use a canning pot or a very large pot with a wire rack. Fill with water almost to top and bring to boil.

2. Meanwhile, wash canning jars and keep them hot (you can keep them in the canning pot until ready to fill).

3. Put the lids and screw-on bands into a saucepan, cover with water, and heat just to a simmer. (Use only the two-part metal lids; do not reuse lids from commercial products such as mayonnaise jars.)

4. Follow the recipe for whatever it is you're canning.

5. Using a ladle and a wide-mouth funnel, fill the hot jars, leaving $1/2$ inch of head space.

6. Wipe any spills from the top rim of the jar.

7. Slide a table knife down inside the side of the jar to release any air bubbles.

8. Using tongs, remove one lid from the saucepan and fit it over the jar top. Then remove a band and screw it onto jar. Careful, it's hot; you may want to use a dishtowel to protect your hands. In recipes this step is often expressed in a shorthand way: "seal."

9. Repeat until all jars are full. Work as fast as you can so that the first jar doesn't cool.

10. Place jars in canning pot (there's a special tool called a jar lifter that makes this easy and prevents hot splashes). Make sure there is enough water in the pot to cover the tops of the jars by at least an inch.

11. Turn heat up to high and bring water to a vigorous boil. Start counting the processing time as soon as water boils. Add one minute to processing time for each 1000 feet above sea level.

12. At end of specified time, remove jars from canner (use the jar lifter) and set them several inches apart on a wire rack or a folded towel to cool.

13. When the vacuum forms, the lids will pop—a very satisfying sound. Occasionally, they don't pop; the test is that the lid is concave and doesn't pop back up when you press on it.

14. You can, if you wish, remove the screw-on bands and use them another time.

15. Refrigerate any jars that don't seal; use within a week. Or freeze them, once the jars are completely cool.

⤳ Dill Bread ⤳

¹/₄ cup finely chopped onion
2 tablespoons dill seed
1 tablespoon butter
1 package yeast
¹/₄ cup warm water
1 cup cottage cheese
2 tablespoons sugar
1 egg
1 teaspoon salt
¹/₄ teaspoon baking soda
2¹/₄ cups flour, or more

Sauté onion and dill in butter over very low heat for 5 minutes. Meanwhile, sprinkle yeast into warm water in large measuring cup; stir to dissolve and set aside. In mixing bowl, beat together cottage cheese, sugar, egg, salt, and baking soda. Add yeast and beat for 2 minutes. Gradually add flour, mixing to make a stiff dough. Cover and let rise until doubled in size. Punch dough down, pat into a greased 8-inch casserole or a 2-quart dish. Let rise until light. Bake at 350° for 30 to 40 minutes. Butter the top with softened butter and sprinkle with salt.

⇥ Dill Pickles ⇤

4 pounds cucumbers, about 4 inches long
1 cup dill seed
21 whole peppercorns
3¹/₂ teaspoons mustard seed
3 cups white vinegar
3 cups water
6 tablespoons salt

Cut cucumbers in half lengthwise. Pack into hot sterilized pint jars. To each jar add 2 tablespoons dill seed, 3 peppercorns, and ¹/₂ teaspoon mustard seed. Combine vinegar, water, and salt in a saucepan and bring to a boil. Pour boiling liquid over cucumbers, leaving ¹/₄-inch head space. Seal. Process in boiling water bath for 10 minutes. (See page 165 for canning instructions.)
Makes 7 pints.

⇥ Dilly Carrots ⇤

These fresh pickles go nicely on an antipasto plate, or alongside sandwiches.

8 to 10 small, young carrots
¹/₂ cup white wine vinegar
¹/₂ cup water
1 teaspoon dill seed
1 teaspoon lemon pepper

Scrape and trim carrots; cut in quarters lengthwise. In saucepan combine vinegar (herb-flavored vinegars, such as basil, thyme, and tarragon, are especially nice here), water, dill, and lemon pepper; add carrots. Cover and simmer for about 10 minutes or until carrots are crisp-tender. Chill for several hours or overnight in liquid. In covered containers, will keep several weeks in refrigerator.
Makes about 1 pint.

⊰ Spicy Winter Squash ⊱

2 to 2¹/₂ pounds banana or Hubbard squash
¹/₂ cup water
1 teaspoon salt
¹/₂ cup sour cream
1 teaspoon dill seed
1 teaspoon onion powder
¹/₄ teaspoon coarsely ground black pepper

Peel squash and cut into 1-inch cubes. Combine in saucepan with water and salt and cook until tender. Meanwhile, toast dill seeds in dry skillet for 2 to 3 minutes, until they are very fragrant. Mix seeds with sour cream and onion powder. Drain the squash and place in serving dish; toss gently with sour cream mixture. Sprinkle with black pepper and serve at once.
Makes 6 servings.

⊰ Lime Dill Dressing ⊱

1 tablespoon dill seed
2 tablespoons lime juice
1 tablespoon vinegar
¹/₂ teaspoon sugar
¹/₂ teaspoon dry mustard
1 tablespoon mayonnaise
¹/₃ cup olive oil
salt and freshly ground pepper to taste

Toast the dill seeds in an ungreased skillet for 2 to 3 minutes, until they are fragrant. Place in blender container and pulse the machine a few times to coarsely grind the seeds. Add lime juice, vinegar, sugar, mustard, and mayonnaise and blend well. Add oil in a steady stream, blending until thoroughly combined. Add salt and pepper to taste.
Makes about ¹/₂ cup.

—Adapted from Renée Shepherd

❧ German Potatoes ☙

3 pounds new red potatoes (see note)
6 strips bacon
2 medium onions, chopped
1 tablespoon dill seed
2 stalks celery, chopped
1 green pepper, chopped
2 tablespoons flour
1/2 cup sugar
salt and pepper to taste
1/2 cup vinegar
3/4 cup water

Cook potatoes; drain and set aside but keep warm. Slice bacon into 1/2-inch lengths. Fry until brown, drain, and reserve. Pour off all but 1 tablespoon of bacon grease. Add onion and dill and cook until onion is golden; then add celery and green pepper and cook gently 1 to 2 minutes, until tender-crisp. Stir in flour, then sugar, salt, and pepper. Slowly stir in vinegar and water; cook until thickened, stirring constantly. Pour hot dressing over potatoes. Mix gently and sprinkle reserved bacon on top.

Note: Use small, whole, unpeeled potatoes if possible. If not available, cube larger potatoes.
Makes 6 servings.

❧ Grilled Salmon with Dill Sauce ☙

Dill Sauce
2 cups plain low-fat yogurt
1/2 cup peeled, seeded, and finely diced cucumber
2 teaspoons dill seed
2 teaspoons sugar
1 teaspoon finely grated lemon peel
2 teaspoons lemon juice
1/4 teaspoon pepper

In medium bowl, combine all ingredients; reserve.

1 1/2 pounds fresh salmon fillets, skin on
2 tablespoons vegetable oil
1 teaspoon onion powder
1/2 teaspoon coarsely ground black pepper

Rub salmon with oil on both sides. Sprinkle flesh side of salmon with onion powder and pepper. Grill salmon, skin side down, on rack over hot coals in covered barbecue for 8 to 10 minutes, or until salmon flakes when tested with a fork. To serve, remove skin from salmon and spoon sauce over fish; pass remaining sauce in small bowl.

You can also broil salmon in oven. Cook, skin-side down, 4 inches from heat source for 8 to 10 minutes or until salmon flakes when tested with a fork.

Makes 4 servings.

—Spice Islands

For Other Recipes Featuring Dill, See:
Dilly Beans, p. 94
Roasted Coriander Corn, p. 140
Greek Chicken Barbecue, p. 177
Mt. Olympus Chicken, p. 184

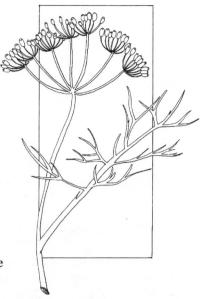

Fennel

Botanical name: **Foeniculum vulgare**
Part used as spice: **Seeds**
Available as: **Whole or ground seeds**

If you shop at greengrocers in large U.S. cities, or travel in Italy, or have Italian relatives, you know fennel as a vegetable. That fat bulb of overlapping stalks that looks like a pregnant celery is known as Florence fennel, or *finocchio*. As we will see in a moment, the love affair between Italians and fennel has been going on for close to five thousand years.

Fennel seeds—the spice—come from another plant, known as common, wild, or sweet fennel. But the two are very close cousins, and if you had Florence fennel in your garden and somehow forgot to harvest it, so that it flowered and went to seed, you could use those seeds the same way.

And if you had fennel in your garden, you'd be glad, for it's a beauty. The attractive foliage, which is soft and amazingly frilly, is very pretty as a garnish or in flower arrangements. And it, like the seeds, tastes like licorice. Somehow, finding that flavor in something green that looks like a fern frond is even more surprising than finding it in a brown seed, and so growing fennel is a lot of fun. I play a game with children: Close your eyes, eat this, and tell me of what it reminds you. Without fail, they exclaim, "Licorice!" And without fail, when I show them what it was they ate, they can't believe it.

Fennel is native to the countries of the Mediterranean, but grows easily in all temperate climates, including my backyard. It is grown commercially in several parts of Europe, Russia, Egypt, India, and China.

It is in the same family as several other plants in this book: caraway, cumin, anise, dill, and coriander. Collectively these are called the Umbelliferae, and all have that distinctive flower head that I think of as an open parasol held wrong side up. Fennel is particularly close to anise in flavor; in a pinch, you could substitute one for the other.

History and Legends

The Romans gave us the Latin name of this plant (don't forget, Latin was their native tongue): *Foeniculum* means "little hay," suggesting that it might have been fed to livestock as well as to more appreciative humans. The word "fennel" is a corruption of the Latin name.

In Greece the fennel plant was called marathon, and there is a great story connected to the name. In 490 B.C. a famous battle was fought between Greeks and the invading Persians on a field outside the town of Marathon, north of Athens; the field was covered with fennel plants.

When the tide of battle seemed to be turning against the Greeks, a Greek courier ran all the way to Sparta for help, a distance of one hundred fifty miles. And that is the origin of the modern, and thankfully shorter, marathon.

Like other plants that have been cultivated by humankind for so many centuries, fennel has developed its share of folklore myths.

- Throughout Europe, superstitious folks hung a piece of fennel over their doorways on Midsummer's Eve, as a protection against the Evil Eye.
- It was used indoors too: Keyholes were stuffed with a paste of fennel seeds and leaves to keep witches out while the family slept safely inside.
- To keep witches from turning milk sour, cows' udders were covered with fennel paste.
- In Greek mythology, Prometheus stole fire from heaven and hid it in a stalk of fennel (mature stems are hollow), so that he could bring it to the mortals on earth without any of the other gods knowing he was giving away this precious commodity.

Fennel was very popular as both food and medicine in ancient Greece and Rome. Citizens of both regions ate the seed for strength and stamina; gladiators mixed it into their foods, soldiers carried the seeds to ease hunger pangs on long marches. Later, Charlemagne, the great ruler of the eighth century, decreed that fennel be grown on all the imperial farms, thus effectively spreading the plant throughout central Europe.

In Renaissance Europe, people sent special messages to one another by using the symbolic meanings assigned to herbs and flowers. Fennel was considered a symbol of flattery, and an Italian expression *dare finocchio* (literally, give fennel) meant to engage in outlandish flattery.

A few hundred years later, in the young United States, mothers of young children slipped a handful of seeds into their pockets as the family left for church. If the children grew restless during the long services, parents distracted them by letting them nibble on the seeds. Reflecting the colloquial name for churches in those days, these were called "meeting house seeds," and fennel was one of them. Other Umbelliferae seeds were also used—dill, anise, and cumin.

We now know that those plants contain a mild sedative, so in addition to distracting squirmy children, they also calmed them down. Without the benefit of modern science, our ancestors figured out what worked.

Those same seeds were also used by adults on fast days, to alleviate hunger pangs . . . just like the Roman soldiers so many centuries earlier.

Medicinal Uses

Fennel has a long history as a healing plant. Since the days of Greece and Rome, it has been prescribed for many, many purposes, some of them valid, some not:

- For scorpion stings and snakebite
- To give strength and stamina
- To make people slim
- As an aphrodisiac
- To give courage and long life
- To ease stomach pains
- For diseases of the lungs, liver, and kidneys
- For earache, toothache, hiccups
- To alleviate coughs, asthma, rheumatism
- As a flea repellent

Pliny, the first-century Roman scholar whose mammoth encyclopedia of the natural world profoundly influenced science and medicine for centuries, described twenty-two ailments that fennel was effective against. Among other things, he wrote that snakes are temporarily blinded when they shed their skin, so they rub against fennel plants, getting some of what he called the fennel "juice" into their eyes and restoring their sight. For the next fifteen hundred years, people used fennel tea as an eyewash, thinking they were improving their vision or even curing cataracts.

The Saxons (fifth-century Britain) believed that nine diseases threatened the world, and that nine sacred herbs were mankind's only protection against decimation; fennel was one of them.

Fennel has had a long reputation as an appetite suppressant and diet aid, dating from the days of the Roman soldiers. Apparently the frantic search for the perfect weight control product is not a twentieth-century fad. In 1650, William Coles, an Englishman, wrote a botanical treatise called *Nature's Paradise.* In it, he said this about fennel:

> Both the seeds, leaves and root of our Garden Fennel are much used in drinks and broths for those that are grown fat, to abate their unwieldiness and cause them to grow more gaunt and lank.

Does it work? It is exactly as effective a diet aid as it is an aphrodisiac: If you believe it works, it will.

One old home remedy involving fennel has been scientifically validated: as a safe treatment for colicky babies. Pioneer mothers fed a mild tea made from fennel and sweetened with honey to fussy babies, and they fell asleep in no time. It works because fennel is both a carminative (breaks up intestinal gas) and a calmative (a mild relaxant). It also works for adults suffering from gas: Crush about a tablespoon of fennel seeds (1/2 teaspoon for babies), steep in a cup of boiling water for 5 minutes, strain, and sweeten to taste.

Another tip for adults: Chew a few seeds to settle your stomach and digest your food after a big meal, or to sweeten your breath after too long a conversation with Jack Daniel's.

Cooking with Fennel

Fennel in all its forms—bulb, stems, foliage, and seeds—is extremely popular in Italy. Cooking the young stems as a vegetable, like asparagus, goes all the way back to the Romans.

The English herbalist John Parkinson, writing in 1640, said: "The leaves, seeds and roots are both for meat and medicine; the Italians especially do much delight in the use thereof . . . The taste being sweet and somewhat hot, helpeth to digest the crude quality of fish and other viscous meats. We use it to lay upon fish or to boil it therewith and with divers other things, as also the seeds in bread and other things." All of which we still do today.

Fennel is so popular with fish it is known as the fish herb; just as Mr. Parkinson says, it does help temper the oily taste of some of the heavier fish. You can use fennel leaves, if you have access to them, or put seeds in the poaching water or baking pan. And if you grow the plant, you can treat your guests to special fennel-grilled fish; at the end of the season, take some of the long stalks and put them on top of the charcoal in the grill; the fish will absorb the aroma.

The seeds taste quite a bit like anise but not as sweet. So they impart a light licorice-y taste that is hard to describe. This sweet-but-not-sweet flavor goes equally well with meatballs, bread, and apple pie.

Whenever possible, use whole seeds. As is true with all other spices, the ground form of fennel, if stored for a long period, tends to lose its flavor. If you don't want the seed itself in your finished dish, but only its flavor, grind up just the amount you need for that recipe.

Use Fennel Seeds with:
- Bread and rolls (as a topping)
- Meatballs, spaghetti sauce
- Tomato dishes
- Sauces for fish and seafood
- Roast pork
- Lentils, cabbage, celery, potatoes, sauerkraut
- Fruit pies, either in the crust dough or the filling

> In a book published much more recently than you would think, it is noted that fennel seeds are good with marinades for wild boar. You probably weren't planning to roast wild boar any time soon—I know I'm not—but it never hurts to know these things.

In commercial food manufacturing, fennel is part of the formula for licorice-flavored liqueurs like Anisette. Most important, however, is its use in flavored sausage. There is an Italian salami so rich with fennel that it is named *finocchiona*. And it is fennel that gives Italian sausage its characteristic flavor. So much fennel is used in Italian sausage, and so much Italian sausage is used in American pizza parlors, that U.S. consumption levels of fennel have increased dramatically in recent years.

Next time you order your pizza with Italian sausage, think back to the Roman gladiators and the snacks they surely made to sustain themselves between matches. With that funny little seed, you all have something in common.

⚜ Green Beans with Fennel and Ginger ⚜

1 tablespoon butter (or 1 teaspoon butter and 2 teaspoons oil)
1 small onion, very thinly sliced
2 teaspoons finely chopped, fresh ginger
1/4 teaspoon crushed fennel seed
1/4 teaspoon salt
1 pound haricots verts or young green beans, trimmed and cut into
    1/2-inch pieces
1/4 cup chicken stock

Heat butter in a large skillet. Add the onion, ginger, fennel seed and salt. Sauté until onions are glazed and translucent. Add beans and stock. Cover and cook only until beans are tender-crisp, about 5 minutes.
Serves 4 to 6.

—Renée Shepherd

∗⟨ Crusty Baked Chicken ⟩∗

¹/₄ cup salad oil
¹/₄ cup apple juice
¹/₂ cup strong black coffee
1 tablespoon fennel seed
¹/₂ teaspoon onion powder
1 teaspoon salt
¹/₈ teaspoon pepper
1 whole chicken

Combine oil, apple juice, coffee, fennel, onion powder, salt, and pepper; pour over chicken and marinate 1 to 2 hours. Roast in 350° oven 1 hour, basting occasionally with marinade.
Serves 4.

∗⟨ Swordfish Italian Style ⟩∗

2 pounds swordfish steak, thickly sliced
2 tablespoons olive oil
¹/₂ cup dry red wine
1 tablespoon lemon juice
¹/₂ teaspoon fennel seed
¹/₂ teaspoon salt
¹/₄ teaspoon pepper
¹/₄ teaspoon garlic salt

Arrange fish in wide, shallow baking dish. Combine remaining ingredients and mix well. Pour marinade over fish, cover, and refrigerate overnight.
Preheat oven to 425°.
Bake, basting occasionally, for 45 minutes, or until fish flakes easily.
To serve, carefully lift fish onto warmed platter; pour sauce over and around fish.
Makes 6 servings.

❧ Greek Chicken Barbecue ❧

2 teaspoons finely grated lemon peel
3 tablespoons lemon juice
3 tablespoons olive oil
1 teaspoon dill seed
¹/₂ teaspoon fennel seed
¹/₂ teaspoon garlic salt (or minced fresh garlic)
4 whole chicken legs (about 2 to 2¹/₂ pounds)

In nonmetal shallow pan or zip-top bag, combine lemon peel, lemon juice, oil, dill seed, fennel seed, and garlic; add chicken and turn to coat completely. Marinate for several hours or overnight. Remove chicken from marinade and place over medium coals; grill until done and browned on both sides (about 30 minutes total). Brush with marinade as chicken cooks; discard remaining marinade.

You can also broil the chicken in an oven. Broil for 15 minutes, 4 inches from heat source, frequently basting with marinade. Turn and broil 10 more minutes or until done. Again, discard any remaining marinade.

Makes 4 servings.

—Spice Islands

❧ Sole in Sour Cream ❧

4 fillets of sole or turbot
salt and pepper
¹/₂ teaspoon ground fennel seeds
1 tablespoon butter
²/₃ cup sour cream

Preheat oven to 350°.

Sprinkle the fish with salt, pepper, and fennel, and put it into a lightly buttered ovenproof dish. Spread the sour cream over the fish and dot with butter. Cover the dish and bake for 25 to 30 minutes. Fish is done when it flakes easily with a fork.

Serves 4.

⋰⋱ Walnut Pastries ⋰⋱

These sweet turnovers are a special treat with coffee or tea.

2¹/₄ cups flour
¹/₂ teaspoon ground fennel seeds
3 teaspoons superfine sugar, divided (see note)
pinch of salt
4 ounces butter
2–3 tablespoons water
1¹/₄ cups walnuts, chopped
seeds from 2 cardamom pods (or ¹/₄ teaspoon ground cinnamon)
2 tablespoons honey
grated rind of ¹/₂ lemon
1 egg, beaten
confectioners' sugar

Combine flour, fennel, 1 teaspoon sugar and the salt in a mixing bowl; with a pastry blender or two knives, cut in the butter until the mixture is crumbly. Add enough water to mix to a soft dough. (You can also use a food processor for these steps.) Form into a ball and chill for 30 minutes.

In a separate bowl mix together the walnuts, remaining sugar, the spice, honey, and lemon rind.

Roll out the pastry on a floured surface and cut out 4-inch circles with a biscuit cutter. Put a spoonful of the walnut filling in the center of each circle and fold over to make a half moon. Moisten the edges lightly with water and press them together with your fingers or the tines of a fork. Prick vent holes in the top with a fork and brush with beaten egg. Transfer the pastries to a cookie sheet and bake in a preheated 375° oven for 15 to 20 minutes. Do not overbake. Cool on a wire rack, then sprinkle with confectioners' sugar.

Note: To make superfine sugar, buzz regular white sugar in the blender.

Variation: Use Poppy Seed filling, page 271, instead of nut filling.

⋰⋱ Mom's Apple Pie with Fennel ⋰⋱

pastry for a 9-inch double crust pie
about 3 pounds tart cooking apples such as Gravenstein
   (7–8 medium apples)
³/₄ cup sugar

¹/₄ cup all-purpose flour or 2¹/₂ tablespoons cornstarch
1¹/₂ teaspoons fennel seed
¹/₄ teaspoon ground cardamom
2 tablespoons butter or margarine

Preheat oven to 400°.

On a floured surface, roll out half of the pastry into a circle about ¹/₈ inch thick; place in 9-inch pie pan and trim off excess around the rim. Roll out remaining pastry into a 13-inch circle. Cover with a damp towel or plastic wrap.

Peel and core apples and cut into thick slices. Measure slices; you should have 8 cups. In a large bowl, stir together the sugar, flour (or cornstarch), fennel, and cardamom. Add the apple slices and mix lightly to coat. Mound apples into the pie pan. Dot with butter.

Fit pastry top over apples. Estimate a 1-inch margin extending beyond edge of pan, and trim away any excess crust. Seal edge of margin to bottom pastry by crimping with the tines of a fork or pressing decorative scallops with your fingers. If you feel fancy, cut excess dough into small apples or leaves and "glue" them to pastry top with a little water. With a sharp knife, cut 5 or 6 vent holes in the top pastry.

Bake pie until pastry is browned and juices are bubbling, about 50 to 60 minutes. If edges of pastry begin to brown too much, cover with a thin strip of foil. Cool pan on a wire rack for at least 30 minutes before serving.

Variation: Instead of fennel and cardamom, substitute ¹/₂ teaspoon Chinese five-spice.

For Other Recipes Featuring Fennel, See:

Scandinavian Bread, p. 48
Italian Rye Bread, p. 56
Indian Potato and Eggplant Jumble, p. 183
Refrigerator Rolls for a Crowd, p. 268
Bouillabaisse, p. 279

Fenugreek

Botanical name: Trigonella foenum-graecum
Part used as spice: Seeds
Available as: Whole or ground seeds

Let's be honest: Fenugreek is not one of the major spices, and you could, if necessary, live the rest of your life without any, but it is nice to know about. And if you ever have a desire to make up your own spice mix for curry, which I hope you will, then you'll need some.

Both the Latin and the common name of this plant come to us from the Romans, who of course spoke Latin as their native tongue. The Romans learned about the plant from the Greeks, who used it to feed livestock, and so they called it *foenum-graecum*, which means "Greek hay." *Foenum-graecum* is retained as the species name, and "fenugreek" is an anglicization of that Latin phrase.

Fenugreek is an annual plant (lives just one year), and a member of the legume family (peas and beans). Like all legumes, it puts nitrogen in the soil, and for that reason is grown as a cover crop in Mediterranean citrus orchards. In some places fenugreek is grown as cattle feed, like hay, but we are more interested in the seeds.

The plant is about two feet high, and produces quite small flowers, from which develop very long (four to five inches), thin, curved pods. Their resemblance to an animal's horn is the reason fenugreek is sometimes called goat's horn or cow's horn. Each pod has from ten to twenty seeds; they are small (about ⅛ inch long), hard, yellowish-brown, and have a diagonal gash that divides the seed into two asymmetrical parts.

In parts of the world where vegetarianism is more the rule than the exception, fenugreek is considered a food. The seeds, which like all legumes are high in protein, are cooked up into a nutritious main dish. We are more likely to use the seeds as a spice; their flavor is essential in curries, and is a tasty addition to stews and hearty soups.

History and Legend

This is one of the oldest cultivated plants known to man; it has been grown in the Nile Valley since 1000 B.C. Papyruses found in Egyptian tombs describe how to cook it as a food and how to prepare it as a medicine (to reduce fevers). The Greeks and Romans, as we have seen, grew it as cattle feed, and also used it medicinally. The Egyptians used it as part of a formula for embalming.

Medicine and Other Uses

Women in Asia eat lots of fenugreek seed because it is reputed to help with menstrual cramps and difficult childbirth, and to increase milk flow after the baby is born. That's another reason it is used as cattle feed: Supposedly it increases their milk, too.

The seeds of fenugreek contain a high proportion (40%) of mucilage, a slippery substance that is used as a natural emollient, meaning something that softens and smooths. (If you've ever eaten stewed okra, or pushed it around on your plate, you've encountered plant mucilage.) Long before they had modern laboratories to analyze plant structures, long before anyone heard the word "mucilage," people used ground fenugreek seeds on chapped lips.

> "When the body is rubbed with it, the skin is left beautiful, without any blemishes."
> —Egyptian medical papyrus, 1500 B.C.

Fenugreek seeds have been used to make a yellow dye. In the Middle Ages, ground-up seeds, made into a paste, were a common "cure" for baldness.

Today the plant is still used in rural areas of Europe and western Asia as cattle food, either by itself or as an addition to regular hay. Fenugreek leaves contain coumarin, which has a sweet fragrance reminiscent of vanilla. Added to hay that has become stale or mildewed, it disguises foul smells. And seed, added to the diet of horses, gives their coats a healthy sheen.

Cooking with Fenugreek

Fenugreek's main claim to fame these days is in curry powder. It is the defining taste in commercial mixes. And if you want to make your own curry powder, you'll want some fenugreek on hand.

The second claim to fame is in the manufacture of imitation maple syrup. Roasted fenugreek seed has an aroma that many have described as similar to that of burnt sugar, and the same chemicals that produce that sugary fragrance also contribute a sweet taste.

The seeds are quite bitter-tasting when raw; it's a good idea to toast them before grinding. But one thing you can do, if you do this sort of thing, is sprout them. The young sprouts are not bitter, and add a nice unusual taste to salads.

The leaves of the fenugreek plant are bitter to Western tastes, although they are sometimes added to vegetable curries in India.

Use Fenugreek in:
- All curried dishes
- Black bean soup
- Vegetable stew
- Beef casserole

⁂ Basic Curry Spice Mix ⁂

Here is a basic medium-hot curry mix, with a hint of sweetness.

3 dried hot chilies
1 tablespoon coriander seeds
2 teaspoons cumin seeds
1 teaspoon mustard seeds
1 teaspoon black peppercorns
1 teaspoon fenugreek seeds
1 tablespoon ground turmeric
1/2 teaspoon ground ginger
1 teaspoon ground cinnamon
1/2 teaspoon ground cloves

Remove and discard the seeds from the chilies (wear rubber gloves to protect your hands). Toast the coriander, cumin, mustard, and fenugreek seeds until they are lightly brown and aromatic; cool and grind to a powder along with peppercorns and chilies. (A small food processor or electric grinder makes the job easier.) Add powdered spices and blend well.

This makes about 1/4 cup of spice mixture, enough for several dishes. It will keep for weeks in a tightly closed container.

Hearty Vegetable Bean Soup

2 tablespoons butter
1 cup sliced onions
2 quarts vegetable or chicken stock
1 tablespoon salt
1/8 teaspoon pepper
2 tablespoons ground fenugreek
2 cups diced potatoes
1 1/2 cups diced carrots
1 cup diced celery
1/4 cup chopped celery leaves
1 tablespoon chopped parsley
1 can (1 pound 4 ounces) red kidney beans

Melt butter in large pan or Dutch oven over low heat. Sauté onions until they are a dark golden color; cooking slowly brings out the sweetness of the onions.

Add broth, salt, pepper, and fenugreek. Stir, scraping up bits from bottom as you do. Add potatoes, carrots, celery, celery leaves, and parsley. Simmer, covered, for 10 minutes, or until vegetables are crisp-tender. Add beans; simmer, covered, another 10 minutes.

Makes 10 cups.

Indian Potato and Eggplant Jumble

1 pound potatoes
1 pound eggplant
2 medium onions
4 tablespoons vegetable oil
3/4 teaspoon fennel seeds
1/2 teaspoon fenugreek seeds
1/4 teaspoon pepper
1/4 teaspoon cayenne
1 teaspoon lemon juice
1 teaspoon salt
pinch ground cardamom
1/2 cup water

Cut the potatoes and eggplant (peeled or not, as you wish) into cubes and chop the onions coarsely. In a heavy pan, heat the oil until it begins to smoke. Add the fennel and fenugreek seeds and cook briefly, until they begin to turn dark. Add the vegetables, lower the heat, and cook for 10 minutes, stirring and shaking the pan.

Mix in the remaining ingredients, cover the pan, and simmer for 15 to 20 minutes, stirring occasionally. Serve hot or at room temperature.

Makes 6 servings.

⤙ Fenugreek Beef Stew ⤚

2 pounds beef stew meat
1/4 cup flour
3 tablespoons vegetable or olive oil
1/2 cup chopped onion
1 can (8 ounces) tomato sauce
1 1/2 cups water
1 1/2 teaspoons ground fenugreek
1 teaspoon salt
1/8 teaspoon black pepper
2 cups sliced carrots
2 cups diced potatoes

Trim excess fat from meat; cut into 1 1/2-inch cubes. Dredge meat in flour. Heat oil in a Dutch oven or heavy saucepan; add beef and brown well on all sides. Add onion; sauté until soft.

Stir in tomato sauce, water, fenugreek, salt, and pepper. Simmer, covered, for 1 hour. Add vegetables, simmer 30 minutes more.

Makes 4 to 6 servings.

⤙ Mt. Olympus Chicken ⤚

2 tablespoons butter
4 boneless chicken breasts
salt and pepper
2 large onions, chopped
1 pound tomatoes, peeled, seeded, and chopped
6 tablespoons white wine
1 teaspoon coriander seeds, crushed
1/4 teaspoon ground fenugreek
1 teaspoon safflower, crushed
1 bay leaf
1/2 teaspoon dried thyme
1 lemon, sliced thinly
4 tablespoons finely chopped dill weed

Melt butter in large, heavy skillet or Dutch oven. Season the chicken with salt and pepper and brown in the butter. When browned on all sides, remove chicken to platter and keep warm. Add onions to pan and cook until golden brown. Add the tomatoes, wine, spices, bay leaf, and thyme. Stir to mix well. Place the chicken pieces on top of the tomato sauce and cover the chicken with the lemon slices.

Cover and simmer for 45 to 50 minutes, or until the chicken is tender. Check sauce occasionally, and add a little more wine or water if necessary. Remove bay leaf before serving.

To serve, spoon out the sauce and spread it over a warmed platter. Arrange the chicken with lemon slices in the center of the sauce. Make sure the lemons are still in position on top of the chicken, and sprinkle the dill over the lemons.

Makes 4 servings.

Five-Spice Powder

Available as: Ground spice blend

This premixed blend of ground spices is used primarily in Chinese cooking, as you might guess from its full name: "Chinese Five-Spice."

The five spices and their relative proportions are (usually):

- Star anise—2 parts
- Pepper (or fagara)—2 parts
- Fennel—2 parts
- Clove—1 part
- Cinnamon—1 part

Sometimes other spices are added to the blend as well: ginger, cardamom, or licorice root. It's still called five-spice powder.

Five-spice is most commonly used in marinades for meat, chicken, or fish, or rubbed into the surface of meat before roasting. The flavor of star anise dominates. This is powerful stuff; use very small amounts.

Fagara is not well known in the West. You may encounter it under other names: Szechuan pepper, anise pepper, Chinese pepper, flower pepper. It consists of the dried berries of a particular kind of ash tree that grows in Asia. Botanically speaking, it is not related to black pepper at all, but the taste is decidedly peppery. Many American manufacturers use white or black pepper instead.

Five-Spice Peanuts

¹/₄ cup water
1 teaspoon salt
¹/₄ teaspoon five-spice powder
2 cups raw blanched peanuts
sesame oil

Preheat oven to 275°.

In a mixing bowl, combine water, salt, and spice. Add peanuts and stir thoroughly.

Spread peanuts in shallow baking pan, add 3 or 4 drops of sesame oil, stir again. Bake for an hour, stirring every 10 minutes or so. Serve warm or cold.

⚜ Hibachi Beef Kabobs ⚜

1½ pounds strip steak or other tender beef
1 small green bell pepper
1 small red bell pepper
2 small crookneck squash
¼ pound small mushrooms
2 teaspoons sesame seed, as garnish

First, make marinade. Trim fat from steak; cut into 1½-inch cubes. Add meat to marinade, turning to coat all sides; marinate in refrigerator 3 hours or overnight.

Cut bell peppers into 1½-inch squares and squash into ½-inch rounds. Thread beef alternately with vegetables onto skewers. Place kabobs over medium-hot coals; grill until browned, brushing often with marinade. Turn and grill until done.

(You can also broil kabobs in oven. Broil for 6 minutes, 4 inches away from heat source, basting with marinade. Turn and broil 5 to 8 minutes or until done as desired.)

Sprinkle with sesame seed to serve.

Makes 4 servings.

Marinade
¼ cup vegetable or olive oil
¼ cup rice vinegar
2 tablespoons soy sauce
2 tablespoons orange juice concentrate
¾ teaspoon five-spice powder
1 teaspoon onion powder
1 teaspoon cracked black pepper

In nonmetal pan or zip-top plastic bag, combine marinade ingredients; reserve.

—Spice Islands

For Other Recipes Featuring Five-Spice, See:
Mom's Apple Pie with Fennel, p. 178

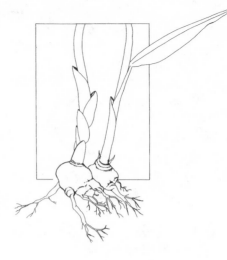

Ginger

Botanical name: Zingiber officinale

Part used as spice: Root (rhizome)

Available as: Fresh, dried, powdered; preserved

Gingerbread men. Ginger snaps. Ginger ale. Ginger beer.

Because the obvious is easy to overlook, we might not at first realize that all these old-fashioned treats are flavored with the spice ginger, the same thing that gives the delicious tang to Ginger Beef in Chinese restaurants, the same thing that turns into hot pink pickles in Japan or sweet tingly candy in Europe.

It may well be that ginger comes in more forms than any other spice (with the possible exception of hot chili peppers), and they all start from the same part of the ginger: the root.

Actually, it isn't really a root. It's technically a rhizome (pronounced

---

An Unusual Houseplant

In commercial plantings, when gingerroot is dug up for the harvest, small pieces of rhizomes are set aside to start the next crop. Each individual nodule, separated from the main root and planted, will grow into a full spreading root within a year. You can do the same in your kitchen, just for fun.

Break off a small piece of fresh gingerroot from the market. Make sure it has one "eye"—the growing node, like the eye on a potato. Fill a pot with good potting soil and plant the ginger piece about an inch below the surface. Keep the soil warm and lightly damp, and in about a month the sprouts will poke up through the dirt.

As the plant grows, treat it like any houseplant: medium filtered light, slightly damp soil. Then, when the plant reaches a good size, you can harvest your crop, if you can bear to part with it.

rye-zohm), a kind of specialized stem that grows underground in a horizontal, mildly zigzag pattern; if you know anyone who grows irises, you've seen rhizomes. But throughout the spice world people speak of "gingerroot," and so shall we. Just try going into your local market and asking the produce manager where the ginger rhizomes are, and see what you get.

Ginger is grown commercially in India, China, Africa, and Jamaica. Jamaican ginger is generally considered the finest, but it is expensive, and most of what is sold to the American market these days comes from India and China.

Ginger in Many Forms

Not so long ago, American cooks shopping for ginger had limited options. Today, ginger in its many forms can be found in ethnic markets around the country, in specialty food stores, and in plain old supermarkets everywhere:

- *Whole raw roots.* This is what most people, including most recipe writers, mean when they refer to "fresh" ginger: a short or long piece of root, light tan in color, with several knobby, gnarled extensions. Spice dealers call it a "hand," because the extensions do sort of look like fat fingers. Nowadays you can find it in the produce section of your favorite market, but just a few years ago most American supermarkets didn't carry it. (Choose pieces that are firm and plump, not shriveled; unless you use it often, buy just enough for one recipe.)
- *Whole fresh roots.* Giving the freshest taste of all, these are roots gathered and shipped when they are still immature; the outer skin is a light green in color. You'll only find these in Oriental markets that carry fresh produce, alongside all those other intriguing vegetables you don't know the names of.
- *Dried roots.* This is one of the most common preserved forms: The whole root is peeled, maybe sliced horizontally, then dried and cut into smaller pieces. Sometimes the pieces are as large as the original "finger" they came from, sometimes they are broken into much smaller bits and then sifted for consistent size.
- *Powdered ginger.* The dried roots are ground into a fine powder. This is probably the form of ginger that is most widely available.
- *Preserved ginger.* Until recently, this product was very familiar in households throughout Europe, where it was called "stem ginger." It is made from fresh young roots, peeled and sliced and then cooked in a heavy sugar syrup. The tender pieces and the syrup are canned together. If you should find an old recipe that calls for "ginger syrup," this is what it means: the syrup from stem ginger. Today if you find it at all it's likely to be in a shop that deals with imported foodstuffs. This is a very old technique for preserving ginger; stem ginger, packed in beautiful ginger jars, was carried to Mediterranean ports in camel caravans, as part of the spice trade.

- **Crystallized ginger.** This is another form of preserved ginger, and it is widely available. Pieces of the fresh root are peeled and cooked in sugar syrup, then air dried, then rolled in sugar. (In case you never thought of sugar as a preservative, why do you think jams and jellies were invented? To preserve summer fruits for the winter.)
- **Pickled ginger.** Fresh gingerroot is sliced thin as paper, then pickled in a vinegar solution. The acid turns the ginger flesh pink, and commercial preparations are often tinted to make the color even deeper. This pickle is served as a small side dish in Japan, where it is known as *gari*, as a way to refresh the palate between courses; a small pile of it usually accompanies sushi.

In the spice industry, only powdered and dried ginger are considered true spices; crystallized and stem ginger are considered candy, and fresh ginger is a condiment. I think that for our purposes that distinction is irrelevant. All those forms impart a ginger flavor to whatever they're added to, and that's all that concerns us. It's a question of convenience, really: Use whatever form you can easily find.

A small personal comment, if I may: Think of the disparity between sushi on one hand and, on the other, warm gingerbread served at teatime. Think of the contrast between imperial Japan and Victorian England. Think of the images that spring to mind when you picture the person who would enjoy visiting a sushi bar in New York City, and the person who loves baking gingerbread men for holiday treats. They will probably never meet, but ginger links them together.

History and Legend

Ginger—the plant—is native to India and China. Its very name comes from the Sanskrit (Indian) word *sringa-vera*, which literally translates to "horn body," meaning "with a body like a horn"—that is to say, like antlers. And a large piece of gingerroot does resemble antlers, in a way. Ginger has been important in Chinese medicine for many centuries, and is mentioned in the writings of Confucius. It is also named in the Koran, the sacred book of the Moslems, which indicates it was known in Arab countries as far back as 650 A.D.

Ginger—the spice—reached the Mediterranean region with the Phoenicians, who traded it to the Greeks and Romans. In fact it was the Romans' second favorite spice (after pepper).

Just as they did with all other spices and other parts of their culture, the Romans brought ginger with them as they invaded the many lands to the north. By the ninth century ginger was so popular in Europe it was included in every table setting, like salt and pepper are today, even though it was certainly not cheap: A pound of ginger was worth the same as a sheep ready for market.

In English pubs and taverns in the nineteenth century, barkeepers put out small containers of ground ginger, for people to sprinkle onto their beer—the origin of ginger ale, now made as a soft drink.

Perhaps the best known use of ginger is in the sweet cake we call gingerbread. This is not an invention of the twentieth century; indeed, gingerbread has been popular for thousands of years. There is some evidence that the first gingerbread cake was made around 2500 B.C., by a baker on the Greek island of Rhodes. The recipe traveled to Egypt and Rome, and thence to all of Europe.

In centuries past it was the fashion to make gingerbread cakes into quite elaborate shapes. In Russia, when the child who would become Peter the Great was born, his father the czar received more than one hundred gingerbread cakes, sculpted into fancy shapes like the imperial coat of arms; some of them weighed more than two hundred pounds. A baker in the court of Queen Elizabeth I was assigned to a special job: molding gingerbread into portraits and three-dimensional models of the guests of honor for royal banquets.

> An I had but one penny in the world, thou shouldst have it to buy gingerbread.
>
> —Shakespeare, *Love's Labour Lost*

Ginger was the first spice successfully introduced to the New World for the purposes of agriculture. Because its rhizomes travel easily without getting broken, and remain viable for a long time, it was a cinch to take some across the Atlantic and plant them in the West Indies, where the climate is right. The experiment was a grand success: In just a few years Jamaican plantations were exporting ginger back to Europe.

Medicinal and Other Uses

We've already learned that ginger was important in Chinese medicine (still is, in fact); it has been used as a medicinal plant for a long, long time, primarily for stomach and digestive tract problems. Dioscorides, the Greek physician from the first century, often mentions it as a way to "warm the stomach" and encourage digestion, but suggests avoiding roots with wormholes . . . good idea, even now.

Over the years ginger has also been used as:

- A plague medicine (Henry VIII of England sent the recipe to the mayor of London)
- A remedy for toothache (chew a piece)
- A way to improve a poor disposition
- A treatment for menstrual cramps (drink ginger tea)
- An aphrodisiac: At the University of Salerno (Italy), medical students during the early Renaissance were taught: "Eat ginger, and you will have love and happiness in old age as in your youth."

Today we know that ginger is a diaphoretic, meaning that it makes you sweat, so as a plague remedy it might not have been so far off. It is also a carminative, which means that it helps break up intestinal gas. So Dioscorides was right, and so were the country healers who suggested chewing a piece after a heavy meal to help digestion. But as far as I know, there has been no scientific verification that chewing a piece of ginger will do anything for a nasty disposition.

It may, however, prove out another piece of folk medicine: that ginger helps prevent motion sickness. In a 1982 research study, volunteers were divided into three groups; one was given ginger, one a well-known over-the-counter product, and one a placebo. Everyone was spun around in a chair for six minutes—or until they asked to stop. Those who took the ginger were the only ones who lasted the whole six minutes.

Ginger, in the form of a compress, has been widely used as a home remedy for congestion, either in the sinuses (put the compress on your forehead) or the chest (on the upper torso). To make the compress, simmer a handful of grated ginger in two quarts of water for 15 minutes, then strain. Wet a clean cloth in the ginger water and wring it out; that damp cloth is the compress. Keep the water hot, and rewet the towel when it starts to cool. When you're all done, you might want to soak your feet in the leftover water; it stimulates blood flow, making them feel warm.

Going outside the realm of medicine for a moment, fishermen have even been known to chew bits of ginger and cover the hook with its juice to attract more fish. Now, does this work? As I think I've said elsewhere, if you believe anything a fisherman tells you, you should check to see if one of your legs is longer than the other.

The essential oil of ginger is used in men's cologne and shaving lotion. The oleoresin extracted from the ground spice is what the soft drink industry uses in ginger ale.

Cooking with Ginger

It has been said that ginger rounds out the flavors of other foods, and adds a note of freshness that other spices do not. That may be one reason why ginger seems so right in so many different kinds of foods: Baked goods, meat and chicken dishes, fish soups, fruit sauces, green salads—all are enhanced with a bit of ginger.

Homemade marmalade makes a beautiful gift. Top the jars with a circle of pretty fabric, and add a gift tag. See recipe section (page 200) for Spice Orange Marmalade.

To cook with fresh ginger, you can either peel a segment and chop into small pieces, or shred it with a grater. Your recipe usually tells you which, but if not, the guiding principle is, what do you want in the finished dish: small bits of ginger, larger slices, or tiny specks? If your answer is "none of the above," try this: Grate fresh ginger into a sieve and press with the back of a spoon, to extract only the juice.

If you have dried ginger (not the powder, but the dried, hard pieces), first bruise it by smacking it with something like the bottom of a jar; this crushes the fibers and opens them up, releasing the flavor.

Use Powdered Ginger with:
- Steaks and chicken: Mix ginger with salt and pepper, rub the mixture over steaks before broiling and chicken before roasting.
- Meatloaf mixtures
- Flour coating for oven-fried chicken
- Homemade applesauce, jams, jellies, and preserves
- Baked fruit desserts like pear crisp and apple pie

❧ Pumpkin Soup ❧

2 tablespoons butter
1/2 cup chopped onion
4 cups chicken broth (see note)
1/4 teaspoon powdered ginger
1/4 teaspoon ground nutmeg
3 cups cooked pumpkin pulp

In a soup pot, melt the butter over medium heat and sauté onion till golden. Add the broth, ginger, nutmeg, and pumpkin. Bring the mixture to a boil. Turn the heat down to low, and simmer the soup for 10 minutes until it is thick, stirring occasionally.

For a completely smooth texture, puree soup in food processor or blender (work in small batches); this is optional.

To dazzle your guests, serve the soup in a carved-out pumpkin.

Note: For a richer (but higher calorie) soup, substitute cream for 1 cup of the chicken broth.
Makes 7 cups.

❧ Ginger-Orange Tea Bread ❧

peels of 2 medium oranges
1/2 cup water
1 1/2 cups sugar, divided
2 tablespoons butter
2 eggs, separated
3 cups sifted flour
3 1/2 teaspoons baking powder
1/2 teaspoon salt
1 teaspoon powdered ginger (see note)
1 cup milk

Preheat oven to 350°.

Remove peels from oranges and cut into thin slivers (or strip peels from oranges with a zester, if you have one). Mix orange peels with water and 1 cup sugar and boil for 5 minutes. (If you use the crystallized ginger, chop it into small pieces and add it to the saucepan at this point.) Cover pan and let cool for at least 1/2 hour.

In mixing bowl, cream butter with remaining sugar; add egg yolks, beating thoroughly. In a separate bowl, combine flour, baking powder, salt, and ginger. Working alternately (a little milk, then a little flour mixture), add milk and dry ingredients to egg mixture. Fold in orange peel mixture.

Beat egg whites until they are stiff. Carefully fold into batter. Pour batter into well-greased bread pans, and bake until a toothpick inserted in the center comes out clean (about 1 hour).

Note: You can also use crystallized ginger; it adds another texture to this bread. Chop into small bits and add to the sugar syrup along with the orange peels.

Makes 1 large or 2 small loaves.

⋅⋇ Indonesian Zucchini Salad ⋇⋅

Serve with grilled meats or chicken as a salad or relish.

1 pound zucchini, cut into matchstick strips
1¹/₂ cups shredded cabbage
1 carrot, coarsely grated
1 tablespoon salt
1 onion, finely chopped
1 large clove garlic, minced
1 tablespoon finely chopped fresh ginger
2 tablespoons finely chopped peanuts or almonds
2 tablespoons vegetable oil
¹/₄ teaspoon red pepper flakes
¹/₂ teaspoon ground turmeric
¹/₂ cup rice vinegar
1 tablespoon firmly packed brown sugar

Garnish:
chopped peanuts
chopped cilantro or parsley

Sprinkle zucchini, cabbage, and carrot with salt. Let stand several hours. Rinse in cold water; drain and pat dry, set aside. Combine the onion, garlic, ginger, and nuts, and set aside.

In a large heavy skillet, heat oil, then add the onion mixture, pepper flakes, and turmeric. Cook over moderately low heat, stirring frequently, for 5 to 8 minutes. Stir in vinegar and sugar and cook an additional 3 to 5 minutes or until slightly thickened. Add the drained zucchini, cabbage, and carrot, stirring until coated with the mixture. Cool to room temperature. Chill for at least 2 hours before serving. Will keep covered in refrigerator for several weeks. Just before serving, garnish with peanuts and cilantro or parsley.

Makes about 4 cups.

—Renée Shepherd

Ginger-Orange Beets

A richly satisfying way to prepare beets that marries several well-matched flavors.

> *6 large beets, cooked in their skins until almost tender and cooled*
> *1 large orange*
> *4 slices bacon, cut into ¹/₂-inch pieces*
> *1 medium onion, diced*
> *1 tablespoon grated fresh ginger*
> *2 tablespoons light brown sugar*
> *2 tablespoons raspberry vinegar*
> *¹/₂ cup chicken stock*
> *salt and freshly ground pepper*
> *¹/₂ teaspoon cornstarch, dissolved in 1 teaspoon water*

Peel and slice beets ¹/₄- to ¹/₂-inch thick. Remove the orange zest (orange part of skin only) from the orange. Cut the zest into fine julienne strips. Squeeze the orange—you should have about ¹/₂ cup juice. In a deep skillet, cook bacon until golden and almost crisp. Discard most of fat. Add onions and sauté until softened—2 to 3 minutes. Add ginger, brown sugar, orange zest and juice, vinegar and stock, and stir. Add beets and cook over low heat for 10 to 15 minutes, stirring frequently. Add salt and pepper to taste. Just before serving, add dissolved cornstarch and water and heat until thickened.

Serves 4.

—Renée Shepherd

Malaysian Chicken and Sweet Potato Kurma

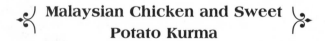

> *¹/₃ cup flour*
> *1 teaspoon ground cinnamon*
> *¹/₂ teaspoon cayenne*
> *¹/₄ teaspoon ground cloves*
> *1 2¹/₂ pound chicken, cut in 8 pieces*
> *¹/₄ cup vegetable oil*

1³/₄ cups onions, cut in 1-inch chunks
1 cup red bell pepper, cut in 1-inch chunks
3 tablespoons curry powder
1 tablespoon garlic powder
2 teaspoons ground ginger
¹/₂ teaspoon salt
3 cups chicken broth
2 pounds sweet potatoes, cut in 1¹/₂-inch chunks
¹/₂ cup coconut milk (see note)

In a large plastic bag combine flour, cinnamon, cayenne, and cloves. Add chicken pieces one at a time, shaking until coated with flour. Reserve remaining flour mixture (about ¹/₄ cup), and combine it with ¹/₂ cup cold water; set aside.

In a Dutch oven or large saucepan heat oil until hot; add chicken pieces in a single layer (don't crowd). Cook until browned, 3 to 5 minutes, on each side; remove to a platter.

Add onions and bell pepper to Dutch oven: Cook, stirring occasionally, until crisp-tender, about 5 minutes. Add curry and garlic powders, ginger, and salt; cook and stir until spices are fragrant, about 1 minute. Add chicken broth and browned chicken; bring to a boil. Reduce heat and simmer, covered, until chicken is nearly tender, about 30 minutes.

Add sweet potatoes; cook until sweet potatoes and chicken are tender, 15 to 20 minutes.

Add the flour-water mixture. Bring to a boil over high heat; cook and stir for 1 minute. Stir in coconut milk. Serve over rice, if desired.

Makes 4 portions.
—Adapted from American Spice Trade Association

Note: Coconut milk has a distinct and unique flavor; there is, unfortunately, no good substitute for it. Canned coconut milk is available from shops that sell Asian foods or the gourmet section of most large supermarkets. Milk can also be extracted from fresh coconut: Make a hole in one of the "eyes" and pour out the milk.

❧ Ginger Beef Strips ❧

1¹/₂ to 2 pounds sirloin or round steak, cut ¹/₂-inch thick
2 tablespoons butter
¹/₄ cup chopped onions
1 tablespoon coarsely chopped blanched almonds
1 teaspoon finely chopped fresh ginger
1 teaspoon chili powder
¹/₄ teaspoon garlic powder
2 cups beef stock
2 tablespoons plum jam
1 tablespoon red wine vinegar
1 tablespoon cornstarch
1 tablespoon cold water
2 tablespoons sherry

Cut steak into 2-inch strips. Melt butter in heavy skillet or wok. Sauté onions until soft. Add meat to pan and brown lightly. Add almonds, ginger, chili powder, and garlic powder; stir to mix. In a small bowl, combine beef stock, jam, and vinegar. Pour over meat, cover pan, and simmer until meat is done. In a small bowl, blend cornstarch with cold water and stir into steak. Simmer until sauce is thick, then add sherry.

Serve with plain white rice.

Makes 6 servings.

❧ Gingerbread ❧

Serve hot or cold with lemon sauce, applesauce, or whipped cream.

¹/₄ cup butter
¹/₂ cup brown sugar
1 egg
¹/₂ cup molasses
1¹/₂ cups all-purpose flour
1 teaspoon baking soda
1 teaspoon ginger
¹/₂ teaspoon cinnamon
¹/₈ teaspoon cardamom
¹/₂ cup buttermilk

Preheat oven to 350°.

Cream butter and sugar until light and fluffy. Beat in egg, then molasses. In separate bowl, sift flour, measure, then sift again with soda and spices. Working alternately, add some of the buttermilk, then some of the dry ingredients, to butter mixture. Pour batter into greased baking pan, 8 or 9 inches square. Bake 30 minutes.

Serves 6 to 8.

⚬⟨ Ginger Peach Freeze ⟩⚬

If the season is right, this is even more delicious when made with fresh peaches.

2 12-ounce packages frozen sliced peaches (see note)
1 pint vanilla ice cream
¹/₂ teaspoon powdered ginger
¹/₄ teaspoon allspice
¹/₄ teaspoon cinnamon
1 teaspoon grated lemon peel

Thaw peaches. Set ice cream out so it defrosts enough to spoon easily. Place peaches in a large bowl, and mash them with a fork or potato masher. Add spices and mix well. Add ice cream. Beat with rotary beater or an electric mixer until smooth. (A blender or a food processor, fitted with steel blade, makes quick work of this.)

Serve in chilled glasses.

To make the dessert ahead of time, spoon into serving glasses and freeze; remove 1 hour ahead and let it get soft and slushy.

Note: To use fresh peaches, you'll need about 2 pounds. Peel peaches, slice, toss them with lemon juice and a little sugar. Cover bowl with plastic wrap and let sit for ¹/₂ hour, to draw the juices. Then proceed as above.

Makes 4 servings.

⚜ Gingerbread Gypsies ⚜

Decoration or dessert? These flavorful and fanciful cookies do double duty.

1/2 cup margarine, softened
1/2 cup packed dark brown sugar
1/4 cup dark molasses
2 cups all-purpose flour
1 1/2 teaspoons ground ginger
1 teaspoon ground cinnamon
1/2 teaspoon ground nutmeg
1/2 teaspoon baking soda
1/2 teaspoon salt
prepared icings for decorating, optional
colored sprinkles for decorating, optional

In large bowl, beat margarine and sugar until light and creamy. Beat in molasses. Combine flour, ginger, cinnamon, nutmeg, baking soda, and salt; beat into creamed mixture until just combined. Form dough into ball. On floured surface, roll dough to 1/8-inch thickness. Cut out shapes.

Bake on ungreased cookie sheet at 350° for 10 to 13 minutes or until lightly browned on bottom. Cool 1 minute on sheet; remove cookies to wire rack to cool completely. Decorate as desired.

You can, if you can bear to miss eating them, make these cookies into tree ornaments. Roll dough to 1/4-inch thickness. Cut out shapes. Bake as directed. While still soft, make a hole for hanging by carefully pushing a skewer through cookie. Decorate as desired.

Makes 3 1/2 dozen cookies or 2 1/2 dozen tree ornaments.

—Spice Islands

⚜ Spice Orange Marmalade ⚜

12 medium oranges
1 1/4 pounds carrots
1/4 cup crystallized ginger
4 1/2 cups sugar

Cut oranges in quarters but do not peel. Remove white membrane in center and any seeds. Peel or scrape carrots. Put oranges, carrots, and ginger through food grinder. (Or, use a food processor with a steel blade to chop the carrots, oranges, and ginger.) Place mixture in large bowl and stir in sugar. Let stand overnight.

Transfer to saucepan and bring slowly to boiling; reduce heat and simmer until thick, stirring frequently. This can take up to 2 hours; watch carefully near the end, to prevent scorching. Pour into hot sterilized jars and process 10 minutes in water bath. (See page 165 for canning instructions.)

Makes about 5 pints.

⁌ Ginger Tea ⁌

If you enjoy a cup of hot tea, try this very refreshing and extremely simple variation.

2 or 3 slices fresh ginger, or 2 to 3 pieces crystallized ginger
1 quart water
3 teabags, or 3 teaspoons loose tea (your favorite kind)

Add the ginger to the water in the teakettle and bring to a boil; remove from heat and let steep for 10 minutes. Remove the ginger and bring the flavored water back to a boil. Add the tea and the ginger water to your teapot and steep 3 to 5 minutes, or until it is done to your preference. (Purists would suggest first prewarming the teapot with hot water from the tap.)

Delicious with sliced lemon and sugar, although if you used crystallized ginger you may not need additional sugar.

Variation: Use this same technique—steeping whole spices in water and using the flavored water to brew tea—with any spice and any kind of tea. Try whole cinnamon, cardamom, cloves, allspice, or mace.

Makes 4 cups.

For Other Recipes Featuring Ginger, See:
Citrus Rum Dressing, p. 41
Pork Vindaloo, p. 79
Cucumbers with Tomato Relish, p. 92
Pak Choi Kimchee, p. 93
Kung Pao Chicken, p. 95
Asian Hot-Sweet Chicken with Broccoli, p. 96
Spicy Pot Roast, p. 100
Peach Chutney, p. 102
Honey Spice Dressing, p. 119
Apple Pot Roast, p. 133
Spicy Pumpkin Pie, p. 133
Molasses Clove Cookies, p. 134
Bishop, p. 134

Horseradish

Botanical name: **Armoracia rusticana**

Part used as spice: **Root**

Available as: **Fresh root; dried root in powder or granule form; prepared horseradish sauce**

Horseradish belongs to the same family as mustard, botanically speaking, and shares many of the family traits. For one thing, if you saw the plant growing, you would notice how similar the flowers are to the flowers of the mustard plant.

For another, their internal chemistry is very much alike. Like mustard seeds, a whole horseradish root has no odor, and for the same reason: Stored separately in its cells are two constituents that, when cell walls are broken, mix together to produce an essential oil that tastes bitter and brings tears to the eyes. Chemically, it's the very same substance—allyl isothiocyanate, or essential oil of mustard—that is in both horseradish and mustard seed, and it has the same properties.

And that brings us to another similarity. Grated horseradish, mixed into a paste and applied as a poultice, has been used as a common home remedy for stiff muscles and chest congestion—just like mustard plasters.

There is even a passing similarity in taste: I'd be willing to bet that if you closed your eyes and tasted fresh horseradish paste next to fresh mustard paste, you might easily get them confused.

The word "horse" is an old English usage that means "rough" or "coarse." So this plant is called horseradish to distinguish it from the regular radish, the red garden vegetable.

At one time the leaves of the horseradish plant were eaten as a vegetable, like mustard greens. Although you don't see too many cooked horseradish greens these days, you could try it if you were to grow horseradish in your garden. And unless you live in the Sun Belt you could certainly do that (grow it, I mean), but only if you're ready for a Big Commitment: Horseradish is a perennial (meaning that it lives from year to year) and lustily multiplies itself from the root stock, spreading in all directions. If you turn your back, it can take over. Then, because the root is so deep and strong, an established plant is very difficult to dig up, and you're more or less stuck.

History and Legend

The horseradish plant is probably native to eastern Europe, and has always been more popular in cold than warm regions. Unlike so many other of our spices, it's not a part of the culinary or medicinal history of the Greeks or Romans, nor does it have a long tradition in Asia. We might even say that horseradish is a "modern" spice—it didn't become well established until the Middle Ages. At that time both roots and leaves were used, as medicine and also as food.

Even now, we associate horseradish primarily with beef and fish, and with mealtimes in England, Germany, and Scandinavia, not the warmer nations of southern Europe. In France it's called *moutarde des Allemandes*—mustard of the Germans.

One old bit of folklore may be of interest in modern times: Carry a bit of horseradish root in your purse, and you will never be poor.

Medicinal and Other Uses

In the past, herbalists (medical practitioners who relied on herbal preparations) used horseradish to treat asthma, whooping cough, chest congestion, kidney stones, gallstones, dropsy, gout, even baldness. Early in this century, it was recommended as the very best treatment for intestinal worms in children.

Horseradish is a very strong stimulant, both internally and externally. Externally, the active ingredient in horseradish, like that in mustard, brings the blood to the surface and warms the skin, which is why horseradish poultices were a popular folk remedy.

Internally, horseradish has the effect of stimulating the digestive juices, and so our habit of eating it with oily fish and rich meats like beef, which are comparatively harder to digest, is not just a matter of taste but of practical benefit also.

Even before vitamin C was fully understood, horseradish was used to prevent scurvy. Now we know that it is a good source of that vitamin: One ounce of fresh horseradish contains twenty-three milligrams, more than a third of an adult's recommended daily allowance.

It may seem strange now, but at one time—and not too long ago, either—horseradish was used cosmetically. Slices of the root were soaked in milk, which extracted the essential oil, and then that milk was used as a facial lotion, for skin that "lacked clearness and freshness of color." Because, as we now know, this oil brings blood to the surface, it surely would give a glow to pale faces. Another cosmetic preparation: Grated horseradish mixed with vinegar was reputed to remove freckles.

Cooking with Horseradish

You may know horseradish only as something that comes in little jars. That's prepared horseradish sauce, and there's nothing wrong with it. But realize that prepared horseradish has the same relationship to horseradish root that prepared mustard has to mustard seeds: Its flavor intensity is predetermined by the manufacturer.

By all means, keep a jar of horseradish sauce on hand; it's very convenient. At the same time, you might want to find a source of either fresh or dried root and experiment with it. Some manufacturers sell dried horseradish both as a powder and as dehydrated granules, which you reconstitute with water (see Frontier Herbs in the Appendix). In horseradish, as in every other kind of spice there is, the fresh taste is superior.

If you are able to find fresh roots, here's how to work with them. Peel off the tough outer skin and grate off a tablespoon or two, just as you would grate a carrot. It is this grating that tears the cell walls and releases the chemicals that form the essential oil that tingles your tongue. Grate just as much as the recipe calls for.

Gentility or Snobbery?

In 1640, the English herbalist John Parkinson said this about horseradish:

> "[used as sauce] by country people and strong labouring men in Germany and in our owne land also, but as I said it is too strong for tender and gentle stomachs."

Did I mention that we can learn a lot about a society from its attitudes toward food?

⚜ Fresh Beet Horseradish ⚜

This wine-red horseradish is especially good mixed with fresh yogurt and served over beet greens, chard, or baked potatoes.

2¹/₂ cups (about ¹/₂ pound) peeled and diced horseradish root
¹/₄ cup mild red wine vinegar
¹/₂ cup rice vinegar
2 small beets, cooked and peeled
¹/₂ teaspoon salt, or to taste
2 to 3 tablespoons sugar, or to taste

In a food processor, process horseradish and vinegars until horseradish is finely ground. Add beets, salt, and 2 tablespoons of sugar, and process until combined. Add more sugar and salt, if needed. Place in a glass jar and refrigerate.
Makes 2 cups.

Note: Without a food processor, finely grate horseradish and beets and combine with vinegars, salt, and sugar.

—Renée Shepherd

⚜ Green Cabbage and Grape Salad ⚜

A unique sweet/tangy coleslaw.

1 quart finely shredded green cabbage
2 cups halved red seedless grapes
3 tablespoons mayonnaise (or 1 tablespoon mayonnaise and 2
*   tablespoons plain yogurt)*
2 teaspoons lemon juice (fresh is best)
2 teaspoons horseradish
¹/₈ teaspoon salt
¹/₈ teaspoon pepper
lettuce
chopped almonds, toasted

Toss cabbage and grapes together. In a separate bowl, combine mayonnaise, lemon juice, horseradish, salt, and pepper; add to cabbage mixture. Toss lightly.
    Serve on lettuce; sprinkle with almonds. Garnish with grape clusters.
Makes 6 to 8 servings.

⤙ Old-Fashioned Baked Beans ⤚

1 pound dried navy or pea beans
¹/₂ teaspoon baking soda
2 cups brown sugar
4 cups tomato juice
¹/₄ teaspoon cloves
¹/₈ teaspoon cardamom
1 tablespoon onion powder (or minced fresh onion)
¹/₂ teaspoon dry mustard
1¹/₂ teaspoons powdered horseradish
¹/₈ teaspoon pepper
8 slices bacon

Pick through beans and remove any debris. Cover beans with cold water and soak overnight. Drain; cover with fresh water and add soda. Bring to a boil, reduce heat to medium, and cook until beans are tender, 30 to 40 minutes. Drain and rinse.

In mixing bowl, whisk brown sugar and all seasonings into tomato juice. Pour juice mixture over beans. Cut bacon into short pieces and fold into beans.

Pour beans into a 3-quart bean pot or casserole. Cover and bake in 300° oven 5 hours. Check occasionally and add hot water if beans become too dry. Remove cover during last 30 minutes of baking.

Makes 10 to 12 servings.

⤙ Tomato Juice Cocktail ⤚

6 cups tomato juice (one 46-ounce can)
6 whole cloves
2 whole allspice
1 bay leaf
1 teaspoon onion powder
¹/₈ teaspoon black pepper
1 teaspoon powdered horseradish
1 tablespoon sugar
3 tablespoons red wine vinegar (see note)

In saucepan combine all ingredients except vinegar. Bring to a boil, then simmer 15 minutes. Strain out spices, and stir in vinegar.

Chill several hours. Serve cold.
Makes about 6 cups.

Note: Herb-flavored vinegar (especially basil) is terrific with this.

For Other Recipes Featuring Horseradish, See:
Beet Surprise Salad, p. 39

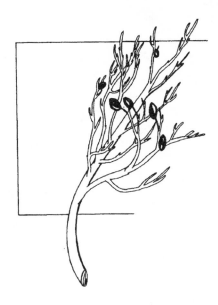

Juniper Berries

Botanical name: Juniperis communis
Part used as spice: Berries
Available as: Whole berries

The juniper that produces the berries we use as a spice is called the common juniper, meaning that it grows everywhere. And indeed the trees can be found growing wild throughout the northern hemisphere, although most of the commercial harvest comes from Europe. This juniper is an evergreen tree with short stiff needles that are wonderfully aromatic, a very tough trunk and limbs, and often a twisted, gnarly silhouette.

The berries, about the size of a small pea, are purplish-black on the tree, often covered with a grayish powdery substance that botanists call "bloom." As they dry, the bloom disappears and the berries become very dark.

The main use of juniper berries is as a flavoring for gin. So closely do we associate the tastes that not only does gin taste like juniper, but juniper tastes like gin. So anything cooked with juniper reminds us of the beverage. For that reason, juniper berries are most appropriate in meat stews or marinades for meats (especially game) that are going to be roasted or barbecued.

The connection between gin and juniper is etymological as well as gustatory. The name "gin" comes from the word for juniper in several European languages, including *genever* (Dutch) and *genièvre* (French).

History and Legend

Many of the historical applications of juniper center around its sharply aromatic foliage. Burning a branch of juniper releases its piney, acrid smell, and that smell has been accorded great powers.

At one time or another juniper was burned to:

- Keep away evil spirits
- Purify the air in temples in preparation for ceremonies
- Drive off snakes and other poisonous creatures
- Dispel the "corruptions of the air" that carried plague
- Confuse and disorient any malicious spirits that might interfere with the soul's progress to heaven (burned at funerals)
- Freshen the air, especially in sickrooms or closed rooms (in cold areas, where windows must be kept shut in winter, juniper branches were burned in the schoolroom stoves to improve air quality)

The Wicked Witch

In rural Europe, there was a long custom of hanging a branch of juniper over the front door of the house to keep out witches. If the smell didn't drive them away, their vanity would. According to the belief, something compelled the witch to stop to count the needles on the juniper branch. But they are so tiny that invariably the witch lost count and had to start over, and became so frustrated that she would just fly away rather than risk having anyone witness her failure.

To this day, juniper is used as a Christmastime decoration in some countries, in remembrance of a legend about Mary and the infant Jesus. As Mary and Joseph fled with the baby into Egypt, trying to escape Herod's soldiers, at one point they were almost overtaken. Mary looked desperately around for someplace to hide, but all she saw was a small juniper tree. At the last moment, the tree spread its limbs and she hid the baby Jesus underneath the branches. When the soldiers approached, they saw only an old man walking with a young woman, and they did not stop to investigate. Thereafter, juniper was dedicated to the Virgin Mary.

Medicinal and Other Uses

Juniper berries were used by the physicians of ancient civilizations to cleanse the body's internal organs of maladies. For example, in the Ebers Papyrus, we find this prescription:

"A remedy to treat tapeworms: juniper berries 5 parts, white oil 5 parts, is taken for one day."

Along the same lines, at one time juniper was prescribed as a diuretic (a substance that increases urination), on the theory that this would help the body "pass off" its unhealthy substances. However, it is now clear that other drugs, even other natural formulations, do this more safely. Certainly you should avoid large amounts if you have any kind of liver problem. Also, it has been shown that juniper can cause contractions of the uterus, and so **it should be totally avoided by women who are pregnant.**

A 1775 book of household remedies, entitled *Toilet of Flora*, suggests making a strong solution of juniper berries and several herbs and soaking your feet in it. Modern men and women, especially if they're on their feet all day, might find this refreshing.

Oil distilled from juniper berries, aside from putting the flavor into gin, is also used in perfumes and lotions, in soap, and in some insecticides. A purple dye can be made from the berries.

Cooking with Juniper Berries

Because of their distinctive taste of gin, juniper berries have limited use. Perhaps the best way to use them is to imagine sauces or marinades that would be enhanced by the flavor of an alcoholic beverage—and then use juniper instead.

> One teaspoon of berries in a marinade gives the flavor equivalent of 1/2 cup of gin.

The flavor is especially appropriate for wild game—venison, duck, pheasant, and so forth. Many cooks like to parboil game in a meat stock before roasting; this helps take away the strong taste that those who do not like it describe as "gamey." A good beef stock, to which juniper, lemon slices, and bay leaves are added, adds flavor while toning down the "gaminess."

Use Juniper Berries with:
- Pot roasts (add to the sauce when slow-cooking)
- Liver pâté
- Pickled meat, such as sauerbraten (add to the brining solution)
- Sauerkraut (in place of caraway seeds), for a different taste

⤳ Juniper Marinade ⤶

1 large onion, sliced
1 clove garlic, crushed
1/2 cup wine vinegar
3 cups red wine
5 juniper berries
12 peppercorns
1 1/2 teaspoons salt
1/8 teaspoon mace
4 whole cloves
1/4 teaspoon dried thyme
2 bay leaves

Combine all ingredients. Cover and let stand overnight. Chill for 24 hours before using.

Use to marinate beef before roasting or grilling; baste with marinade while cooking.

To tenderize game meat, marinate meat in refrigerator 1 to 3 days. Then grill or roast as desired.

The marinade itself can be stored (in a jar with a tight lid) for several weeks in the refrigerator, but once you have used it on meat, it must be discarded.

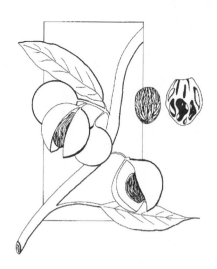

Mace

Botanical name: Myristica fragrans
Part used as spice: Aril (covering around the seed)
Available as: Whole blades or ground spice

The same tree that gives us nutmeg also produces the spice known as mace; it's the only two-for-one deal in the spice world.

Mace is the outer covering of the large, hard pit that lies within the seed cavity of the fruit of the nutmeg tree. (See chapter on Nutmeg.) When the fruit is ripe it splits open, exposing the bright red "net" around the seed. That net (its technical name is aril) is the spice we call mace.

The aril is removed from the seeds by hand and spread out to dry. As it dries, it develops its characteristic aroma but loses its bright red color.

As you will see in the chapter on nutmeg, the trees have for many years been cultivated in two distant parts of the world: Indonesia, Sri Lanka, India, and other parts of the East Indies; and Grenada and other islands of the Caribbean, sometimes referred to as the West Indies.

Over time, the trees have evolved slightly different characteristics, and some of the differences show up in mace. Mace from East Indian nutmegs is more orange; from West Indian trees, a yellowish brown. Also, the mace from the West Indian trees is more solid, less holey, than the East Indian. Mace is much, much lighter in weight than nutmegs. A pile of East Indian fruits large enough to make one hundred pounds of nutmeg produces just one pound of mace.

Other trees that are related to nutmeg also have an aril covering their seeds, and sometimes those are used to substitute for true mace or to dilute it. These are called Bombay mace or wild mace, and even though there is a faint resemblance in taste, these false maces are much coarser and definitely inferior. Price is a good guide: If you ever find mace priced at a significant discount from prices you've seen before, it may not be genuine.

History and Legend

As you might expect, the history of mace is intimately tied up with nutmeg. It appears that the two items were treated as separate spices from the beginning. Pliny, the Roman scholar who wrote about natural history in the first century, mentions a tree that had two spices, but it's not clear whether he meant nutmeg or something else. It is a matter of record, however, that the Arab caravans that ended up in Constantinople in the sixth century had both mace and nutmeg among their cargo of spices.

Mace was highly regarded in England in the fourteenth century; one pound of mace would buy three sheep. In fact, mace has always been more expensive than nutmeg. Back in the time when the Dutch controlled the Spice Islands, one colonial administrator in Amsterdam, who had obviously never seen the tree, sent out orders that the colonists should plant fewer nutmeg trees and more mace trees. Wouldn't you like to have been present when the plantation supervisor received that directive?

Cooking with Mace

Whole mace (the dried filaments are called blades) is not easy to crush into a powder at home. You may find it works better to soak a few blades in a liquid and then add the liquid to your recipe (rather like working with whole saffron). Ground mace is as easy to use as ground cinnamon.

Mace or Nutmeg—Which to Use?

There are minor and subtle differences—primarily the fact that mace is stronger—but basically nutmeg and mace are much more alike than they are different. So why would anyone choose mace over nutmeg, especially since it is more expensive?

Well, for one thing, ground mace is lighter in color than ground nutmeg, so it would be the better choice if you were cooking something where you wouldn't want dark flecks—such as a pound cake or a white sauce for fish.

Another instance where whole mace is clearly preferable to whole nutmeg is in making potpourri (see page 126). The essential oils that give nutmeg its fragrance and taste are carried in thin veins inside the nutmeg; the only way to extract the flavor is to grate or crush the nutmeg so that those veins are exposed. A whole nutmeg, ungrated, has practically no fragrance and would do you no good in a potpourri.

Blades of mace, on the other hand, do have a fragrance. Also, they are an attractive color (especially the more orange hue of mace from the East Indies). In a potpourri designed around autumn colors, whole mace would be a very pleasant addition.

In most recipes, the two are, for all practical purposes, interchangeable. Note, however, that mace is sweeter, so you would need less of it than nutmeg to accomplish the same end.

Use Mace with:
- White or light-colored cakes and cookies
- Pudding
- Homemade doughnuts
- Oyster stew and other cream-based or clear soups
- Chicken pie
- Cream sauces for vegetables
- Homemade jelly

⋅⅊ Spicy Carrot Pickles ⅊⋅

¹/₂ tablespoon whole allspice
¹/₂ tablespoon whole mace
¹/₂ stick cinnamon
¹/₂ tablespoon whole cloves
1 pint distilled white vinegar
2 cups sugar
3 pounds carrots

First, make pickling syrup: Tie whole spices into cheesecloth bag and add to saucepan along with vinegar, sugar, and enough water to cover. Simmer 15 minutes, then remove spice bag.

Meanwhile, scrape carrots and cut in strips to fit pint jars (allowing for ¹/₂ inch head space). Cook in the syrup until just heated through. Pack hot carrots lengthwise into hot sterilized jars. Cover with hot syrup. Seal jars and process 10 minutes in boiling water bath. (See page 165 for canning instructions.)

Makes 5 to 7 half-pints.

⤙ Mace-Blueberry Muffins ⤚

For a special occasion, serve muffins hot from the oven with Strawberry Butter.

2 cups all-purpose flour
3 teaspoons baking powder
1/2 teaspoon salt
3 tablespoons sugar
1/4 teaspoon mace
1 egg
1 cup fresh or frozen blueberries (see note)
3/4 cup milk
1 teaspoon vanilla extract
3 tablespoons butter, melted

Preheat oven to 425° and prepare muffin tins: Butter the bottoms of the cups or line with paper baking cups.

Sift flour, measure, and sift again with salt, sugar, and mace. In separate bowl, beat egg lightly; stir in berries, milk, vanilla, and melted butter. Add milk mixture to dry ingredients. Fold together very lightly, just until dry ingredients are moistened, 10 to 15 strokes.

Spoon batter into muffin cups until two-thirds full, and bake 20 to 25 minutes. Serve hot.

Note: If you use frozen berries, thaw first, then drain, discarding any juice.
Makes 12 muffins.

Strawberry Butter
Mix equal parts butter and strawberry preserves; melt in microwave or double boiler. Spoon into serving bowl and chill for 1/2 hour, or until mixture solidifies.

⤙ Waldorf Salad ⤚

Dressing
1/4 teaspoon dry mustard
1/4 teaspoon ginger
1/8 teaspoon mace
dash cardamom
1 teaspoon grated fresh lemon peel
2 teaspoons lemon juice
1/2 cup mayonnaise or plain yogurt
1 tablespoon light cream or milk, if needed

Salad
> *¹/₂ cup chopped celery*
> *¹/₂ cup chopped walnuts or pecans*
> *¹/₄ cup raisins*
> *3 cups diced apples*

Garnish:
> Seedless grapes

Combine ingredients for dressing in blender: mustard, ginger, mace, cardamom, lemon juice and peel, mayonnaise. Thin with milk if dressing seems too thick.

In large mixing bowl, toss celery, nuts, and raisins together. At last minute (so they don't turn brown), dice apples, add to bowl, and immediately cover with dressing. Mix well. Cover bowl with plastic wrap and refrigerate if not serving immediately.

Serve on chilled salad plates lined with red-leaf lettuce. Garnish with small clusters of red and green seedless grapes.

Serves 6 to 8.

⊰ Apple Cider Squash ⊱

> *1 package frozen winter squash (or 1¹/₄ cups fresh, peeled, and cut*
> *into chunks)*
> *2 tablespoons melted butter*
> *¹/₂ teaspoon salt*
> *¹/₈ teaspoon mace*
> *¹/₈ teaspoon cinnamon*
> *dash pepper*
> *¹/₃ cup apple cider*

Preheat oven to 350°.

Butter a 1¹/₂-quart casserole; place squash in casserole. In separate bowl, blend melted butter and seasonings into cider, and pour mixture over squash. Cover and bake 45 minutes.

Serves 4.

❧ Hawaiian Grilled Pork Chops ❧

1/2 cup pineapple juice
1/2 cup vegetable or olive oil
1/4 cup soy sauce
2 tablespoons lemon juice
1 teaspoon dry mustard
1/2 teaspoon ginger
1/8 teaspoon mace
1/4 cup brown sugar
8 pork chops, 1-inch thick
fresh pineapple slices

Combine all ingredients, except pork chops and pineapple. Arrange pork chops in a flat baking dish, pour marinade over, and cover. Marinate in refrigerator for several hours, turning once or twice.

Prepare charcoal grill for cooking. Place chops on grill 6 inches from coals; sear on both sides. Knock coals down and to the side; cover grill, if possible, and cook slowly until chops are well done, 30 to 40 minutes. Baste with marinade during cooking.

Serve with slices of fresh pineapple, grilled for a few minutes.
Serves 4.

❧ Raspberry Sauce ❧

Luscious over vanilla ice cream, frozen yogurt, cheesecake, or lemon pound cake.

2 10-ounce packages frozen raspberries
3 tablespoons cornstarch
1/2 cup sugar
1/4 teaspoon salt
1/8 teaspoon ground allspice
1/4 teaspoon ground mace
2 tablespoons butter

Place raspberries in a small sieve placed over a bowl, to catch the juice. When berries are thawed, measure the juice and add enough water to make 1 1/2 cups liquid. Put juice-water mixture in saucepan. In small bowl, mix cornstarch, sugar, salt, allspice, and mace; stir into liquid. Cook over medium heat until sauce thickens; stir constantly.

At this point you may wish to puree the berries and press the puree through a fine sieve, to remove the seeds.

Add drained raspberries (or raspberry puree) to juice in saucepan, along with butter. Simmer 3 minutes.

Chill (sauce is thicker as it cools). Store, in covered container, in refrigerator for up to one week.

Makes 2¹/₂ cups.

For Other Recipes Featuring Mace, See:

Swedish Fruit Soup, p. 38
Caraway Pound Cake, p. 59
Jasmine Tea Bread, p. 112
Mulligatawny, p. 156
Ginger Tea, p. 201
Shrimp Pie, p. 243
Spicy Banana Nut Bread, p. 317

Mustard Seeds

Botanical name: Brassica hirta; B. nigra; B. juncea
Part used as spice: Seeds
Available as: Whole or ground seeds

If you're on good terms with vegetables, you already know and love many of the members of the genus *Brassica*: Broccoli, cabbage, cauliflower, Brussels sprouts, turnips, and even radishes are in what botanists refer to as the mustard family. Also in that family are plants that we grow for their leaves: arugula, with its peppery bite; several kinds of Oriental greens; and just plain mustard greens.

If you ever lived anywhere in the South, you know mustard as a green vegetable with a sharp, tangy taste. But you may not know that a very close relative of that same green plant is the source of the yellow mustard that we so joyously squirt on hot dogs at the ballpark. Whereas the first type of mustard is grown for its leaves, the second is grown especially for the seeds. The plants make flowers, the flowers make seeds, and the seeds are harvested to make . . . well, mustard. But here, the mustard path separates into three options.

As consumers we can buy mustard in three different forms: whole seeds, dry powder, and prepared mustard (the yellow stuff in the jar). The seeds and the powder most closely fit the definition of spices, so they will be the focus of this chapter, but I will also tell you a little about prepared mustard.

Whole Seeds
You are most likely to encounter whole seeds if you make pickles. They are part of every commercial blend of mixed pickling spices that I know of, and usually included as well in pickle recipes that enumerate the spices individually. Toasted, they also add their unique flavor to many other dishes, which we will learn about in the section on Cooking with Mustard.

Three species of mustard plants are grown for mustard seed, and since the differences among them are easiest to see in their seeds, this is as good a time as any to introduce you to the three types. Let me warn you: The names are all goofed up.

1. White mustard (*Brassica hirta*, sometimes *Brassica alba* or *Sinapis alba*) produces seed that is not literally white but actually beige, the color of straw. With its milder flavor, this is the one that is most common in the United States, both in pickling spice and in ballpark mustard. White mustard seeds have good preservative qualities, another reason they are used in pickling.
2. Black mustard (*Brassica nigra*) is much more pungent than white mustard. The seeds are dark, dark brown; in fact, in some parts of Europe these were sometimes called brown mustard. This type gets very tall (eight to ten feet) and readily drops its seed, making commercial harvest difficult. Because of this, black mustard has practically disappeared from the world marketplace.
3. Brown mustard (*Brassica juncea*) is more pungent than white, less so than black. There are actually two *juncea* varieties, called "brown" and "Oriental." Oriental seed is not really brown but quite pale in color, rather like white mustard; it is mostly used in Japan. Brown mustard seeds are very dark, hard to distinguish from black seeds; in fact, they are often called "black mustard." However, you could easily tell the difference if you were looking at the plants, for the brown is about half the size of the black, which makes it possible to be harvested mechanically. Because of this, brown mustard has virtually replaced the black in all commercial plantings.

Although scientists think the mustard species are native to the Mediterranean region (southern Europe, the Middle East, and western Asia), the plants grow quite well in almost all temperate climates, and now there are commercial fields in many countries. Most of what we consume was grown in Canada or the northern U.S.: Montana and the Dakotas.

Powdered Mustard

In a process not unlike milling wheat, the seeds are ground very finely and then sifted and screened several times to remove all debris. The end result is a very fine powder about the consistency of flour, and indeed it is sometimes referred to as mustard "flour."

Dry mustard may be made completely from white mustard seeds, or a mix of white and brown; the mix is hotter. Unless the label says otherwise, the powdered mustard we buy in the supermarket is probably white mustard.

The interesting thing about mustard flour is its chemistry. On its own, mustard powder has no aroma. That is because its familiar flavor is locked into separate cells in the form of two constituents: a glucoside and an enzyme, which combine in a chemical reaction to produce the essential oil that gives mustard its taste. That chemical reaction is triggered by water. So the only way we can get flavor out of powdered mustard is to wet it; then we must wait five or ten minutes for the full flavor to emerge.

The best liquid to use for this is plain tap water. If you use boiling water, you will kill the enzyme, producing a mild, bitter taste. Mixing the flour with vinegar stops the enzyme action, so full flavor will not develop. But once the essential oils have formed, then you can add the other things to enhance flavor: vinegar, wine, beer, salt, herbs, etc.

The final taste of the mustard is affected by the liquid added:

Water produces a sharp, hot taste.
Vinegar produces a milder, English-style flavor.
Wine produces a pungent, spicy flavor.
Beer produces an extremely hot taste.

Mustard Tip

The moral of this story is: If you intend to add powdered mustard to something you are cooking, first stir in a bit of tap water, let it sit for 10 minutes, then add the paste to your dish.

Prepared Mustard

A few hundred years ago, when national prosperity allowed Europeans the luxury of time to think about good food, people in different countries developed ways to produce a flavorful condiment from mustard flour, and distinctive products evolved; even now we speak of French, English, and German mustard, all with different tastes.

- *French mustard.* In the town of Dijon in France, mustard makers developed a particularly fine recipe using white wine and several herbs; the exact formula, unchanged for centuries, is secret. In 1634, the Dijon manufacturers were given an exclusive: They would be the only source of true French mustard, and in return had to wear "clean and sober clothes" and put their names on the products. They decided to set up just one retail shop, where all manufacturers would sell their wares, to forestall any complaints about inferior mustard. Grey-Poupon, founded in 1777, is still a familiar manufacturer of Dijon mustard.

> "A tale without love is like beef without mustard: an insipid dish."
>
> —Anatole France

- *English mustard.* Although mustard was made in England since the days of the Roman conquerors, it wasn't always in the physical form we now know it. In the time of Shakespeare, mustard seeds were roughly ground, then mixed with honey or vinegar and cinnamon and formed into balls for storage and commerce. Then around 1720 a woman in Durham, England, figured out a way to grind the seeds into fine powder and then sift it even finer—in effect, inventing powdered mustard. In Britain today you will still hear people speak of "Durham mustard."

  But mustard didn't become a large industry in England until the beginning of the nineteenth century, when a young man named Jeremiah Colman, who owned a grain mill, decided to experiment with milling mustard seeds. Over the next few decades he developed a process that ground the seeds into very fine flour, and added a new touch: The ground flour was sifted through silk cloth that was woven right on the spot. Today Colman's dry mustard, in the familiar bright yellow, square tins, is still made in the same place where Jeremiah's first mill was located.

- *German mustard* is dark and hearty, flavored with several herbs. The full seed, including the coat, is used, which produces the darker color.

- *American mustard*—ballpark mustard—is, as you already know, made from white seeds, and so its flavor is relatively mild. The formula contains some vinegar, which acts as a preservative, which is why it can stay in your refrigerator for eons without going bad. Its yellow color, by the way, comes from turmeric, not mustard powder.

- *Chinese mustard.* The hot mustard you get in Chinese restaurants is simply mustard powder and water—nothing else. You can easily make it at home; stir in enough lukewarm water to make a paste, give it 10 minutes to develop the flavor. Mix up just enough for a meal, since it doesn't store well.

Many specialty mustards are available these days, flavored with Champagne, beer, herbs, other spices, tomato paste, honey, just about anything under the sun. Browse the shelves the next time you're in the supermarket; you'll be amazed.

History and Legend

Mustard seeds were used by the Chinese thousands of years ago, and the ancient Greeks considered them an everyday spice. The Greeks' technique was to crush the seeds and sprinkle them on food—not, as we have learned, the best way to get the flavor.

As part of their meal rations, Roman soldiers carried the seeds throughout Europe as early as 50 B.C. Mustard, the garden plant, is very easy to grow, and seeds that fall to the ground stay viable for years. Doubtless the soldiers' cooks dropped a few seeds along the way, and today wild mustard reseeds itself so vigorously it is considered a weed in many places.

The Romans also gave us the name "mustard." They often mixed ground mustard seeds with "must," which is the name for grape juice in a certain stage of winemaking, and called the concoction *mustum ardens,* meaning "burning must"—because it was must that burns the tongue. Over the years *mustum ardens* was slurred into "mustard."

A Zen Story About Mustard

Once a small baby died for no reason that anyone could discover. The grieving mother took the baby to the wise man of the village, pleading for him to restore the child to life. The wise man told her to bring him some mustard seed from a house where no one—no child, no parent, no grandparent, no husband, no wife, no servant—had ever died, and he would use that seed to revive the baby.

The young mother ran frantically from house to house throughout the village, growing more desperate as each visit failed to produce what she sought.

At last she understood: Death cannot be avoided; every household will be touched by it at some point. With a sad heart but calm soul, she thanked the wise man for his lesson.

At about the same time as the Romans were dropping mustard seeds in Gaul and Britain, the Arabs were introducing mustard to Moorish Spain, as they did with so many other spices, and thus it became known to other countries in southern Europe in quick order. The difference here is that, unlike many of the true spices from the Orient, mustard would easily grow in European soils. So it was one spice that ordinary people (not just the wealthy) could enjoy, because they could grow it for themselves.

When Europeans explored and settled the New World, mustard was one of the food items they brought with them; again, since it grows so easily in temperate climates, it caught on quickly. In early California the

Spanish priests deliberately dribbled mustard seeds along the way as they moved from mission to mission—or so the story goes—making it easy to find their trails in later months.

Mustard seeds have earned an interesting place in spice folklore:

- In Scandinavia, seeds were mixed with ginger (another hot spice) and cool spearmint and given as a prescription to women considered frigid.
- In India and Denmark, the seeds were once considered to have magical powers; they were scattered around on the floors of a house to keep evil spirits away.
- If a young German bride sewed mustard seeds into the hem of her wedding gown, she would be the dominant partner in her marriage.

And of course there are several places in the Bible where mustard seeds are used as a metaphor for something extremely small.

Medicinal and Other Uses

It's easy to forget, in these days of chrome-plated medicine, that for most of its history, the human race has had to rely on the plants growing around us for healing; that those old remedies have been around much, much longer than prescription drugs. One of those remedies that you may have heard of is the mustard plaster; it was still very much in use well into the twentieth century.

But mustard's contribution is much older than that; it has been used as a medicine since ancient times. Pythagoras (fifth century B.C.) and Hippocrates (fourth century B.C.) both spoke of its effectiveness for a wide range of ailments, including scorpion bites. In fact, it held such an important place in medicine in those days that the Greeks believed it had been created by Asclepius, the god of healing, as a gift to mankind.

Our friend Pliny the naturalist, in the first century A.D., suggested mustard seed as a good way to "overcome lassitude in females." We don't know exactly what he meant; the word lassitude suggests a kind of dreamy, languid weariness, and certainly women in all ages have had plenty to make them weary, but it is also possible he was referring to fainting spells.

It isn't very surprising that something with such strong properties would have been used to treat all manner of problems. At one time or another, physicians of the day have prescribed mustard for scorpion stings or snakebite (presumably because the mustard bites back), epilepsy, toothache, hair falling out, black-and-blue bruises, stiff neck, scratchy voice, and failing memory.

One old treatment that may sound strange actually makes sense:

Culpeper, the English herbalist of the seventeenth century, suggested drinking a mustard blend to counteract poisonous mushrooms. We know today that mustard is an emetic (will make you vomit), so if you took enough and acted quickly enough, you might indeed get rid of the poison. But a lot of what Culpeper suggested is goofy, and you should never blindly follow his advice.

And then there is the well-known mustard plaster, an old home remedy for rheumatism, neuralgia, arthritis, and the like. Because mustard seed is a rubefacient (an irritant), it has the effect of drawing blood to the surface of the skin, warming and easing stiff muscle tissue. But it does burn, and **you need to be careful if you intend to try this**.

To make a plaster, mix mustard powder (or grind up some seeds, if that's all you have) with water to make a paste, and spread the paste on a thin cloth. Lay a second clean cloth on your body, then the mustard cloth, then cover it with a third clean cloth. Don't put the paste directly on the skin, because it can actually burn; in any case lift the plaster every five minutes and check your skin for redness.

Another interesting old idea: a mustard seed footbath. It will warm your feet (very soothing when you have a cold), and that same footbath is reported to help with headaches too. (Once again, there is modern verification to this. Migraine sufferers have learned that warming their hands and feet draws blood away from painfully dilated blood vessels in the head.) Dissolve 1/4 cup powder or crushed seeds in 1 pint boiling water, then add another pint of hot tap water, and soak your feet for about 5 minutes. Just remember to be careful. Use common sense: If you feel a burning sensation, that's the signal to stop.

In addition to home remedies, mustard plants have other uses. In rural areas, all the mustards have been grown as a crop for cattle, and also as green manure (to be tilled under as a soil enhancer). In California honeybee country, mustard is grown for its flowers. The honey is light-colored and reported to be very mild flavored.

Crafts and Gifts

Each year for some time now, I have made up a large batch of special mustard from dry mustard powder for Christmas gifts. The one year I missed, I heard nothing but whining for months. It is hot and spicy and sweet all at the same time, and it is delicious on grilled sausages. Heck, it's even delicious on your finger.

The recipe I use is in the cooking section of this chapter (page 232), but you do not have to limit yourself to that one. What I hope to do is introduce you to the idea of making specialty mustards. Once you discover how good they are, I'm guessing you'll explore your cookbooks for other recipes.

Most homemade mustard needs to sit for a few weeks to develop its

Gourmet mustard from your kitchen. Present it to friends as a special gift, if you can bear to part with it; caution them to keep it in the refrigerator.

flavor, so if you're making yours for holiday gifts, start a month or so early. Also, be aware that many of these mustards need to be refrigerated. Be sure to add a line to the jar label, or attach a gift tag noting, "Keep refrigerated." In the refrigerator, in a jar with a good lid, they keep indefinitely.

Cooking with Mustard

When your recipe calls for adding powdered mustard to a dish, remember that you'll get the mustardiest flavor if you first stir in some water and let it rest for 5 to 10 minutes. Just to give you a sense of perspective, one teaspoon of dry mustard produces about the same flavor concentration as a tablespoon of prepared mustard.

Use Dry Mustard in:
- Barbecue sauce, cocktail sauce for seafood
- Salad dressings
- Deviled eggs
- Baked beans
- All kinds of meat dishes
- Chowders and bisques
- Beets, succotash
- Deviled crab
- Mayonnaise dressing for fruit salads
- Sprinkle on baked chicken or beef instead of pepper

Use Whole Mustard Seeds in:
- Pickles, relishes, chutneys, and similar mixtures
- Cabbage, sauerkraut, beets (add to the cooking water)
- With cooked vegetables in place of caraway or dill seeds (toast the seeds first)

In India, a common garnish is whole seeds that have been cooked in hot oil. The heat destroys the enzymes and so the taste is not hot like mustard but nutty, more like poppy seeds. This distinctive taste is a key ingredient in some Indian dishes, and well worth experimenting with in other foods.

Commercially, mustard is used in manufacturing canned deviled ham, luncheon meats, and all sorts of pickles. Mustard powder, especially that made from white seeds, acts as an emulsifier, binding together oil and vinegar, and as such is used in the commercial manufacture of mayonnaise.

⤙ Cheesy Herb Crackers ⤚

1 cup flour
1/2 teaspoon baking powder
1/2 teaspoon dry mustard
1/4 teaspoon salt
1/4 teaspoon cayenne
1/4 cup butter, at room temperature
1 cup finely grated Swiss cheese
1/4 cup finely chopped toasted almonds
1 tablespoon diced garlic chives (or regular chives)
2 to 3 tablespoons milk

Sift together flour, baking powder, mustard, salt, and cayenne. In a separate bowl, mix together butter and cheese. Add flour mixture, blending with fingers or a pastry blender. Mix in almonds and garlic chives. Add milk 1 tablespoon at a time, stirring with a fork, until dough holds together. Shape into a log about 1 inch in diameter. Wrap in plastic wrap and chill for several hours.

Preheat oven to 400°. Slice the dough into rounds about 1/4-inch thick and place them on ungreased baking sheets. Bake 10 to 12 minutes or until lightly browned.

Makes about 3 dozen.

⚔ Spiced Raisin Sauce ⚔

Nice with ham, pork chops, or baked chicken.

1 cup brown sugar
1¹/₂ tablespoons cornstarch
¹/₈ teaspoon dry mustard
¹/₈ teaspoon ground cloves
¹/₄ teaspoon ground allspice
¹/₄ teaspoon ground cinnamon
¹/₂ cup vinegar
2 cups water
1 cup seedless raisins
2 tablespoons butter or salad oil

Combine brown sugar, cornstarch, and spices in top of double boiler. Blend in vinegar and water. Cook over medium heat, stirring constantly, until sauce comes to a boil. Add raisins, reduce heat, and simmer until sauce is thickened and smooth and raisins are plump, about 10 minutes. Stir in butter or oil, and serve hot.

Store unused sauce in covered container in refrigerator.

Makes 4 cups.

⚔ Miami Mustard ⚔

Use this rich mustard sauce in chicken salad, meatloaf sandwiches, or to-die-for hamburgers.

1 tablespoon dry mustard
2 tablespoons dry white wine
1 cup mayonnaise
¹/₄ cup heavy cream
dash hot sauce

In a small bowl, combine dry mustard and white wine. Let stand for 30 minutes. Whisk in mayonnaise, cream, and hot sauce; blend thoroughly. Cover and refrigerate until used.

Makes 1¹/₄ cups.

❖ Carrot-Cabbage Coleslaw ❖

1 large cabbage
2 carrots
4 stalks celery
1 medium onion
1 large green pepper

Grate cabbage and carrots; dice celery, onion, and pepper. Mix all ingredients together in a large bowl. Pour hot dressing over vegetables and stir well. Chill. Salad will keep in refrigerator for up to two weeks.

Dressing
1 teaspoon mustard seed
³/₄ cup olive oil
³/₄ cup red wine vinegar
1¹/₄ cups sugar
1 teaspoon salt

Combine all ingredients for dressing and bring to a boil.
Makes about 4 quarts.

❖ Healthy Vegetables ❖

1 tablespoon butter
1 tablespoon mustard seeds
1 zucchini, sliced or julienned
2 carrots, sliced or julienned
2 onions, coarsely chopped
1 green pepper, seeded and cut into chunks
¹/₄ cup hot water
salt and pepper

Melt butter in heavy skillet over medium heat; add mustard seeds and sauté 1 to 2 minutes, until they become fragrant. Be careful not to burn.

Increase heat to high and add vegetables. Cook and stir vigorously for 1 minute, till vegetables sizzle and brown around the edges. Add water to pan and cover tightly. Reduce heat to low. Cook until vegetables are done but not mushy, about 5 minutes. Season with salt and pepper to taste.

Serve with brown rice.
Serves 6.

-ᢞ **East Indian Potatoes** ᢣ-

¹/₄ teaspoon mustard seeds
3 tablespoons vegetable oil
1 large onion, sliced thin
1 fresh chili pepper, finely chopped (see note)
¹/₂ teaspoon grated ginger
¹/₂ teaspoon turmeric powder
4 large potatoes, peeled and cubed
1 medium tomato, seeded and chopped
1 teaspoon salt

Sauté mustard seeds in hot oil until they crackle. Add onions and sauté until golden brown. Add chili pepper, ginger, and turmeric and cook for 1 or 2 minutes.

Add potatoes to pan and stir to coat with seasonings. Add a small amount of water, so potatoes don't stick, and simmer until potatoes are just barely tender, about 10 minutes.

Fold in tomatoes and salt and cook another 5 minutes. Serve hot with your favorite curry.

Note: Use rubber gloves when handling fresh chilies; don't rub your eyes. If you like extremely hot foods, include the seeds; if not, don't.
Makes 4 to 6 servings.

-ᢞ **Mustard Tarragon Burgers** ᢣ-

1 pound ground turkey or lean ground beef
2 tablespoons applesauce
1 teaspoon onion powder (or 2 teaspoons minced fresh onion)
1 teaspoon dry mustard
¹/₂ teaspoon dried tarragon, crumbled
¹/₂ teaspoon pepper

Combine all ingredients in mixing bowl; cover and chill in refrigerator 10 minutes, or until ready to cook.

Prepare charcoal grill or preheat oven broiler. Shape meat into 4 patties and cook about 5 minutes on each side, or until done to your liking.
Serves 4.

—McCormick/Schilling

⤚⟨ Chicken with Mustard-Orange Sauce ⟩⤛

1 chicken, cut into serving pieces
3 large oranges
1 teaspoon salt
1 teaspoon dry mustard
1 teaspoon paprika
1/4 teaspoon Tabasco sauce
1/3 cup vegetable oil
1 4-oz. can sliced mushrooms or 3/4 cup sliced fresh mushrooms

Heat oven to 400°. (If you like your chicken extra-crisp, bake at 425°.) Place chicken skin-side-down in single layer in shallow baking pan.

Slice one orange, unpeeled, into rounds and set aside for garnish. Grate rind from remaining oranges until you have 2 tablespoons of peel. Squeeze oranges for juice; you should have 1/2 cup. In mixing bowl, combine juice and rind, salt, mustard, paprika, Tabasco, and oil; mix well. Pour sauce over chicken; use spoon to make sure each piece is well coated.

Bake 45 minutes, basting occasionally. Turn chicken over, sprinkle mushrooms onto chicken. Baste again and bake 15 minutes longer. Remove chicken to hot platter and spoon sauce over top. Cut reserved orange slices halfway through (from one edge to center), twist, and arrange twists around the edge of the platter.

Makes 4 to 6 servings.

⤚⟨ Hot-Sweet-Spicy Mustard ⟩⤛

6 ounces dry mustard (about 2 cups)
1/2 teaspoon pepper
1/4 teaspoon white pepper
1/2 teaspoon cayenne
1/2 cup water
3 eggs
2 cups sugar
1 1/2 cups vinegar
1 teaspoon salt
1/2 cup butter or margarine (1 stick)

Mix together the mustard powder and the three peppers. Gradually mix in water until you get a thick paste; you may need a bit more or less than 1/2 cup. Set aside.

Beat the eggs very well. Add to top of double boiler with sugar, vinegar, salt, and margarine. Cook over low heat until sugar is dissolved and margarine melted.

Stir half of the egg mixture into the mustard mixture; blend well, then return this to the double boiler, mixing thoroughly. Simmer until thick, about 15 minutes. Pack into jars, seal, and chill. The mustard is considerably thicker when it cools.

Store in refrigerator. Keeps indefinitely, especially if you hide it.

Makes about 4 cups.

For Other Recipes Featuring Mustard, See:

Nutmeg

Botanical name: Myristica fragrans
Part used as spice: Seed
Available as: Whole nutmeg or ground

The beautiful evergreen tree from which we get both nutmeg and mace is native to the Banda Islands, which are part of the larger island group called the Moluccas, which in turn are part of the modern country of Indonesia. The Moluccas are the same as what Europeans once called "The Spice Islands" (see map, page 24). The term "Banda nutmeg" is still used today to denote a spice of particularly high quality.

Indonesia still supplies nutmeg to the world spice market; but other countries also have commercial plantations, especially the tiny Caribbean island of Grenada. How the nutmeg tree traveled halfway around the world from the East Indies to the West Indies is part of the overall history of the spice trade, as we will see shortly.

The nutmeg tree, which gets to be as much as seventy feet tall, blooms with small yellowish flowers—small, that is, in relation to the fruit that develops from them. The flowers have a sweet fragrance, and so do the leaves if you crush them, but we are most interested in the fruit—or, to be more exact, the seed inside.

The fruit, which has the mottled yellow coloration of a pear but the approximate shape of a small peach, splits in half when it is ripe, revealing the seed that is the source of both nutmeg and mace. The first thing you see when the fruit opens up is a holey, stringy covering over the seed like a net. In botanical terms, this net is called an aril; in the nutmeg it is bright red. (The nutmeg aril is also a spice in its own right; see the chapter on Mace.) Underneath the aril (and visible through its holes) is a dark, shiny, hard pit, and inside that is an oval-shaped kernel or seed. That inner seed is the nutmeg.

In days past, plantation workers waited until the fruit was so ripe it fell to the ground. In Grenada they still do this, but elsewhere the fruit is usually picked from the tree before it falls.

Workers on the ground open up the fleshy fruit (sometimes the fruit is used to make a preserve, but most often it is simply discarded), exposing the seed. First they carefully peel off the arils (see Mace chapter for the next steps), and then the hard seed pits are spread out on drying racks. After several weeks, the inner seed has dried so thoroughly it rattles when someone shakes it, and that's the signal that it is ready.

The outer seed coat is cracked open and the nutmeg inside is removed. In some cases it is treated with lime, just as in the old days (see History, below), although now the motive is to protect against insect infestation rather than against potential smugglers.

In the spice trade, nutmeg is labeled "East Indian" or "West Indian," meaning that it comes from, respectively, Indonesia and nearby islands, or Grenada.

History and Legend

It was the Arabs, who dominated the spice trade for so many centuries, who first brought nutmeg to the West in the sixth century. Nutmeg was among the wares in their caravans from the East Indies to Constantinople, and before long it had become established throughout Europe.

In the twelfth century, to prepare for a visiting dignitary, nutmegs were piled in the streets and set on fire. The aromatic fumes and smoke covered up, for a while, the powerful stench that characterized most cities in those days before sewage systems.

Certainly nutmeg had made its way into Great Britain by the twelfth century, when the poet Chaucer wrote:

> There springen herbs grate [great] and smalle
> The licoris and the setewole
> And many a clove gilofre
> And nutemuge [nutmeg] to put in ale
> Whether it be moist or stale.

Is Chaucer telling us that nutmeg was added to ale of poor (stale) quality, to improve its taste? Maybe. In any case, the combination of nutmeg in alcoholic drinks continues to this day.

When Vasco da Gama reached the Moluccas in 1512 and claimed them for Portugal, he realized he had discovered the native habitat of the costly nutmeg. But Portugal didn't get to enjoy that wealth for long. In 1602 the Netherlands managed to gain control of the East Indies, and immediately set out to construct a monopoly.

They strictly controlled the area in which nutmeg trees could be grown and the number of trees, and made it clear to the native population that anyone who collected nutmegs and tried to sell them would be executed. For a time, convicted criminals from Holland were shipped to the Bandas to work in the nutmeg plantations as incarcerated labor.

The Dutch were especially worried because the part of the fruit that is used as the spice is also the tree's seed. Anyone could, in theory, buy a whole nutmeg, plant it, and grow their own tree—or a whole orchard of trees. To protect against this, the Dutch ordered that all the harvested nutmegs be bathed in lime, which would prevent them from ever sprouting.

The local birds, however, paid no attention. The nutmeg fruits were a favorite of pigeons, who would get to the ripe fruit before the agricultural workers could pick it. The birds enjoyed the fruit and then flew away, later scattering the seed wherever they happened to be—perhaps on another island. In this way, the seeds spread throughout the East Indies.

The Dutch persisted. They dispatched workers to search out renegade trees and destroy them. In years when the harvest was particularly good, they even burned large piles of nutmegs, to keep the supply low and the price high.

But in spite of all these precautions, French visitors managed to smuggle some nutmegs out and start a trial plantation on the island of Mauritius, off the east coast of Africa near Madagascar. (See the chapter on Cloves for the full story of this daring raid.)

In the end, all the rigid Dutch controls came to naught, for in 1796 the British took over the Moluccas and spread the cultivation of nutmeg to other East Indian islands. When these experiments proved successful, the British decided to try growing nutmeg trees in some of the Caribbean islands then under control of the Crown: St. Vincent, Trinidad, and finally Grenada.

And that is how nutmeg came to the tiny nation that now calls itself the Nutmeg Island. So important a crop is nutmeg in Grenada that the national flag bears a stylized image of a nutmeg in one corner, and the entire flag is done in nutmeg colors: green (leaves), yellow (fruit), and red (aril).

There is even a nutmeg footnote to American history. In the early nineteenth century, traveling peddlers sometimes substituted fake nutmegs, carved of wood, for the expensive spice; this fraud was so notorious in New England that Connecticut came to be called the Nutmeg State. Nowadays, the labor involved in making a small carving is such that a "fake" nutmeg would cost far more than the real thing.

Medicine and Magic

Through the years nutmeg has been considered to have quite strong magical powers, both for better health and better sex. For example:

Tuck a nutmeg into your left armpit when going to a social outing on a Friday night, and many admirers will seek your attention. Young men were further advised to carry a small vial of oil of nutmeg on such an occasion and at the proper moment anoint their you-know-what, for virility that would last all weekend long. The source of this knowledge? A monk, in the sixteenth century.

Nutmegs have also been used as amulets, to protect from all manner of disaster. In 1147, St. Hildegard stated quite positively that if you were given a nutmeg on New Year's Day, and if you always carried it in your pocket, you would be safe from all harm; if you had a very serious fall, you would not break even the tiniest bone. Others have believed that a nutmeg in the pocket will prevent boils, and one worn as a necklace will keep rheumatism at bay.

In many old medical books and herbals, nutmeg is often suggested as a treatment for many ailments, ranging from plague, liver and stomach problems, scarlet fever, and apoplexy to hemorrhoids, freckles, and bad breath.

Some of those old prescriptions speak specifically of the narcotic effect that nutmeg seemed to have. Thus a mild dose was suggested to help people sleep, a larger dose as a sedative for someone suffering convulsions.

Modern laboratory analysis has confirmed this narcotic action. One of the alkaloid constituents of nutmeg, a compound called myristicin, is actually hallucinogenic in sufficient quantities. **This is nothing to fool around with; large amounts can be fatal.** In the amounts you would use in cooking, however, there is no danger.

Nutmeg has no legitimate medicinal applications today.

Cooking with Nutmeg

Generally, we associate nutmeg with sweet spicy dishes. Indeed, it is wonderful in sweet breads like banana or apricot bread, in cakes and cookies, and in fruit pies; and of course it's indispensable in holiday eggnog. But nutmeg also adds a surprising and delicious note to many other dishes.

Here are a few ideas that may be new to you.

- Mix ¼ teaspoon ground nutmeg into ¼ cup softened butter; use for corn on the cob.
- A stunningly simple dressing for fruit salad: Vanilla yogurt, straight from the carton; grate nutmeg on top.
- Serve premium vanilla ice cream in tall goblets, with a few sliced fresh strawberries for garnish, and grate a few grains of nutmeg over each serving.

- Serve fancy hot chocolate at your next wintertime party. Along with the chocolate, set out small bowls of whipped cream and several whole nutmegs with a grater. It may be the first time some of your guests have ever seen whole nutmeg.

Use Nutmeg with:
- Applesauce
- Fruit desserts: pies, cobblers, etc.
- Fruit sauces for cakes
- Pineapple desserts and molded salads
- Puddings and custards, and sauces for them
- Lemon desserts such as mousse and custard
- Pumpkin pie
- Pears with a lemon/nutmeg sauce
- Rice pudding
- Candied yams
- Green leafy vegetables: cabbage, cauliflower, kale, and especially spinach
- Tomatoes, green beans, corn, eggplant, onions
- Mashed potatoes
- Onion sauce
- Cheese dishes
- Brunswick stew, beef stew, vegetable stew
- Oyster stew, clam chowder
- Lamb dishes
- Soups: black bean, tomato, pea, potato, split pea, chicken

> Whole nutmeg keeps for years and, even though it looks as if it would be hard as a rock, is actually very easy to grate.
>
> So you have no excuse. Get yourself one of the several types of graters on the market, and get in the habit of grating the nutmeg right into the dish you're cooking. It really is better, and besides, it's fun.

Essential oil is processed from nutmegs (often broken ones are used for this) and used in manufacturing perfume, soaps, and lotions.

⋖ Island Rice Salad ⋗

¹/₄ cup mayonnaise
¹/₄ cup plain yogurt
¹/₂ teaspoon nutmeg

1 cup uncooked rice
¹/₂ cup raisins
¹/₂ cup chopped almonds
¹/₂ cup pine nuts

Garnishes:
Avocado
Canned mandarin oranges, drained

In small bowl, combine mayonnaise, yogurt, and nutmeg; set aside.

Cook rice with 2 cups water and ¹/₂ teaspoon salt. When rice is done, quickly fold in the mayonnaise mixture. The hot rice will absorb most of the dressing.

Let the rice cool and then fold in raisins and nuts; mix well. The rice should be just moist enough to hold together; if necessary, add a bit more mayonnaise.

Mold mixture into 12 small balls.

To serve, line salad plates with frilly lettuce leaves. Place 3 rice balls in the center. Add 3 avocado slices and several orange segments to each plate, in an attractive arrangement. Pass a serving bowl of sour cream dressing.

Makes 4 servings.

Sour Cream Dressing

1 cup sour cream
¹/₄ cup orange marmalade
1 tablespoon crystallized ginger, finely chopped

Use blender or food processor to blend ingredients thoroughly. Chill until ready to use.

Makes 1 cup.

⊰ Sweet Potato Vichyssoise ⊱

1 tablespoon butter
1 large coarsely chopped onion or the white of 2 large leeks, thickly sliced
6 cups chicken broth
3 cups diced, peeled sweet potatoes
¹/₄ teaspoon freshly grated nutmeg
salt and pepper
low-fat sour cream

Melt butter in large saucepan; sauté onion over medium heat until onion is transparent. Add broth, potatoes, nutmeg, and salt and pepper to taste. Simmer, covered, until potatoes are tender.

Set soup in refrigerator to cool, then puree in blender. You can do this much in advance.

To serve, reheat and pour into individual serving bowls. Add one spoonful sour cream to each serving and grate a few grains of additional nutmeg directly onto the sour cream.

Makes 6 servings.

❧ Sautéed Cabbage and Apples ☙

This reheats well.

> *2 large tart apples*
> *¹/₃ cup butter*
> *8 cups coarsely shredded cabbage*
> *¹/₄ cup chopped onions*
> *1 teaspoon seasoned salt*
> *¹/₂ teaspoon nutmeg*
> *3 tablespoons cider vinegar*
> *2 teaspoons sugar*
> *dash cayenne*
> *¹/₄ cup chopped pecans or walnuts (optional)*

Peel, core, and chop apples. In large heavy skillet or pan, melt butter. Add apples, cabbage, onions, salt, and nutmeg. Cover and cook over low heat 20 minutes, stirring frequently.

In small bowl, combine vinegar, sugar, and cayenne; add to cabbage. Cook 5 minutes longer.

Just before serving, sprinkle nuts over top.

Serves 4 to 5.

❧ Spinach Fritters ☙

Rich with corn and cheese, this spinach mixture can be cooked on the griddle as fritters or baked in a casserole.

> *3 eggs*
> *1 16-ounce can whole kernel corn, drained*
> *¹/₄ cup fresh parsley, minced*
> *¹/₂ pound spinach leaves, chopped*

1 cup grated cheddar cheese
1 green pepper, chopped
¹/₈ teaspoon freshly grated nutmeg
¹/₂ cup canned mushroom soup, undiluted
rolled oats
vegetable oil for griddle

In large mixing bowl, beat eggs. Add all other ingredients except rolled oats, and mix well. Fold in enough oats to thicken batter to dense consistency for griddle frying.

Heat griddle and spread on a thin layer of oil. Drop batter in large spoonfuls, flatten with spatula. Cook until brown on one side and then turn to brown on the other.

Serve with peanut sauce (recipe follows).

Serves 6.

Variation: To serve this as a casserole, add the following to the batter:

¹/₂ cup sweet pickles, chopped
1 small can pimientos, drained and chopped
¹/₂ cup tomato chunks (peeled and seeded)

Pour mixture into buttered casserole and bake at 375° until top browns.

Peanut Sauce
1 small onion, minced
2 tablespoons peanut oil
1 tablespoon brown sugar
1 tablespoon lime or lemon juice
¹/₄ cup peanut butter
1 cup rich chicken stock

Sauté onion in oil over very low heat until golden brown. Add other ingredients and mix very well. Store in refrigerator until ready to serve.

Makes about 1 cup.

❧ Creamed Spinach ❧

1¹/₂ pounds fresh spinach, or 2 10-ounce packages frozen spinach
1 tablespoon olive oil
1 tablespoon butter or margarine
1 large onion, finely chopped
4 cloves garlic, minced
2 tablespoons all-purpose flour
³/₄ cup half-and-half or light sour cream
¹/₄ teaspoon ground nutmeg
1 cup Parmesan cheese, divided
salt and pepper to taste

For fresh spinach: Wash, trim off thick stems, and slice leaves into narrow strips. Put damp spinach into a large pan, cover, and cook over medium heat until leaves are wilted (2 to 3 minutes).

For frozen spinach: Defrost, use your hands to squeeze out excess moisture, and chop if whole leaves.
    You should have 2 to 2¹/₂ cups chopped cooked spinach.

In a large heavy skillet, melt the oil and butter together. Add onion and garlic and cook over medium heat until onion is soft. Sprinkle flour over the onions, stir in well. Remove pan from heat and gradually blend in the half-and-half (or sour cream) and nutmeg.
    Add the spinach and return to high heat, stirring, until bubbling vigorously. Remove from heat and mix in ¹/₂ cup of the cheese and the salt and pepper.
    Transfer to hot serving dish and sprinkle with the remaining cheese.
Makes 4 to 6 servings.

❧ Danish Meatballs ❧

1 cup soft bread crumbs
1 egg, well beaten
1 cup applesauce, divided
¹/₂ cup catsup, divided
1 teaspoon salt
¹/₄ teaspoon nutmeg
¹/₈ teaspoon pepper
1¹/₂ pounds lean ground beef
¹/₄ cup minced onion
¹/₄ cup white wine, or water

Preheat oven to 425°.

Thoroughly mix the bread crumbs, egg, ¹/₂ cup applesauce, ¹/₄ cup catsup, salt, nutmeg, and pepper. Fold in meat and onion, blending well.

Form into 1-inch balls. Bake in large, shallow pan for 15 minutes. Spoon off excess fat. Mix together remaining applesauce, catsup, and wine, and pour over meatballs. Bake 10 minutes longer.

Serve with hot buttered noodles.

Makes 6 servings.

-ᘒ Shrimp Pie ᘒ-

2 cups bread crumbs
1 cup milk
2 cups cooked, shelled shrimp
2 tablespoons melted butter
1 teaspoon salt
¹/₂ teaspoon black pepper
1 teaspoon Worcestershire sauce
2 tablespoons sherry
¹/₈ teaspoon mace
¹/₄ teaspoon nutmeg

Preheat oven to 375°.

Soak bread in milk. Fold in shrimp, butter, and seasonings. Place in a buttered 1-quart baking dish and bake for 30 minutes.

Makes 4 servings.

-ᘒ Nutmeg Butter Cookies ᘒ-

1 cup butter, softened
¹/₂ cup sugar
1 egg
1 teaspoon vanilla
3 cups sifted all-purpose flour
¹/₂ teaspoon baking powder
¹/₄ teaspoon salt
1¹/₄ teaspoons ground nutmeg

Cream butter and sugar together until light and fluffy. Beat in egg and vanilla. In separate bowl, sift together flour, baking powder, salt, and nutmeg. Blend this into butter mixture.

Shape into 2 or 3 long rolls, 2 inches in diameter. Wrap in foil or waxed paper. Chill thoroughly, at least an hour.

When ready to cook, preheat oven to 425°.

Slice dough into rounds about 1/4-inch thick and place on ungreased cookie sheet. (If you prefer, pack dough into cookie press and press into desired shapes.) Bake until lightly brown, 5 to 7 minutes; don't overdo it.

Makes about 6 dozen cookies.

⤜ Deep Dish Apple Pie ⤛

uncooked pastry for one-crust pie
6 cups sliced tart apples
3/4 cup sugar
1/4 cup flour
1 teaspoon cinnamon
1/4 teaspoon nutmeg
1/4 teaspoon cloves
2 tablespoons water
1 teaspoon brandy extract
2 tablespoons butter
2 sticks cinnamon (optional)
cinnamon sugar

Preheat oven to 350°.

Prepare pastry; set aside.

In large bowl, combine apples, sugar, flour, cinnamon, nutmeg, and cloves; mix with your hands to cover apples well. Butter a 1 1/2-quart shallow baking dish and pour in apples. Sprinkle with water and extract; dot with butter.

Roll pastry to 1/8-inch thickness. Place on top of baking dish. Allow for 1/2-inch overhang, and trim away the excess. Fold the overhang back and under the edge of the casserole dish so that it does not pull away from the side as it cooks; use your fingers or tines of a fork to make a decorative pattern on the edges. Cut two or three steam vents in top of pastry; insert cinnamon sticks upright in vents, if you wish. Sprinkle top with cinnamon sugar.

Bake 15 minutes; reduce temperature to 350° and bake 30 minutes longer or until top is nicely browned.

Serve warm or cold with cheddar cheese or ice cream.

Serves 8.

For Other Recipes Featuring Nutmeg, See:

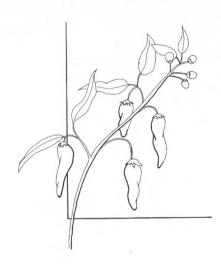

Paprika

Botanical name: **Capsicum annuum**
Part used as spice: **Fruit**
Available as: **Powder**

The spice we know as paprika is the dried, powdered fruit of a particular type of Capsicum (see chapter on chili peppers). In the fifteenth century, European explorers found capsicums growing in the New World and took some seeds home with them. There, grown in quite different circumstances, the plants gradually evolved. The Europeans seemed to prefer milder tastes, and so only the seeds of mild chilies were saved from year to year. This process of selection, plus the physiological effect of different soils, elevations, and climate, combined to produce considerably different peppers—milder, less piercing, sweeter.

It is from these mild peppers that we get paprika. The peppers are harvested when they are fully ripe, dried, and then ground into powder. In some cases the seeds and inner ribs are removed; in other cases, only the seeds. The first group produces paprika that has no bite; the second group has a rich pungency but still not the fierceness of hot peppers.

In Europe, the two main centers for growing paprika were—and still are—Hungary and Spain. In the past, Hungarian paprika was stronger and richer and Spanish paprika was quite mild. As a general rule, this is still true, although with controlled breeding they are becoming more alike. In fact, to maintain the stronger taste that consumers expect, some spice companies now add a bit of cayenne to Hungarian paprika.

The newest producer of paprika peppers is California, where the state's agricultural belt provides the long growing season that these peppers need. In fact, most of the paprika that Americans consume comes from peppers grown here in this country.

Medicinal Uses

All the capsicums have a long history of medicinal applications (see the chapter on Chili Peppers). Paprika has an additional distinction: its high content of vitamin C. In 1937 a Hungarian scientist won the Nobel Prize for isolating this vitamin in paprika peppers. Unfortunately, the very high heat of modern drying processes destroys most of this vitamin.

Vitamin A is another, happier story. Paprika, the spice, is a very good source of beta carotene, which is converted in the body to vitamin A. One tablespoon of paprika gives a woman all the vitamin A she needs for the day, and 84 percent of a man's recommended daily allowance.

Cooking with Paprika

In the kitchen, paprika has two functions: flavoring and garnish. If all you want to do is add a little bright color to the stuffed eggs you're taking to the church picnic, you'll probably prefer the milder type of paprika. It's not hard to find: This is the "basic" paprika on your grocer's shelves.

If you are interested in something with a richer and deeper taste, try to locate paprika from Hungary. In fact, if you want to make European dishes like goulash and paprikash, it's definitely worth the effort. Real Hungarian paprika makes a difference in these dishes.

Of course even the milder varieties of paprika add a little flavor. And if you want a richer taste but can only find domestic paprika, just use twice the amount called for.

> Like the other capsicums (cayenne, chili powder, red pepper flakes), paprika loses vitality quickly—even more than most spices. Store it in a container that has a tight lid, and keep it away from heat and light. In very hot weather, store it in the refrigerator.

An interesting quality of paprika is its ability to serve as an emulsifier. As every schoolchild knows, oil and water do not mix. But each of them does bond, at least temporarily, with paprika. So if paprika is part of a salad dressing, the two will blend into a smooth mixture. It's not a permanent bond, but lasts long enough to get you through dinner.

Commercial food manufacturers use paprika in processed meat products, in cheeses, tomato sauces, soups, chili powder, etc. Often its main purpose is to add color. If you buy a food item that is red, orange, or reddish brown, and the label lists among its ingredients "Natural Color," that's probably paprika.

❧ Mushroom Soup Paprika ❧

¹/₂ pound fresh mushrooms
1 tablespoon butter or margarine
1 teaspoon paprika
1 tablespoon all-purpose flour
2 tablespoons finely chopped parsley
4 cups beef broth
1 egg yolk
1 cup sour cream

Clean mushrooms and slice them thinly. Melt butter in heavy saucepan; add mushrooms and paprika and sauté until mushrooms are golden brown, about 5 minutes. Sprinkle mushrooms with flour and parsley. Gradually stir in beef broth and simmer slowly for 30 minutes.

You can do this much of the recipe ahead of time. Refrigerate soup; reheat when ready to serve.

Beat egg yolk slightly, then blend with sour cream. Place this mixture in bottom of soup tureen or serving bowl. Pour the hot soup over it gradually, stirring constantly. Serve immediately.

Makes 6 servings.

❧ Red Rice ❧

2 tablespoons oil
1 cup long-grain white rice
1 teaspoon salt
1 teaspoon paprika
2 pimientos, diced
2 cups boiling water

Heat the oil in a heavy skillet that has a lid, and sauté the rice until it starts to become transparent. Sprinkle the salt and paprika over the rice and mix in thoroughly; cook for about 30 seconds. Stir in pimientos and boiling water, cover the skillet, and reduce heat to very low. Cook until all the water is absorbed, about 30 minutes. Don't peek.

Makes 3 cups.

⋅❦ Garden Chicken Paprika ❧⋅

3 pounds chicken, cut into pieces
salt and pepper
2 tablespoons butter, divided
2 tablespoons olive oil, divided
1 clove garlic, minced
1 large onion, chopped
3 cups sliced mushrooms
1¹/₂ tablespoons paprika
1¹/₂ cups chicken stock
2 anaheim chile peppers, roasted, skinned, seeded, and coarsely
  chopped
2 tablespoons flour
1 cup low-fat sour cream

Garnish:
3 tablespoons fresh chives or parsley, chopped

Pat chicken dry. Season with salt and pepper. In a large skillet, heat 1 tablespoon each butter and oil. Add chicken pieces and sauté until golden brown on both sides. Remove chicken from pan and set aside; pour off excess fat.

Add garlic and onions to skillet and sauté until light golden. Push onions to one side of pan, add mushrooms and sauté until soft; if needed, add more butter and oil. Sprinkle onions and mushrooms with paprika, stirring until coated. Add chicken stock. Bring to a boil, scraping up bits from the bottom of pan as it cooks.

Return the chicken to skillet along with chile peppers. Cover pan and simmer until chicken is tender, about 25 to 30 minutes, spooning pan juices over chicken occasionally. Remove chicken to a platter and keep warm.

In a small bowl, whisk the flour into the sour cream, then stir into simmering stock. Simmer 5 to 7 minutes longer, stirring until sauce is thickened. Return the chicken to skillet and simmer for a few more minutes, spooning sauce over the pieces.

Serve over noodles. Garnish with chopped chives or parsley.
Serves 4.

—Renée Shepherd

⚜ Scallops in Sherry ⚜

1 quart scallops, quartered
1 cup sherry
1/2 cup olive oil
1 cup chopped green pepper
1 cup onion, minced
1 tablespoon capers
2 teaspoons paprika
1 teaspoon salt
1/2 teaspoon minced garlic

Place scallops in a shallow baking dish. Combine remaining ingredients and pour over scallops. Broil, stirring occasionally, until scallops are lightly browned, 10 to 15 minutes. Serve over rice.
Serves 6.

⚜ Hungarian Goulash ⚜

1 green pepper
2 tomatoes
4 tablespoons tomato paste
1 cup water
1/4 cup chopped onions
3 tablespoons butter
3 pounds beef shoulder roast, cut into 1 1/2-inch cubes
1 tablespoon paprika
1/2 teaspoon coarse-ground black pepper
2 teaspoons seasoned salt
6 anise seeds
dash cayenne
3 slices bacon

Remove core and seeds from pepper and chop into small chunks. Peel and seed tomatoes and cut into wedges. Mix pepper and tomatoes with tomato paste and water; set aside.

In large skillet or Dutch oven, sauté onions in butter until golden brown. Lift onions from pan and set aside. Add beef to skillet and brown on all sides. In a small bowl, mix paprika, pepper, salt, anise seed, and cayenne; sprinkle this spice mixture over meat.

Return browned onions to skillet. Pour tomato mixture over meat in skillet. Place bacon strips over meat. Cover and simmer 2 hours or until meat is tender. If sauce becomes too thick, add water.

Serve over hot cooked noodles.

Serves 4 to 6.

❧ American French Dressing ☙

1¹/₂ cups olive oil
¹/₂ cup vinegar
³/₄ teaspoon salt
2 teaspoons sugar
1 teaspoon paprika
¹/₄ teaspoon garlic powder
¹/₄ teaspoon white pepper
¹/₂ teaspoon dry mustard

Combine all ingredients in jar; shake vigorously. For best flavor, make at least 1 hour ahead, to allow flavors to blend. Store in covered jar in refrigerator; keeps indefinitely. Shake well before using.

Makes about 2 cups.

For Other Recipes Featuring Paprika, See:

Rosy Caraway Cheese Dip, p. 56
Chicken-Caraway Simmer, p. 58
Hot Texas Red Chili, p. 78
Persian Lamb, p. 141
Bengali Beef Stew, p. 152
Chicken with Mustard-Orange Sauce, p. 232
Potato Soup, p. 260
Paella, p. 280
Arroz Con Pollo, p. 281
Carolina Rice and Shrimp Supper, p. 308

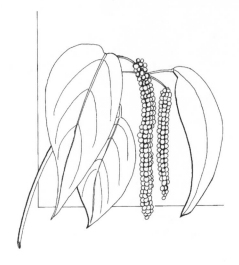

Pepper

Botanical name: Piper nigrum
Part used as spice: Dried fruit
Available as: Whole or ground peppercorns

I invite you to try something: Walk into the kitchen (or wherever your family normally has its meals), sit down at the table, and pick up the pepper shaker. Sprinkle a little bit into your hand, or on a plate, and look closely at it while you think about this:

- For those small black grains, kingdoms have been ransomed, cities have been plundered, and entire economic systems have developed, flourished, and then failed. Bold men have risked, and sometimes lost, their lives. Privateers have grown wealthy, and thieves have been put to death.
- For those small grains, adventurous sailors from Europe's capitals raced each other to find a sea route to the Spice Islands of the East, whose location was only hazily understood. Among them, one sea captain dared to sail a westward course to the eastern islands—and discovered the New World.

You are, in a sense, holding the entire turbulent history of spices in your hand. For there can be no doubt that pepper is the most important spice known to humankind, both past and present. It is now, and ever has been, the king of spices.

Types and Grades of Pepper

Black pepper comes from the fruit of a vine that grows in humid tropical forests, approximately twenty degrees either side of the equator. The plant is native to southwestern India, but has been cultivated for many centuries in other parts of Asia with similar climates: Malaysia, Indonesia, Thailand, Vietnam, Sri Lanka. Today there are also commercial plantings in tropical Africa and South America, especially Brazil.

The vine produces thin, droopy clusters of small white flowers, about three inches long, which are followed by long clusters of between twenty and thirty berries. The berries are green at first, turning to red when fully mature. How and when these berries are harvested and processed determines whether the final result is black, white, or green peppercorns.

Black Pepper. The berries are picked when they are full size but still not quite mature; they are still green, just starting to turn red. The berries are spread out to dry, either in the sun or in kilns; as they dry they turn dark and the outer skin becomes wrinkled. The inner part of the berry, the seed, is still pale-colored, which is why ground black pepper shows bits of white with the black.

White Pepper. The berries are allowed to ripen fully, then picked. They are soaked in water for approximately a week, which loosens the outer covering of the berry and makes it easy to remove in a threshing process. The large inner seed, which is naturally a pale gray, is then dried in the sun, which bleaches it white.

The true relationship between black and white pepper was not always understood. For a long time botanists assumed there were two different plants. Then, from a fourteenth-century treatise titled *The Nature of Things*, comes this imaginative explanation of how black pepper gets black.

"Pepper is the seed or fruit from a tree which grows on the south side of Caucasus Mountains [wrong, although some trade routes did pass through this range in southern Russia], in the hottest sunshine. The pepper forest is full of poisonous snakes that guard it. When the fruit is ripe, people come and set fire to the forest. The snakes flee, but the smoke and flames blacken the pepper fruits and make their taste sharper."

Green Peppercorns. These are picked from the vine when they are still green. Because they are not dried in the conventional way, they will rot if not preserved in some fashion. Until recently, the most common way was to pickle or can them in jars or bottles. Recently, some manufacturers are using a quick dehydration process and then treating the berries with a preservative: freeze-dried peppercorns.

What about taste? White pepper is somewhat milder in flavor, but as a practical matter the primary reason for choosing it rather than black is aesthetic: You would use it when cooking something you wouldn't want black flecks in—a white sauce, for instance. In Europe, white pepper is more popular for everyday use; in the United States, it's black.

Green peppercorns have a slightly different flavor, a taste that many describe as "fresh."

Pepper is grown commercially in many areas of tropical Asia, and the various types and grades of pepper recognized by the modern spice trade take their name from the areas where they grow or the ports from which they are traditionally shipped. Tellicherry pepper, usually considered the finest of all, is named for the port town of Tellicherry, on the northern end of India's Malabar Coast. Number one in terms of volume is Lampong, named for the Lampong district of the island of Sumatra. Other types of pepper include Singapore, Penang (in Malaysia), Malabar, Acheen (in Sumatra), and Sarawak (on the coast of Borneo). A relatively new type is called Brazilian, and indeed it is grown in Brazil, the first Western nation to enter the field.

Other Peppers: Long Pepper, Grains of Paradise, Pink Peppercorns

In addition to pepper in white and basic black (from the plant *Piper nigrum*), there are other spices referred to as pepper. They are not so familiar to most of us, but interesting to know about.

Pink peppercorns have a peppery taste and look like peppercorns in size and shape, but not color—they are truly pink. But they are not related to black pepper.

They come from a plant known as the Brazilian pepper tree, which is a relative of poison ivy. Some research has shown that people with a sensitivity to poison ivy don't tolerate this pepper well, and pink pepper was not officially approved by the FDA until fairly recently. You are most likely to find it in a mixture of whole peppercorns, where its function is mostly decorative: The pretty color makes the mixture a visual treat in a clear container. In France, pink peppercorns are considered a gourmet flavoring.

Long Pepper. This spice is closely related to black/white pepper, and grows in roughly the same area and in roughly the same way. There are two species: *Piper longum* and *Piper officinarum*, both originally from India.

Long pepper was far more significant in the past than it is now. The pepper mentioned in the ancient Sanskrit papers of India, some three thousand years ago, was probably long pepper. Historians also believe that when Alexander the Great led his troops eastward from the Mediterranean into India, he may have been the first Westerner to taste pepper, and that too was probably long pepper.

In India, long pepper was known as *pipali*; when it was brought into Persia by traders, the name was mispronounced as "pipari," which eventually came to be the name of all types of pepper, and is the source of the genus name *Piper*.

From Persia (in what is now the Middle East), long pepper made its way to ancient Greece and Rome. The Roman historian Pliny, in the first century, complaining about the high cost of pepper, wrote that long pepper cost almost four times more than black pepper; this indicates to us that it held gourmet status at the time.

Today long pepper is mostly a historical curiosity in the West, although it is still used in India in curries and sauces.

Grains of Paradise. This spice comes from West Africa. The seeds of a flowering plant in the same family as ginger, grains of paradise is not related to true pepper but has something of its taste, and was used as an inexpensive substitute for it during the years when pepper was out of the reach of ordinary people.

The plant produces yellow or pink flowers, which then form a fruit that contains as many as one hundred seeds. The seeds are harvested and dried, turning black on the outside but still white inside. They are smaller than black peppercorns but have a peppery taste with an undertone of ginger; when ground, they look remarkably like black pepper.

Before the age of the great sea explorations, African traders brought this spice on caravans across the Sahara to Tripoli in northern Africa, where it became part of the general spice trade of the Mediterranean. Then when the European explorers opened up ports on the western coast of Africa, this pepper substitute was brought to Europe directly by Portuguese traders.

Enslaved Africans included grains of paradise among the plants they took with them to the Caribbean islands, and the spice was cultivated there for a time.

In Europe this spice was often used by makers of wine and beer to give an extra kick to their products. When it became clear that the purpose was to disguise inferior taste, King George III of England imposed a stiff fine on any brewers who possessed grains of paradise and an even stiffer fine on pharmacists who supplied it to them.

Today grains of paradise is a common cooking spice only in its native land—West Africa.

History and Legend

Today, when a year's supply of pepper costs about the same as two loaves of good bread, it's hard to imagine the importance that pepper held in earlier centuries.

We can think of it as a classic example of the law of supply and demand. In the days when meat spoiled before it was all eaten, the demand was high for anything that would cover up the rancid taste. At the top of the list: pepper, the spiciest of spices. But the supply was limited, because of the long, dangerous, and costly journey from India westward. Pepper was literally worth its weight in gold: It took an ounce of gold to buy an ounce of pepper.

As such a valuable commodity, pepper was a driving economic force in much of the world's history. For instance:

- Starting in ancient Greece and Rome, and on through much of the Renaissance years in Europe, taxes—and official bribes—were paid in pepper.
- In the first century A.D., the scholar Pliny wrote about pepper, saying it was too expensive—one hundred times its actual cost by the time it reached Rome. Why, he wondered, would anyone pay such exorbitant prices for something that tasted so bad?
- Alaric, king of the Visigoths, gathered his troops on the outskirts of Rome in A.D. 410 but promised to spare the city if he was paid a ransom: five thousand pounds of gold, three thousand pounds of pepper, and thirty thousand pounds of silver. The gold and silver were on hand, but the city leaders had a hard time finding that much pepper. (P.S.: He eventually plundered the city anyway.)
- In the Middle Ages, pepper was used as money. Serfs could buy their freedom for one pound of pepper. Tenants on feudal estates paid their rent in pepper; this led to the custom of handing over one single peppercorn as a ceremonial payment, signifying the long-term relationship between landowner and tenant, a practice that endures today in the British expression "peppercorn rent," meaning something of inconsequential value.
- The English theologian known to history as the Venerable Bede, at his death in A.D. 735, left instructions for distributing his worldly goods among his brother monks; among his few treasures, a small supply of pepper.
- Workers on the docks where the trading ships were unloaded were not allowed to wear any clothes that had pockets, to prevent them from stealing a few grains of this most valuable commodity.

In England in the Middle Ages, commerce was controlled by a system of guilds, rather like modern unions. As far back as 1180, there was a Guild of Pepperers in London, to which all spice merchants belonged. The fact that they were called pepperers is testimony to the primacy that pepper held among all the spices. One of their responsibilities was to set standards for spices so that customers could be assured they were receiving the real thing; anything so costly was vulnerable to adulteration with inferior-tasting look-alikes. A few hundred years later, the guild members became known as grocers, from the term *vendre a gros,* meaning "sell wholesale."

Medicinal and Household Uses

The three primary chemicals in pepper—piperine, piperidine, and chavicin—produce the fiery flavor and "bite" that your tongue knows as pepper. All three are classified as irritants (they stimulate mucous membranes) and diaphoretics (they make you perspire). Both properties can be beneficial.

If you have a cold or hay fever, especially if your chest or nasal passages are congested, the irritation of the mucous membranes will help you cough or blow your nose and clear out the congestion. So make up a batch of good warm soup and put lots of pepper in it. Perspiration is a natural cooling process, so any foods that increase perspiration are very popular in hot climates.

The same property in pepper that makes your nose run also stimulates saliva, so pepper has been thought to improve your appetite.

For many years pepper has been used as a home remedy for indigestion, nausea, and constipation. Centuries-old medical texts suggest that ancient physicians considered pepper something of a cure-all; it was prescribed for fevers, cholera, jaundice, arthritis, hemorrhoids, ringworm, and toothache, among others.

In parts of Africa, pepper is considered a mosquito repellent: When you eat a lot of it, so the theory goes, your skin emanates a peppery odor that keeps mosquitoes away.

Organic gardeners, take note: Piperine, the main alkaloid in pepper, is a natural insecticide and can be effective against harmful insects in your garden. Mix a teaspoon of ground pepper in a quart of warm water, and spray the affected plants.

An old book of household hints suggests making up a mixture of milk, sugar, and pepper and setting it out in shallow dishes to catch and kill flies. Similarly, homemakers were advised to sprinkle winter clothing with pepper in the summer to deter moths.

Cooking with Pepper

The Historical Perspective

It is possible, without being too cute about it, to track the economic ebbs and flows of modern history through our eating habits. Let us consider pepper from this angle.

We know that, early on, its main function was to disguise the foul taste of meat once it was past its prime. We also know that, since the days of ancient Rome and Greece, through the Middle Ages, and well into the Renaissance years, pepper was astronomically expensive. Only the very wealthy could afford it. Therefore, if you were able to serve food highly spiced with pepper in those years, you were signaling your financial status.

As pepper became more affordable with the opening up of multiple trading centers, gradually its use spread down through the socioeconomic layers and became less of a status symbol.

Then, starting in the seventeenth century, tastes changed. Under the gastronomic influence of France, well-to-do Europeans developed a liking for fresh, raw foods. The mask of spices, once a sign of wealth, became a symbol of lower station. Whereas once only rich people could afford it, now only poor people—unable to afford really fresh foodstuffs—needed it.

One thing we know about fashion—all kinds of fashion—is that it moves in circles. Today pepper is no longer reserved for the wealthy, but at the same time it is not scorned as a sign of poverty.

The Modern Perspective

After many centuries as the king of spices, pepper is still the most popular spice in the world; by itself it makes up approximately one-fourth of the world's trade in spices. Americans consume about four ounces a year per person, which makes us the number one market for pepper.

In fact, pepper is such a common and popular seasoning that it would be rather silly for me to tell you what to use it with. But here are a few ideas that might be new to you:

- Add a bit of ground pepper to hot cooked fruits.
- Pepper accentuates the flavor of cinnamon and cloves. Add a pinch to any recipe that has either or both; for instance: pies, fruit cobblers, mulled wine, hot chocolate.
- For a quick, nutritious, low-fat lunch: A bed of sprouts or shredded lettuce, a large scoop of low-fat cottage cheese, chunks of red and green bell pepper (or any fresh veggie you have on hand), and two or three turns from the pepper grinder.
- A pinch of pepper keeps sweet potato dishes like candied yams from being overpoweringly sweet.

- A striking garnish for brightly colored cream soups like tomato, beet, or carrot: a spoonful of sour cream, covered with coarsely ground pepper. Grind the peppercorns into a small dish and use a spoon to place the pepper on just the right spot.
- For a special dinner, make pepper butter balls to accompany steamed or poached fish. Soften butter and shape into very small balls, about 1/2 inch in diameter. Roll in freshly ground pepper, then refrigerate until very firm. Serve several to each guest, placing them alongside the fish.
- Use the same technique to make pepper-covered balls of cream cheese; serve with fresh or lightly poached pears.

Buy whole peppercorns and grind them as needed. There really is a distinct difference in taste between freshly ground pepper and the other stuff. Whole peppercorns keep their flavor practically forever; preground pepper quickly loses it and becomes bitter.

It's a very simple matter. Invest in a small pepper grinder (most cost just a few dollars) and keep it handy, full of whole peppercorns; soon you won't remember having it any other way. You don't need one of those long monsters that restaurant waiters carry tucked under their arms; they have to be long so the waiter can get to your salad without leaning into the food. At home, you won't have that problem.

⊰ Peppered Pistachios ⊱

1/4 cup sugar
1/2 cup shelled pistachios
2 tablespoons crushed peppercorns

Pour sugar into nonstick pan and place over medium heat. Cook without stirring until sugar caramelizes. Remove from heat and add in nuts and peppercorns, stirring to coat thoroughly.

Pour coated nuts into a wide, shallow pan that you have coated with butter. As soon as they are cool enough to handle, break up the large clusters of nuts into individual pieces; if they get too cool you may need to chop them apart with a kitchen knife. Serve at room temperature.

Makes 1/2 cup.

❧ Potato Soup ❧

White pepper adds taste but no color, especially appropriate in this lovely pale soup.

4 large potatoes
2 large onions
1/2 teaspoon salt
1 1/4 cups water, divided
4 cups milk
2 cups cream
3 tablespoons flour
1/2 cup (1 stick) butter (optional)
1/2 teaspoon white pepper
1/2 teaspoon paprika

Peel potatoes and cut into small bits. Peel and chop onion. Simmer potatoes and onion, along with the salt, in 1 cup of water, about 15 minutes, or until potatoes are tender. Drain and rinse. (See note.)

Return potatoes and onions to saucepan, add milk and cream. Mix flour with 1/4 cup cold water; stir into soup. Simmer over low heat until soup is thickened.

Slice butter, if desired, into 8 portions. Place one slice of butter in each of 8 bowls, and ladle in the hot soup. Sprinkle pepper and paprika over top of soup.

Note: If you prefer a smooth soup, at this point puree potatoes, along with a small amount of the milk, in blender or food processor. Stir the puree into the milk and cream in pan, and proceed with recipe.

Makes 8 servings.

❧ Radish Salad ❧

Especially pretty if made with a mix of red and Daikon (white) radishes.

1/4 cup vinegar
3 tablespoons olive oil
2 teaspoons salt
1/2 teaspoon freshly ground pepper
1 pound radishes, sliced
1 tablespoon minced fresh parsley

Combine vinegar, oil, salt, and pepper in mixing bowl. Let stand at room temperature for 2 hours. Add radishes; toss well. Let stand for 30 minutes more. Just before serving, sprinkle with parsley.

Makes 6 to 8 servings.

⚔ Sherried Beef Stir-Fry ⚕

Gorgeous color and delicious flavor.

1/2 cup dry sherry
3 tablespoons soy sauce
1 tablespoon minced garlic
3 tablespoons packed brown sugar
1 tablespoon cornstarch
1 teaspoon ground ginger
1/4 teaspoon white pepper
3/4 pound tender beef steak, fat trimmed and cut into narrow strips
3 tablespoons peanut or vegetable oil, divided
1 1/2 quarts sliced bok choy or Swiss chard (1 medium head)
1 large red bell pepper, cut in 2-inch strips
2 teaspoons sesame seed, to garnish

In bowl or zip-top bag, combine sherry, soy sauce, garlic, brown sugar, cornstarch, ginger, and white pepper. Add beef, turning to coat all sides; marinate in refrigerator at least 15 minutes. Drain meat; reserve marinade.

In large skillet or wok, heat 2 tablespoons oil over medium-high heat. Stir-fry meat until browned, about 3 minutes. Remove meat from pan. Add 1 tablespoon oil to skillet; add bok choy and red bell pepper and stir-fry for 1 or 2 minutes until tender-crisp. Return beef to pan; add marinade and stir-fry just until sauce has thickened and glazed.

Makes 4 servings.

—Spice Islands

⚔ Pepper Steak (Steak au Poivre) ⚕

Many people believe this famous dish is France's greatest contribution to good food.

1 1/2 to 2 pounds sirloin or top round steak, cut 3/4-inch thick
2 teaspoons freshly ground pepper or cracked whole peppers
3 tablespoons butter or margarine, divided
salt
2 tablespoons finely chopped onions or shallots
1/2 cup beef stock
2 to 4 tablespoons brandy, cognac, or Madeira

Set your pepper mill for a coarse grind and lightly cover both sides of the meat with pepper; or, place whole peppercorns between two pieces of waxed paper and crack with a rolling pin. Press pepper into the meat with your fingers. Chill at least 1 hour.

Melt 1 tablespoon of the butter in a large, heavy frying pan over high heat. Add meat and sauté quickly on both sides; the outsides should be well browned and the inside still slightly pink. Season with salt to taste and remove steak to a hot platter.

Melt another tablespoon of butter in the pan, add the onions, and sauté until golden. Add stock and boil until liquid is reduced by half. Add 2 tablespoons of brandy and bring back to a boil. Stir in remaining tablespoon of butter. Spoon sauce over steak.

For the traditional dramatic presentation, bring the platter to the table along with a metal cup in which you have heated the additional 2 tablespoons of brandy. Light the brandy, and carefully spoon it, flaming, over the meat.

Makes about 4 servings.

⁍ Pfeffernusse ⁌

Believe it or not, these German cookies really do have black pepper in them, and they're delicious.

1 cup firmly packed light-brown sugar
1/2 cup butter or margarine, softened
2 eggs
1 teaspoon vanilla extract
1 teaspoon lemon extract
1 teaspoon anise extract (see note)
1 teaspoon baking powder
1 teaspoon ground cinnamon
1/2 teaspoon salt
1/2 teaspoon pepper
1/8 teaspoon ground nutmeg
1/8 teaspoon cloves
2 3/4 cups sifted all-purpose flour
confectioners' sugar

Using large mixing bowl or bowl of electric mixer, cream sugar and butter together until fluffy. Beat in eggs and extracts.

Add remaining ingredients (except confectioners' sugar) to flour and sift again. Gradually add flour mixture into egg mixture, mixing well after each addition. Cover dough and refrigerate 2 hours.

Preheat oven to 375°.

Shape teaspoonfuls of dough into ovals, and place 1 inch apart on ungreased cookie sheets. Bake 10 minutes. Remove from baking sheets, place on wire racks, and sprinkle with confectioners' sugar while cookies are still warm.

Note: If unable to find anise extract, or if you simply prefer a slightly crunchy texture, substitute 1 tablespoon toasted anise seeds, roughly ground.

Makes approximately 5 dozen cookies.

—McCormick/Schilling

For Other Recipes Featuring Pepper, See:

Shrimp Pie, p. 243
Hungarian Goulash, p. 250
American French Dressing, p. 251
Bouillabaisse, p. 279
Paella, p. 280
Arroz Con Pollo, p. 281
Sesame Green Beans, p. 289
Molokai Ribs, p. 299
Carolina Rice and Shrimp Supper, p. 308
Persian Beef Patties, p. 310

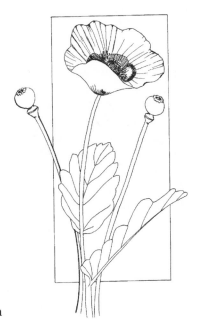

Poppy Seeds

Botanical name: **Papaver somniferum**

Part used as spice: **Seeds**

Available as: **Whole seeds**

Let us start by clearing up something that may be bothering you. The same plant that produces the poppy seeds we cook with also produces opium, but *the seeds are perfectly safe.*

The opium is found in the tissues of the outer walls of the immature seed pod. To extract it, the seed pod is slit in several places and a sticky resinlike material oozes out; when it dries it is scraped off and stored for processing (both legal and illegal) into opium and its derivatives: morphine, codeine, and heroin.

This gooey material, which contains more than twenty narcotic alkaloids, is present only during a certain phase in the plant's life; the seeds have virtually no alkaloids, because they do not appear until the seed head matures, and by then the narcotic alkaloids are no longer present.

The only way for opium to reach the seeds is accidental: If the person making the slits cuts all the way through the outer wall, then the gooey stuff will drip inward instead of outward, making it inaccessible and therefore worthless. As you might imagine, great care is taken to see that this does not happen.

However, there have been some reports in recent years of people getting a false-positive reading on drug tests after having poppy seed muffins for breakfast. The tests are sophisticated and ultra-sensitive, and apparently pick up minute amounts of the alkaloids that have somehow been transferred to the seeds. This doesn't happen often, but on the side of caution you might want to have a bran muffin on the morning of a drug test instead of one with poppy seeds.

In this chapter we will in all respects concentrate on the culinary uses of poppy seeds—the tiny, crunchy, slightly sweet, totally innocent seeds.

Poppies are native to Asia and the eastern Mediterranean, but the plants grow easily in most temperate climates. The poppy seeds we get in America, which seem to be black but in reality are slate blue, come from Europe, primarily the Netherlands.

The seed pods are gathered when they are completely ripe and have started to turn brown. Sometimes the entire stalk is cut, and they are piled into irregular pyramids like haystacks. In other areas the seed pods are cut from the stalk and spread out to dry in the sun.

One pod may have thirty thousand seeds; they are so small it takes almost a million of them to make a pound.

History and Legend

Poppies were grown and used—and abused—by all the ancient civilizations. The Sumerians (in what is now Iraq) wrote about it in 3500 B.C. The Egyptian scroll known as the Ebers Papyrus, produced in 1500 B.C., speaks of poppy. Three Greek physicians whose writings determined the course of medicine for many centuries—Hippocrates (400 B.C.), Theophrastus (300 B.C.), and Dioscorides (A.D. 100)—all speak of using opium to treat dysentery, cholera, malaria, and other painful illnesses.

But what of poppy seeds? The food value of the seeds and their oil was well known to those same civilizations. A popular sweet treat in ancient Rome was a dense mixture of roasted seeds and honey; the historian Pliny, who described everyday life in first-century Rome, explains how to make it.

The same Ebers Papyrus that documents medicinal use of opium in 1500 B.C. also details the use of poppy seed oil in cooking. Galen, a Greek physician from the second century A.D. whose treatises recorded medical practices of the day, suggests adding the seeds to flour for a slightly sweet bread dough—proof, if more were needed, that there is very little new under the sun.

Red poppies have long been the symbol of battlefield valor. Those of us of a certain age can remember the red crepe paper poppies sold by veterans to honor the war dead, and the famous poem about poppies "in Flanders fields" commemorates the soldiers lost in a fierce World War I battle there.

In Roman mythology, poppies play a part in the story of Ceres, the goddess of agriculture (our word "cereal" comes from her name). Ceres's daughter, Persephone, had been abducted by Pluto and taken to the underground; devastated by her grief, Ceres became so depressed she couldn't sleep. When it became clear that her inattention to her duties meant that no crops were growing, Somnus, the god of sleep, was dispatched to solve the problem. He made poppies spring up wherever she stepped, and soon she fell asleep among the flowers. Thereafter, earthly mortals made a special burnt offering of poppy seed pods to Ceres and planted poppies among the rows of corn in her honor.

The Latin name of this plant testifies to its sedative qualities: *Somniferum* means "makes you sleep."

Medicinal Use

It is difficult to separate the legitimate medicinal use of opium and opium products from the abusive. Physicians from the first century to the twentieth have used opiates such as morphine to help patients suffering intense pain. At the same time, so powerful are these products that stories of patients becoming addicted to their medication also date back through the centuries.

The story of the medical aspects of the opium poppy is long and tortured. However, since our focus in this chapter is the seeds of the poppy, and since the seeds themselves have very little medical tradition, we can move on to the more pleasant side of poppy seeds: their taste.

Cooking with Poppy Seeds

Poppy seeds add a nice crunch and a mild sweetness to many dishes. Probably you are most familiar with them in baked goods: mixed into the dough for muffins or cake, or used as a topping on breads, rolls, and bagels. Those are indeed fine uses for the seeds, but there is no reason to stop there.

Use Poppy Seeds in:
- Buttered noodles
- Salad dressings
- Fruit salads

Poppy seed bread. Loaves, twists, rolls—any kind of bread is improved with a topping of crunchy, faintly sweet poppy seeds.

- Coleslaw
- Macaroni salad
- Mashed potatoes
- Steamed vegetables, especially cabbage, spinach, carrots, onions, zucchini
- Piecrust
- Breads, rolls, bagels, muffins
- Cakes, strudel, coffee cake

Crushed seeds are the basis of fillings for coffee cakes or pastries. Start by mashing the seeds into a crunchy paste. You can use a spice grinder or a mortar and pestle, or put the seeds between two pieces of waxed paper and scrunch them with a rolling pin or the bottom of a glass.

In India, crushed seeds are used in curries to thicken the broth.

> Poppy seeds are, you may be surprised to learn, a pretty good source of protein. One tablespoon has 1.6 grams, the same as an ounce of beans. The protein is incomplete on its own but complete when combined with grains—as, for example, a topping for whole wheat rolls or a filling for Danish pastry.

Poppy seeds have a high content of vegetable oil (more than 50 percent), and a fine cooking oil is made from them. It is very stable, and takes much longer than olive oil to become rancid. It is common in Europe and Asia, and perhaps someday will be widely available in the United States as well.

Although by far the largest share of commercially grown poppy seeds is used for culinary purposes, by either home cooks or large manufacturers, there are a few other uses. The whole seeds are included in many bird seed mixtures, and the oil from the second pressing is used in the manufacture of soaps and of artists' oil paints.

⊰ Refrigerator Rolls for a Crowd ⊱

2 packages yeast
2 cups warm water, divided
1/2 cup sugar
1 teaspoon salt
1/2 cup butter
3 eggs, divided
6 cups flour
poppy seeds

Dissolve yeast in 1 cup warm water, in large measuring cup or small bowl. In saucepan, bring another cup of water to boiling; add sugar, salt, and butter and heat until butter is melted and sugar dissolved.

Pour sugar mixture into a large mixing bowl and cool to lukewarm. Meanwhile, beat 2 of the eggs. Add yeast mixture and beaten eggs to large bowl. Gradually add in flour and beat well.

Refrigerate overnight, or for several hours. Shape into rolls and let rise 1 hour. Beat remaining egg and paint egg wash over rolls; generously sprinkle poppy seeds over all. Bake at 400° for about 15 minutes. *Makes 100 to 140 rolls, depending on size.*

Variations: Use sesame seed or fennel seed instead of poppy seed.

Note: You can make your own brown-and-serve rolls with this recipe. Form rolls and partially bake, cool, then freeze. Thaw as many rolls as you need for one meal, and brown in 400° oven. This recipe also makes two loaves of bread; divide dough in half, shape into loaves, put into greased bread pan, let rise until doubled, bake at 400° till browned on top and hollow on bottom when tapped (about 40 minutes).

Cabbage Combination

¹/₂ head of cabbage
2 cups celery, thinly sliced
2 cups chopped apples, cut in ¹/₂-inch cubes
1 cup coarsely chopped pecans

Cut cabbage into small cubes and steam for 1 minute. Place in large mixing bowl, and chill in refrigerator. Meanwhile, prepare apples: Core but do not peel, and cut into small chunks. Submerge in salt water until ready to mix into salad, then drain and rinse.

When cabbage is cold, add celery, apples, and nuts to salad bowl; toss well. Pour dressing (see recipe on page 270) over salad and mix thoroughly.

To serve, line salad plate with a large leaf of lettuce. Using ice cream scoop or 1-cup measuring cup, put a mound of salad on the lettuce. Garnish generously with minced parsley.

Dressing
¹/₂ pint sour cream
3 ounces cream cheese
¹/₂ teaspoon poppy seeds
dash turmeric
¹/₂ teaspoon salt
dash onion salt

Combine all ingredients in blender; mix thoroughly.
Serves 8 or more.

—Renée Shepherd

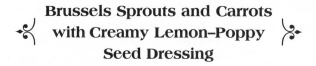

Brussels Sprouts and Carrots with Creamy Lemon–Poppy Seed Dressing

5 tablespoons olive oil
3 tablespoons fresh lemon juice
1¹/₂ teaspoons poppy seeds
1 teaspoon minced garlic
¹/₂ teaspoon Dijon mustard
¹/₄ teaspoon salt
pinch of cayenne pepper
1 egg
8 carrots, cut into ¹/₂-inch slices
1 pound Brussels sprouts, trimmed
1 tablespoon chopped scallions

Whisk oil, lemon juice, poppy seeds, garlic, mustard, salt, and cayenne pepper together until well blended. Heat a saucepan of water to boiling. Add the egg in shell; cook for one minute only. Break the egg into the sauce and whisk to blend.

Steam the vegetables until tender-crisp (about 15 minutes), drain; pour sauce over vegetables and toss with vegetables to blend. Sprinkle the scallions over the top and serve. Serve hot or at room temperature.
Serves 4 to 6.

—Renée Shepherd

❧ Poppy Seed Noodles ❧

1 package (12 ounces) egg noodles
2 to 3 quarts boiling water
2 tablespoons salt
3 tablespoons butter
2 tablespoons poppy seed
1 tablespoon powdered chicken stock base (or 1 bouillon cube,
*   crumbled)*

Cook noodles in boiling salted water until tender. Drain and rinse in hot water. Melt butter, add poppy seeds and chicken stock base. Pour over noodles and toss until thoroughly mixed. Serve immediately.

Makes 8 servings.

❧ Poppy Seed Pastries ❧

A versatile spread for many baked goods.

²/₃ cup poppy seeds, ground
¹/₃ cup toasted almonds, ground
2 teaspoons sugar
3 tablespoons honey
pastry as in Walnut Pastries (see page 178)

Mix together the poppy seeds, almonds, and sugar, then add the honey to form a thick paste. Use instead of the walnut filling in the Walnut Pastries recipe.

Variations: This sweet mixture can be used as filling in many kinds of sweet pastries and buns.

For example, make a poppy seed coffee cake. Here are abbreviated instructions. Roll out one-fourth recipe of Refrigerator Roll dough (page 268) into a rectangle, spread with softened butter and poppy seed filling. Bring long sides together so you have a thick roll, then bring ends together so you have a circle; carefully transfer to baking sheet. Use a razor or sharp knife to cut diagonal slashes in the dough in several places, and let rise until double. Paint dough with an egg wash, and bake at 375° until brown, about 30 minutes.

Or, follow recipe for cinnamon rolls (page 111), except spread dough with poppy filling.

❧ Poppy Seed Cake ❧

4 eggs, separated
1 cup butter or margarine
1 cup sour cream
1¹/₂ cups sugar, divided
¹/₃ cup poppy seed
1 teaspoon baking soda
2 cups sifted cake flour

Preheat oven to 350°.

Separate eggs while they are cold, but then let eggs, butter and sour cream come to room temperature.

Beat egg whites until almost stiff. While continuing to beat, gradually add in ¹/₂ cup sugar; beat until whites hold stiff peaks. Set aside.

In a separate large bowl, cream together butter and the remaining sugar until light and fluffy. Add egg yolks, one at a time, beating well after each addition. Stir in poppy seed, mixing well.

In another bowl, blend baking soda and sour cream. Working alternately and in small batches, add the sour cream mixture and the flour to the butter mixture, mixing after each addition. Gently fold in the stiffly beaten egg whites.

Spoon batter into an ungreased 9-inch tube pan and bake for 1 hour. Use a sharp knife to loosen cake around sides and carefully turn out on rack to cool. Serve while still warm; top with chilled Raspberry Sauce (see page 218).

❧ Fresh Fruit with Poppy Lime Topping ❧

¹/₂ cup plain nonfat yogurt
1 tablespoon honey
2 teaspoons lime juice
¹/₂ teaspoon vanilla extract
¹/₂ teaspoon poppy seed
6 cups chopped fresh fruit

Combine first 5 ingredients in a small bowl. Divide fruit into 4 serving dishes. Spoon yogurt mixture over fruit.

Makes 4 servings.

—McCormick/Schilling

Saffron

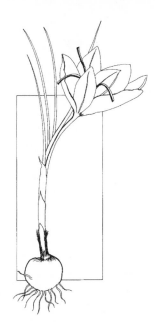

Botanical name: **Crocus sativus**

Part used as spice: **Stigma (from inside the flower)**

Available as: **Dried stigmas, whole or powdered**

Saffron is the most expensive spice in the world. Once you know how it is grown and harvested, you will see why.

First, return to Part I of this book and remind yourself about the sex life of flowers: the wonderfully designed interplay between the male stamens and the female pistil with its three components—ovary, style, and stigma.

The pistil of the saffron crocus has one style that branches into three distinct stigmas. They are bright orange in color, about an inch long and quite thin, and droop downward outside the flower. The spice we call saffron is these stigmas, collected and dried.

Each crocus plant makes one, occasionally two, flowers; the entire flowering period lasts only about fifteen days. The flowers have to be picked by hand, which, because the plants are only about a foot high, is backbreaking work. Then the stigmas must be pulled out from the flowers—again by hand—and spread out to dry. It takes some 75,000 flowers, more than 200,000 tiny threadlike stigmas, to make one pound of dried saffron. One entire acre of crocus plants yields only 10 pounds of saffron.

To make matters worse, the plants will reliably produce flowers for only three or four years, after which the fields must be dug up and replanted.

All that intensive harvesting labor, and all that agricultural investment, combine to make saffron astronomically expensive: At this writing, a single ounce of it was $165. For comparison, an ounce of ground turmeric from the same source was 36 cents and an ounce of whole mustard seed was 22 cents.

Spice Crimes

Anything that commands such a high price presents a serious temptation to the unscrupulous. There is no such thing as "bargain" saffron; if you are ever offered saffron at a ridiculously low price, it has undoubtedly been adulterated with other things.

Saffron in powdered form can easily be diluted with powder made from less expensive materials: turmeric, flower petals from pot marigold or safflower, even corn silk. That is one reason many people prefer to buy, and reputable dealers prefer to sell, the whole form of the spice: You always know what you're getting.

This particular culinary deception is nothing new. The Greek historian Pliny, in the first century A.D., warned that saffron was easily tampered with. In the Middle Ages in Europe, when saffron was worth more than gold, all spice merchants had to have their saffron offerings inspected, and the penalty for cheating was death. Dishonest dealers were burned at the stake, along with their impure goods.

The crocus that gives us saffron is native to the areas around the eastern Mediterranean, what we now call the Middle East. From there it spread to the ancient cultures of Greece and Rome, and also eastward to India and China as part of the spice trade.

Saffron Look-Alikes

Do not confuse *Crocus sativus* with the plant called meadow saffron (*Colchicum autumnale*), which is not a crocus at all and has nothing to do with saffron. Meadow saffron is poisonous; a gout medication is made from it, and cattle who eat it along with the meadow grasses in which it grows are likely to die.

Another possible source of confusion is safflower. This plant is sometimes called Mexican saffron, and petals from its dried flowers have in the past been used fraudulently to dilute genuine saffron. Although safflower makes a very nice cooking oil in its own right, it has no connection to saffron.

The Arabs, who gave us its name (the Arabic word for yellow is *za'-faran*), are also responsible for introducing saffron into Europe. They cultivated it in Moorish Spain around 950, from whence it spread into Italy and France by the eleventh century; even now saffron is best known in the dishes of those countries.

In the thirteenth century the Crusaders brought saffron back to England with them from the lands of the Middle East. The plant grows easily in Great Britain, and for a time after the Crusades enterprising farmers attempted to grow saffron in a large scale. The town named Saffron Walden, in Essex, was the center of this production;

the name endured, even though the agricultural venture did not.

Today, most saffron sold in the United States is grown in Spain; other significant producers include Portugal, Italy, France, Turkey, and India. In the region of India known as Kashmir is a fertile valley named Happy Valley, with vast plantations of crocuses; five thousand acres of purple crocuses all blooming at once must be a sight to see.

History and Legend

About as far back as we have written records, there is evidence of saffron being used as perfume, medicine, and a cooking spice.

- It is mentioned in the Bible (The Song of Solomon) and in the epic poem *The Iliad*, written some three thousand years ago.
- It was known in the countries of the Mediterranean four thousand years ago; a fresco on the palace at Knossos, Crete, which has been dated at 1700 B.C., shows a worker gathering saffron threads from crocuses planted in containers.
- It is described in the Ebers Papyrus, a record of Egyptian medicine written about 1500 B.C.

Wealthy Egyptians scattered the flowers on the floors and tables at elegant banquets; and Roman emperors, who indulged every fancy and endeavored to outdo one another in extravagance, bathed in saffron-scented water. Other Roman noblemen made special saffron-stuffed pillows to get a good night's sleep after a heavy feast and awaken without a hangover. For extra hangover insurance, they also drank a goblet of saffron water *before* indulging.

Today we mostly think of saffron in terms of color and taste, but in earlier times its fragrance was equally valued. Cleopatra used it in her cosmetics and perfumes, and throughout the ancient lands of the Mediterranean, saffron was used as a kind of air freshener in crowded public buildings such as theaters and temples. The flowers of saffron crocus were strewn on the floors, saffron oil was dripped onto the seats of wealthy patrons, and it is reported that the Roman emperor Hadrian ordered a torrent of saffron water to be flooded down the theater steps during a performance.

Use in cooking began in those ancient civilizations too. In Rome, special occasions were celebrated with a ceremonial saffron cake. Saffron rice has been part of the wedding feast in India for centuries, and European bakers once made special saffron buns at Eastertime as a gift for their best customers. In medieval England, banquet cooks prepared large balls of a meat mixture and then coated the outside with saffron; the golden balls were served to the nobility and their guests of honor.

In parts of Asia, it is still the custom to welcome special guests with a sprinkle of saffron water.

Saffron as Medicine

The first medical reference work we know of is a book of Chinese medicine, written about 2600 B.C. In it, saffron is prescribed as an overall tonic, especially for those who felt themselves in need of stimulation and stamina—as for instance on their wedding night.

Hippocrates, known as the Father of Medicine, included it among his medicinal plants in the fourth century B.C. The Roman scholar Celsus, who compiled an encyclopedia of scientific knowledge in the first century A.D., wrote that physicians in his time used saffron to treat abdominal complaints and counteract several types of poison.

In 1597 John Gerard, author of one of the most-quoted herbals (a reference work describing herbs and their medicinal uses), wrote, "For those at death's door, and almost past breathing, saffron will bringeth forth breath again." Soon after, another English herbalist, Nicholas Culpeper, warned that too much saffron was dangerous: "Some have fallen into an immoderate convulsive laughter, which ended in death." Not all physicians of that time agreed; in 1670 J. F. Hertodt of Germany wrote an entire book about saffron, which he titled *Crocologia;* in it he expounded at some length on his belief that a bit of saffron would cure any ailment known to man or woman.

According to the Doctrine of Signatures, which depends on the theory that physical characteristics of a plant indicate what illness it is good for, saffron with its intense yellow color was a perfect treatment for jaundice, which turns the skin yellow.

In the 1920s a medical examiner in London remarked on what was then a common treatment for measles: saffron tea mixed with brandy.

This is as good a time as any to remind you: Just because something appears in one of these old medical books doesn't mean you should do it. It is not recommended that you try saffron mixtures for measles or any other health problem today. In large amounts, larger than you would ever use in cooking, saffron is harmful to humans. Fortunately, its high price adequately discourages experimentation of this sort.

Saffron as a Dye

The stigmas of the saffron crocus contain an orange pigment (which in honor of the plant has been given the name crocin) that is so intensely colored one drop of it will turn one hundred fifty thousand drops of water yellow.

In many early cultures yellow was the color of royalty, and saffron was much in demand to dye the robes of the ruling classes in ancient Greece and early Ireland. Kings of Persia (in today's Middle East) also dyed their shoes yellow. In Greek mythology, the gods and goddesses wore yellow robes, and the mortals on earth sprinkled walkways, floors, and tabletops with crocus petals to invite the gods' favor.

Since the time of Buddha's death in the fifth century B.C., the distinctive saffron yellow has been the official color for robes of Buddhist priests, who consider it a symbol of piety.

Until King Henry VIII ordered them to stop, Irish peasants used saffron to dye their bed linens. Their reasons were twofold: The old bit of folklore that whoever came in contact with saffron gained strength, and the more pragmatic reason that nonwhite sheets would not need laundering so often. Whether Henry's intention was to promote better hygiene or to reserve the saffron color for nobility is a matter of debate.

In ancient Rome, women used saffron to dye their hair, and it has even been used to make canaries a brighter yellow, by dissolving some of the spice in their drinking water.

Cooking with Saffron

As we have already learned, saffron has been a favorite spice in cuisines of the Mediterranean region for centuries. John Evelyn, an Englishman who in 1699 wrote a book describing the food plants of his day (*A Discourse on Salads*), said this about saffron: "Those of Spain and Italy generally make use of this flower, mingling its golden tincture with almost everything they eat." And this is still approximately true today.

Saffron is essential in:

- Paella (Spain)
- Bouillabaisse (France)
- Arroz con pollo (Spain)
- Risotto (Italy)

In fact it goes extremely well with all dishes of rice, chicken, fish, and shellfish, especially in combination with garlic. It is also used by bakers in Europe, especially the Scandinavian countries, to color and flavor special breads, cakes, and cookies.

How to Work with Saffron

Because saffron is so intense in its color and flavor, only a tiny amount is needed in most recipes; the trick is to get that small bit evenly dispersed throughout the dish.

If you start with whole threads of saffron, first soak them for ten minutes or so in a bit of the liquid that is part of the recipe—water, broth, whatever. In just a few minutes in warm liquid, the dried stigmas expand and release their color and flavor into the water. Put the liquid and the threads into the dish. Of course you can also pulverize the threads in a grinder, but this is harder because generally you use such a small amount.

If you start with ground saffron, you can just add it to your dish according to the recipe. When making bread or cookies, for instance, sift the saffron along with the flour and other dry ingredients, so that the spice is evenly distributed throughout the mixture.

Saffron is very sensitive to light; it affects color, taste, and fragrance. Now that you've spent so much money to buy the saffron, be sure to store it in a container that closes tightly and keep it in a cool, dry spot.

Saffron has a very distinctive taste; nothing else is quite like it. If all you care about is the rich, golden color, save yourself some money and use turmeric instead. But in dishes where the flavor of saffron is traditional and expected—bouillabaise, paella, arroz con pollo—there is no adequate substitute. And if you don't put the saffron in saffron bread, you really must call it something else.

❧ Easy Saffron Bread ❧

1 cup milk
3 tablespoons sugar
2 tablespoons butter or margarine
2 teaspoons minced onion
2 teaspoons salt
1/8 teaspoon crushed saffron pieces
2 packages active dry yeast
1 cup warm water
4 1/2 cups all-purpose flour
 caraway seed

In microwave or saucepan, heat milk to just below boiling. Add sugar, butter, onion, salt, and crushed saffron; stir till butter is melted and sugar is dissolved. Cool to lukewarm.

Meanwhile, sprinkle yeast over warm water in a large mixing bowl; stir until dissolved, and let sit about 5 minutes until bubbly. Stir in milk mixture. Add flour one cupful at a time; stir after each addition until well blended.

Cover and set in warm place. Let rise to more than double its bulk, about 40 minutes. Meanwhile, butter a 1 1/2 quart round or square casserole dish. Stir batter down and beat vigorously for 30 seconds. Turn into casserole dish, smooth top, and sprinkle with caraway seed. Bake in 375° oven for 60 to 80 minutes.

Makes 1 loaf.

❧ Saffron Rice ☙

⅛ teaspoon crushed saffron threads
2 cups boiling water, divided
1 cup long-grain white rice
2 tablespoons olive oil
1 teaspoon salt

Steep the saffron in ½ cup boiling water for 5 minutes. Keep rest of water boiling.

Lightly sauté rice in oil in large covered skillet or saucepan. Add salt, saffron water (strained), and balance of the boiling water. Cover tightly, reduce heat to very low, and simmer until done (about 20 minutes).

Serves 4.

❧ Bouillabaisse ☙

This classic fish stew has lots of ingredients, but isn't as hard as it may appear at first glance. Save it for a special Saturday night supper party.

1 carrot
1 pound fresh tomatoes
4 rock lobster tails, 7 to 8 ounces each
5 pounds assorted fish (such as perch, cod, sole, red snapper)
1 cup chopped onions
¼ teaspoon minced garlic
2 teaspoons parsley flakes
24 individual pieces saffron
1 bay leaf
¼ teaspoon dried thyme
⅛ teaspoon whole fennel seed
1 teaspoon grated orange peel
¼ teaspoon pepper
⅓ cup olive oil
1 8-ounce bottle clam juice
1 tablespoon lemon juice
water
French bread
fresh parsley, minced

Peel carrot and cut into small cubes; peel, seed, and chop tomatoes. Cut lobster tails into large pieces. Cut fish into 2-inch pieces.

Put all ingredients (except French bread and fresh parsley) in a large saucepan or kettle. Cover with water; cook over high heat for 8 minutes; reduce heat and simmer 8 minutes longer.

To serve, cut French bread into 1/4-inch slices and toast them. Put one slice of toast in bottom of each individual soup bowl and ladle soup over. Garnish with parsley.

Serves 8 to 10.

❧ Paella ❧

1 teaspoon whole saffron
1/4 cup warm water
3 chorizos (Spanish sausage)
1/3 cup vegetable or olive oil
2 whole chicken breasts
4 chicken legs
1 cup chopped onion
1 clove garlic, minced
2 14-ounce cans chicken broth
1 teaspoon pepper
3 1/2 teaspoons salt
1/2 teaspoon dried tarragon
1/2 teaspoon paprika
1 can (28 ounces) whole tomatoes, including juice
2 cups uncooked rice
1 1/2 pounds shrimp
12 clams, in the shell
6 mussels, in the shell
1/2 package frozen peas
1 can artichoke hearts

Steep saffron in warm water. Cut sausage into 1-inch lengths and sauté them until grease is released. Drain sausage on paper towels; discard grease.

In very large skillet, Dutch oven, or paella pan, brown chicken in oil; remove chicken from pan. Add onion and garlic to pan and cook until golden brown. Add chicken broth, pepper, salt, tarragon, paprika, and juice from tomatoes. Drain out saffron and add saffron water to pan. Bring to a boil, add rice and tomatoes, and cover.

Cook about 10 minutes. Add sausage and chicken; simmer 30 minutes. Arrange shrimp, clams, and mussels around chicken pieces. Cover and steam until shells open. Sprinkle peas throughout rice and cook just until they are bright green. Add artichokes, cook just until they are heated through.

Serves 4 to 6.

Arroz Con Pollo
(Chicken with Rice)

1 chicken, cut into serving pieces
salt
3 tablespoons olive oil
1 large onion, chopped
1 clove garlic
1 medium green pepper, chopped
1 can (19 ounces) stewed or diced tomatoes
1/3 cup sherry
1/4 teaspoon pepper
pinch saffron
1/2 teaspoon paprika
2 whole cloves
1 bay leaf
1 1/4 cups uncooked long-grain rice
1 cup water
1 pimiento, cut into narrow strips
fresh cilantro

Sprinkle chicken with salt, and brown on all sides in oil in large saucepan or Dutch oven over medium heat. Reduce heat, add onion, garlic, and green pepper; cook until soft and golden. Add remaining ingredients except pimiento and cilantro.

Increase heat to high and bring to a boil; reduce heat, cover, and simmer on very low heat about 30 minutes, until rice has absorbed all liquid. Garnish with pimiento strips and cilantro leaves.

Serves 4 to 6.

For Other Recipes Featuring Saffron, See:
Chicken Livers with Allspice, p. 41
Indian Rice, p. 70

Sesame Seeds

Botanical name: Sesamum indicum

Part used as spice: Seeds

Available as: Whole seeds

Sesame seeds are important to cooks of the world in two respects: the seeds themselves, and oil that is derived from them.

The sesame plant is an annual, meaning that it goes through an entire life cycle in one year and must be planted anew each year. It grows to be about three feet tall, and produces white flowers and then squarish pods about an inch long. The seeds inside the pods are what we are interested in.

When the pods are ripe, they burst open rather dramatically, with a popping sound, and the seeds fly in all directions. This is Mother Nature's way of making sure that seeds get thoroughly scattered. This works well as a way of perpetuating the plant, but not so well from the standpoint of those whose goal is to harvest the seeds.

To overcome this, commercial growers pick the seed pods while they are still green and put them through a drying process. In recent years, they have also developed a variety that has nonshattering pods.

In their natural state the seeds have an outer covering that is light or dark brown; when the outer hull is removed, the inner seed is creamy white. A few large mail-order houses carry unhulled seeds, but most of what you will find for sale are the hulled seeds.

In the supermarket if you find seeds that are light brown in color, they are in all likelihood white seeds that have been toasted, rather than unhulled seeds. Sometimes in Oriental markets you will find jars of sesame seeds that are a mix of colors—white, brown, and very dark brown. The colors represent different degrees of toasting.

Most of the world's commercial sesame crop is used for making sesame oil. It is a high-quality vegetable oil that keeps for a very long time without

Sesame seeds are very nutritious. One ounce of seeds has as much protein as one cup of milk. Vegetarians, take note: the protein is considered incomplete (low in lysine), but combines very well with legumes, which are high in lysine but low in the amino acids that sesame contains; in other words, good complementarity. The oil content of the seeds also is a source of vitamin E.

Sesame oil, since it is a vegetable product, has no cholesterol and is high in polyunsaturates.

going rancid. It has long been the main cooking oil in the Far East; now, as Asian dishes become more popular in this country, more Americans are becoming acquainted with it as well. In addition, it is used commercially in the manufacture of margarine and bottled salad dressings.

Sesame seeds are almost 50 percent oil. The oil is extracted by compression, in several steps. The first, which is a cold pressing, pro-

The classic tale known as *The Thousand and One Nights* includes the story of "Ali Baba and the Forty Thieves."

Ali, you may remember, hiding in fear of his life from the thieves, witnessed an amazing scene: The chief thief shouted "Open Sesame!" at what appeared to be the face of a cliff, and the cliff wall opened to reveal a treasure-filled cave. When the robbers were safely gone, Ali Baba tried the same command—Open Sesame—and slipped inside the cave, leaving with a few gold coins.

His wicked brother, Cassim, discovered the coins, bullied the secret password out of Ali Baba, and went to the cave himself. Once inside, he closed the cave opening with the command "Close Sesame" while he searched through the treasure. Suddenly, he heard forty horses approaching. In his haste to get away, Cassim forgot the password to open the cave door.

"Open, barley!" he shouted. Nothing. "Open, wheat!" Nothing. He went through every grain he could think of, but he did not think of sesame in time, and the thieves found him inside, and killed him.

Now, the interesting question for us to ponder is this: Why was sesame the magic word? Some folklorists think this story is based on a bit of human psychology, that sometimes the most common things slip out of our mind. If that is the case, it would indicate that sesame was a staple in every household of Arabia.

Or it could be, some have suggested, that the sound of the cave door opening is the same sound the sesame pod makes when it pops open.

duces a clear oil of high quality. Then the remaining pulp is heated and pressed two more times; this yields a cloudy oil that must be purified.

Oil from raw hulled sesame seeds is pale in color and practically odorless; it is used as a cooking oil. Sesame oil with the characteristic flavor that we associate with Chinese dishes is made from seeds that have been toasted; it is used mostly as a flavoring and is added to dishes at the end of their cooking.

History and Legend

The sesame plant is native to the islands of Indonesia, where it has been cultivated for nearly five thousand years. From there it spread to other areas: China, Japan, India, and then, through ancient trading routes, to warm-climate areas in Africa and the Middle East.

It is one of the world's oldest spices, possibly *the* oldest. We know, for instance, that:

- A drawing on an Egyptian tomb that is four thousand years old shows a baker adding sesame seeds to dough.
- More than thirty-five hundred years ago, in the area historians call Mesopotamia (now Iraq), sesame was an established crop, cultivated for the oil in its seeds. A written record of this crop was made around 1600 B.C., but the plant may have been used long before then.
- In about 1550 B.C., Egyptian physicians prepared a record of all the medicinal preparations then known, including all the plants used to treat illness. Among the medicinal plants listed: sesame.
- In the 1960s, archaeologists in Turkey uncovered the ruins of a fortified city occupied between 900 and 700 B.C. Among their findings: the pulp that remains after sesame seeds are pressed for their oil. This city was part of the ancient kingdom of Urartu, called Ararat in the Old Testament.
- Two scholars of ancient Greece, who established much of the foundation of scientific knowledge, both include sesame among their writing: Theophrastus, known as the Father of Botany, in the fourth century B.C., and Dioscorides, a physician in the first century A.D.

Since ancient times, sesame has been used both for its seeds and the oil from the seeds. Starting in the first century A.D., sesame from what is now Pakistan was shipped through the Red Sea to Europe. A few centuries later, seeds were exported to Venice through Alexandria, Egypt, where the plant was widely grown. Marco Polo, writing in 1298, noted that sesame oil was widely used in Persia (which we now call Iran) because they had no olive oil there.

In the first century B.C., Greek soldiers on long marches ate sesame seeds for energy. Ignorant of nutritional analysis, they did not know that the seeds were a source of both protein and fat, only that they were easy to carry and did not spoil. In other words, possibly the world's first K-rations.

The climate of tropical Africa is very hospitable to the sesame plant, and it easily took hold there, spreading from Egypt and the Arabian peninsula south and west to Ethiopia, Kenya, and Tanganyika, and then on to the states of west Africa. Many Africans used the seeds—which they called *benne*—as a basic food crop, like wheat or rice elsewhere. When Africans were forcibly taken to the New World as slaves, they brought the seeds with them. The plant thrived in the warm states of the American South, where even today sesame seeds are sometimes called benne seeds.

Any plant that has been grown over such a wide geographic range for so many centuries as sesame is bound to have much folklore associated with it.

- The Assyrians, who inhabited the land we now call Iraq about twenty-five hundred years before the birth of Christ, had their own version of how the earth was created: Their gods ate a mighty feast and drank large amounts of sesame wine to fortify themselves for the serious work of creating the universe.
- Yama, the Hindu god of death, is believed to be responsible for creating sesame. The seeds have long been used by Hindus in burial ceremonies, to represent immortality. Small piles of seeds are offered to nourish the soul on its journey.
- The ancient Romans made special funeral cakes of sesame, rice, and honey.
- An old Arabic recipe for a sweet treat with aphrodisiac qualities calls for chopped dates, sesame seed, and licorice root, mixed with honey.
- Even older is a formula used by the women of ancient Babylon (now Iraq): Sesame seeds blended with honey were believed to heighten desire and increase fertility.
- In Africa, the seeds are symbols of good luck.
- Ibn Baithar, an Arabic botanist and physician who lived in the Moorish-held region of Spain in the thirteenth century, suggested a blend of sesame and olive oils for those afflicted with dandruff.

Medicinal and Other Uses

Sesame oil has long been used as a laxative, and a paste made from ground seeds mixed with water was an old remedy for wounds and bleeding sores. In the fourth century B.C. an Indian physician used a sesame poultice to help heal incisions after surgery.

Pliny, in the first century A.D., prescribed sesame oil for earaches, and the leaves of the plant were once simmered to make a compress for sore eyes. Today, sesame has no significant medicinal applications that I am aware of.

Sesame oil is an emollient, and was favored by none other than Cleopatra as a skin softener and moisturizer.

To produce sesame oil, seeds are pressed and then compressed a second and sometimes a third time. The solid material that remains is a dense "mash" that is rich in protein; it is added to cattle feed and, in rougher times, was included in the diet of the poor people in countries where sesame is an important crop.

In China and India sesame oil is burned as lamp oil.

Cooking with Sesame Seeds

You may be most familiar with sesame seeds as a topping for bread and rolls; if you've ever been to a fast-food hamburger place, you've had sesame seed rolls. Indeed, the largest share of seeds imported into the United States goes into the manufacture of hamburger buns.

Using these nutritious seeds atop bread is not a new idea; John Parkinson, who was responsible for the gardens of medicinal plants for King James I of England in the early 1600s and whose writings preserve the botanical knowledge of that day, noted: "The seed in ancient times was much used in bread for a relish and makes it sweet, as also in cakes with honey as poppy seeds."

And it remains true today. The most common use of the whole seeds is in baking: bread, rolls, cakes, and cookies. The extremely sweet candy known as *halvah*, popular in Jewish households, is made with sesame seed. So is a sweet confection called *niu bi tang*, sometimes served as dessert in Chinese restaurants in this country.

Another form of sesame, in addition to seeds and oil, is tahini, a thick, oily paste made from ground-up seeds. It looks a lot like, and tastes vaguely like, peanut butter; you might think of it as sesame butter. It is a common kitchen staple in countries of the Middle East, where it is used as an ingredient in cooking and by itself as a spread like butter.

As ethnic cooking of all kinds spreads across America, you may have encountered tahini in restaurants featuring Greek, Lebanese, and other cuisines of the Mediterranean. It is part of the recipe for *hummus*, a thick spread made of chickpeas, usually served as an appetizer, and *baba ghanouj*, a similar spread made from roasted eggplant.

The flavor of sesame seeds is much enhanced by toasting; they become slightly sweet and very nutty—an excellent substitute for any kind of nut your recipe calls for but you happen to be missing.

The best way to toast the seeds is also the easiest: Cook them on medium heat in a dry frying pan (no oil). It takes just a few minutes, but keep a sharp eye on them, for they burn easily.

Use Sesame Seeds in:
- Bread and rolls, sprinkled on top before baking
- Piecrust; mix into dough
- Crumb topping for baked fruit desserts like crisps and cobblers
- Flour coating for fried or sautéed chicken
- Breading mixes for fish
- Breadcrumb topping for vegetable casseroles

Sprinkle Toasted Sesame Seeds on:
- Baked potatoes
- Sliced fresh tomatoes
- Cream cheese (cover a whole block of cheese with seeds, serve with crackers)
- Green salads
- Steamed vegetables
- Cream soups (especially those with good color contrast, such as beet, spinach, or pumpkin)
- Fruit salads

⊷ Benne Wafers ⊶

Benne is the African name for sesame, brought to America by the slaves and still used in parts of the South.

¹/₂ cup sesame seeds
¹/₂ cup butter (one stick), at room temperature
¹/₄ teaspoon Worcestershire sauce
2 cups grated cheddar cheese
1 cup flour
¹/₄ teaspoon dry mustard
¹/₄ teaspoon salt
¹/₄ teaspoon cayenne

Toast the sesame seeds in dry frying pan or 350° oven; set aside. Beat butter until fluffy; add Worcestershire and beat again to blend. Fold in grated cheese, mixing thoroughly.

In separate bowl, combine flour, mustard, salt, and cayenne; fold in sesame seeds. Gradually add the flour mixture to the cheese mixture; blend well.

Roll dough into walnut-size balls and place on an unbuttered baking sheet. Flatten each slightly with a fork. Bake at 350° for 12 to 15 minutes until lightly brown.

These zesty crackers keep well for several days in an airtight container.

Makes about 30.

⋊ Crunchy Chicken Salad ⋉

2 tablespoons sesame seeds
Mustard-Soy Dressing (recipe follows)
1 carrot
1 cucumber
1 bunch green onions
3¹/₂ to 4 cups shredded cooked chicken
2 cups finely shredded lettuce
1 cup bean sprouts
³/₄ cup roasted salted almonds, divided
salt and pepper

Toast sesame seeds in frying pan over medium heat with no oil; crush in shallow bowl using the back of a spoon; set aside.

Prepare Mustard-Soy Dressing; set aside.

Prepare vegetables. Peel or scrape carrot, cut into thin strips the size of matchsticks. Wash wax from cucumber but do not peel; cut in half lengthwise and discard seeds if they are large; cut cucumber flesh into matchstick strips. Cut onions into 2-inch strips, including green tops. Measure each vegetable separately; you should have 1 cup of each.

In a large salad bowl, combine chicken, lettuce, carrot, cucumber, onions, bean sprouts, ¹/₂ cup of the almonds, and sesame seeds.

Stir dressing, then pour over salad; mix gently. Season to taste with salt and pepper. Garnish with remaining ¹/₄ cup almonds.

Makes 4 to 6 servings.

Mustard-Soy Dressing

¹/₄ teaspoon dry mustard
¹/₄ teaspoon liquid hot pepper seasoning (like Tabasco)
1¹/₂ teaspoons soy sauce

2 tablespoons salad oil
1 tablespoon sesame oil
2 teaspoons lemon juice

Combine all ingredients; mix well.

⋖ Sesame-Topped Vegetables ⋗

¹/₂ English cucumber, unpeeled
3 large carrots
3 cups cauliflower pieces
¹/₂ cups sesame seeds
2 cloves garlic, minced
¹/₂ cup minced shallots
¹/₃ cup salad oil
¹/₂ cup white vinegar
¹/₄ cup sugar
soy sauce

Julienne-cut cucumber and carrots into matchstick slivers. Break cauliflower into smaller pieces. Set vegetables aside.

In a wide frying pan over medium heat, toast sesame seeds, shaking pan frequently, until golden (1 to 2 minutes); set aside.

Over medium heat, sauté garlic and shallots in oil until shallots are soft. Increase heat to high and add vinegar, sugar, cauliflowerets, and carrots. Cook, stirring, until vegetables are tender-crisp, about 10 minutes. Fold in cucumber and cook just until heated through. Season to taste with soy.

Transfer to a serving dish and sprinkle with sesame seeds. Serve warm or at room temperature.

Makes 6 to 8 servings.

⋖ Sesame Green Beans ⋗

1 pound fresh green beans
10 large mushrooms
³/₄ cup boiling water
¹/₈ to ¹/₄ teaspoon pepper
soy sauce or salt
1 tablespoon sesame oil
1 large pimiento, cut into strips

Wash beans and remove ends. With a sharp knife, cut beans lengthwise into thin slivers. Clean mushrooms and slice thinly.

Place beans and mushrooms in a large saucepan, cover with boiling water. Cover and cook over medium heat until beans are tender to bite (6 to 8 minutes). Immediately remove from heat; drain well.

Sprinkle bean mixture with pepper and season to taste with soy, then drizzle with oil. Toss to distribute seasonings. Transfer to warm serving dish; garnish with pimiento strips.

Makes 4 servings.

⚜ Sesame Spinach ⚜

Subtle oriental seasonings are perfect with fresh spinach, and sesame finishes the dish.

1¹/₂ tablespoons soy sauce
1 teaspoon sesame oil
¹/₂ teaspoon sugar
2 tablespoons peanut oil
2 cloves garlic, finely chopped
2 teaspoons freshly grated ginger
6 scallions, finely chopped
1 very large bunch fresh spinach, washed and drained

Garnish:
1 tablespoon toasted sesame seeds

Thoroughly mix soy sauce, sesame oil, and sugar. Set aside. Heat peanut oil in a large skillet, and add garlic, ginger, scallions. Sauté over medium heat until softened, 2 to 3 minutes. Add spinach and stir-fry until cooked through but still a bit crispy, about 2 to 3 minutes. Add reserved soy sauce mixture and heat through. Remove from heat, sprinkle with sesame seeds, and serve immediately.

Serves 3 to 4.

—Renée Shepherd

⚜ Chicken Baked in Buttermilk ⚜

1 egg
1 cup buttermilk
3 pounds boneless chicken breasts
1 cup cornflakes

¹/₄ cup sesame seeds
2 tablespoons butter
1 teaspoon Worcestershire sauce

Beat the egg well and combine it with buttermilk in wide bowl or casserole dish. Add chicken to buttermilk mixture, turning to cover all sides. Cover the bowl and marinate in refrigerator at least 1 hour.

Crumble the cornflakes and mix with the sesame seed. Drain chicken from milk and coat with cornflake mixture. Place chicken in ungreased shallow baking dish. Melt the butter together with the Worcestershire sauce and pour over the chicken. Bake 1¹/₄ hours in a 350° oven.
Serves 6.

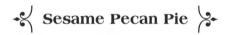

Sesame Pecan Pie

pastry for 9-inch pie, uncooked
¹/₄ cup sesame seeds
3 eggs
³/₄ cup sugar
¹/₄ teaspoon salt
¹/₃ cup melted butter
1 cup light corn syrup
1¹/₂ teaspoons pure vanilla extract
1 cup pecan halves
whipped cream (optional)

Line a 9-inch pie plate with pastry. Toast sesame seeds in 350° oven (or stovetop on medium heat in dry frying pan) until golden brown. Sprinkle seeds evenly over bottom of pastry shell.

Beat eggs with rotary beater or electric mixer until light and fluffy. Add sugar, salt, butter, corn syrup, and vanilla; continue to beat until well mixed. Fold in nuts, and pour batter into pie pan.

Bake in 350° oven until knife blade inserted in center comes out clean (about 1 hour). Serve slightly warm or cold. Whipped cream, just barely sweetened, sets off the rich taste of this pie very nicely.
Serves 6 to 8.

For Other Recipes Featuring Sesame Seed, See:
Asian Hot-Sweet Chicken with Broccoli, p. 96
Hibachi Beef Kabobs, p. 187
Sherried Beef Stir-Fry, p. 261
Refrigerator Rolls for a Crowd, p. 268

Star Anise

Botanical name: Illicium verum (sometimes Illicium anisatum)
Part used as spice: Dried fruit
Available as: Whole or ground

The spice we call star anise is, botanically speaking, no connection what-soever to the herb/spice we call anise. If it were possible to view the two side by side, you could see in an instant that they are not related. Anise is about 1¹/₂ or 2 feet tall, has very frilly foliage and a flower cluster that looks like a parasol upside down; the small seeds form at the very tip ends of each flower stalk, and at the end of the season the whole plant dies.

Star anise is a full-fledged tree, growing as tall as fifty feet. Its leaves are broad and leathery, somewhat like a magnolia (which makes sense, since it is part of the magnolia family). It is a perennial (lives from year to year) and will produce flowers and fruits for one hundred years. The flowers are set on the branches individually, rather than in clusters; the fruits that form when the flowers die give us our spice.

Yet, in spite of these profound differences in the plants, the aroma and the taste of the spices they produce are very, very similar. How could that be?

Think back to what we learned in Part I about essential oils and their constituent chemicals. As it happens, anise and star anise both contain the same three chemicals (although not in exactly the same propor-tions): anethole, which contributes the licorice taste; chavicol, which adds a peppery tang; and anisaldehyde, which tastes like vanilla. And that is why their taste is so similar.

Now, if you're wondering why it is that two plants so far apart in their botanical alliance would have the same chemicals, I would say (1) excel-lent question, and (2) I have no idea; that's something you'll have to take up with Mother Nature.

A word of caution: If you should happen to be traveling in the Far East and come across a plant known as Japanese star anise (*Illicium lanceolatum*), don't buy it. Even though it is in the same genus as regular star anise, it has some extra constituents that make it poisonous. In Japan it is used to make a pesticide for commercial agriculture. Do not experiment with it. Buy star anise only from legitimate spice companies.

The star anise fruits are picked when they are full size but still green, and then dried in the sun. As they dry, the fruits open out into a star shape. There are eight segments to the star, each one shaped like a miniature canoe and containing one seed. (The Chinese name of the spice means "eight points.") When you purchase whole star anise, frequently some of the segments are broken off and the seeds have fallen away. Fear not—it is the segments themselves that have the stronger flavor, and so if some seeds are missing you won't lose much.

The tree that produces these fruits is native to southern China and Vietnam. It has been successfully transplanted to parts of Central America where the climate is similar, but the commercial production of the spice is still centered in China.

Medicinal and Other Uses

In the Far East, as elsewhere, people have for centuries used the plants growing around them in various medicinal formulations; what is different about Eastern medicine is that these natural formulas have not been totally supplanted by more modern techniques. Star anise has been (and still is) used to relieve colic, flatulence, and rheumatism. Chewing a piece of an anise pod after a heavy meal to sweeten the breath is another old practice that is still in use.

In Japan, the bark of star anise trees is an essential part of a special incense burned in temples, and so the trees are planted in temple courtyards, where they are convenient for harvesting the bark.

Crafts with Star Anise

Usually we think of spices in terms of their fragrance and their taste. Star anise has one very important extra benefit: good looks. A perfect pod of star anise, with all eight points of the star intact, is a very pretty sight.

And for many people that visual charm is the most important reason for using star anise. You can get anise flavor from other sources; there is no substitute for the pretty little star in craft projects.

Project: Package Decorations

At various places in this book you will find many ideas for homemade gifts featuring spices: Trivet (page 106), hotpad (page 35), jam or preserves (page 193), to name a few. For these and any other spice-related gifts (such as a new cookbook), make your gift extra-special by adding spices to the giftwrap.

The highly decorative look of star anise pods makes a wrapped package especially pretty, while at the same time giving a little hint to what's inside.

Here we show two spice-trimmed packages, one using star anise and one using whole cinnamon sticks. I'm sure you will come up with many other pretty ideas.

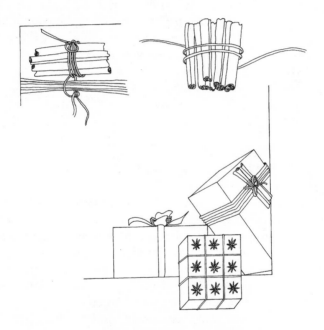

Decorate packages with whole spices. Tie several cinnamon sticks into a bundle, then tie the bundle into the middle of your bow. For a different look, tie ribbon around package in a grid pattern, then glue on star anise.

Project: Potpourri

In the chapter on cloves you will find a full description of the process of making potpourri (see page 126). Here we look at the extra decorative flair that star anise adds to potpourri mixtures.

With its dark color and exotic woodsy look, star anise seems most appropriate in potpourris that have a fall or winter theme—for instance, the mixture shown here.

❧ Midwinter Magic ❧

3 cups very small cones, such as alder or hemlock
1 cup star anise pods
1 cup dried orange peel, broken into chips
1 cup oakmoss
2 drops pine oil
2 drops bergamot oil
2 drops clove oil

Mix the oakmoss and the oils; stir gently. Keep in tightly covered jar for two days, until the fragrance is fully absorbed. Gently mix in the other ingredients. Age the mixture in a covered container for two to three weeks, then it's ready to display in your home or package up for gifts.

To make this especially festive, spray a few of the anise pods with gold paint before mixing them in. When you display your potpourri in its container, make sure some of these golden stars are visible.

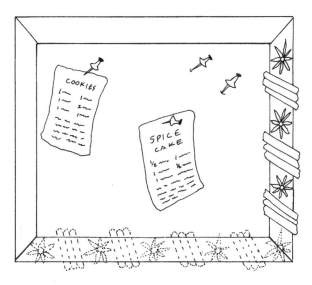

Spice-decorated bulletin board for your kitchen. Buy a bulletin board in desired size; flat frames work best. Choose whole spices with an attractive appearance (here we used cinnamon sticks and star anise). Lay the spices out in various patterns until you are satisfied with the results, then glue them in place.

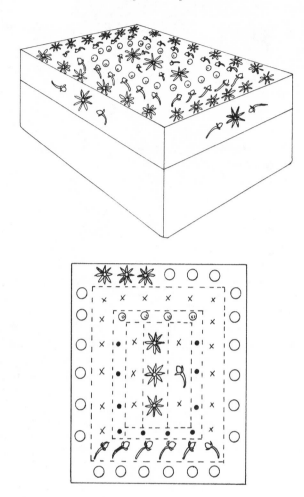

Decorated recipe box. Whole spices, glued to the top of a simple recipe box, turn a utilitarian item into a unique gift.

Layout for spice box. We used whole allspice, cloves, and star anise for the pattern here. Mark the pattern on the lid of the box with pencil, and glue the spices in place.

Project: Kitchen Bulletin Board

Many people find it handy to hang a small bulletin board in the kitchen, as a place to keep new recipes, shopping lists, reminder notes, and so forth. With hardly any work at all, you can turn an ordinary utilitarian board into something special by decorating the frame with spices.

Experiment by placing clusters of spices in various combinations around the frame; here we've used whole star anise pods and short lengths of cinnamon sticks. You can cover the entire frame or concentrate on just the corners. Once you get a look you like, glue the spices in place with either a hot glue gun or a drop of superglue.

Decorated recipe box. This box, with its rounded top, takes on the look of a magical treasure chest in miniature when decorated lavishly with whole spices.

Project: Spicy Recipe Box

First, find your box. In stationery or office supply stores, look for the boxes designed to hold index cards, either the 3 × 5 or the 4 × 6 size; they may be plastic, metal, or wood. Some kitchen departments carry what are essentially the same boxes, with additional decorations proclaiming "Recipes." Sometimes you can find wonderful old wooden boxes of an appropriate size in antique and secondhand stores.

Next, collect your spices and work out your design. On a plain piece of paper, sketch out the dimensions of the top of the box, and move the spices around on that rectangle until you have a design you like (see page 296). Then, glue the spices onto the box, with a glue gun or strong household glue.

This can be a wonderful personalized gift: a shower gift for a new bride, a housewarming present, or a celebration of "memories of our great meals together" for someone moving to a new home in a distant state. Make the box as pretty as you can. Include lots of blank recipe cards, and a few of your own favorite recipes.

Cooking with Star Anise

As a cooking spice, star anise is far more prominent in Asia, where the tree is indigenous, than in the West. It is used in Chinese cuisine with duck and pork, and by the Vietnamese to flavor their very versatile beef-noodle soup known as *pho*.

> If you have ever encountered Chinese five-spice powder you have met star anise without knowing it, for it is the principal flavor of that special blend. (Five-spice powder has its own short chapter in this book.)

The fundamental flavor of star anise and aniseed are so close that they are for all practical purposes interchangeable. Manufacturers of commercial products—baked goods, candies, soft drinks, chewing gum, toothpaste, cough syrup, lotions, perfumes, and the like—use one or the other depending on world market prices. In your kitchen, you too can successfully substitute one for the other in any recipe if need be. However, note that many people consider the taste of star anise stronger and somewhat harsher than anise, so go easy with it.

Use Star Anise in:
- Barbecued or roasted chicken
- Poached fish or shellfish; fish stews
- Light soups based on clear broth
- Rice pudding
- Steamed cabbage, braised leeks

⋖ Star Anise Cashews ⋗

4 cups water
1/2 cup coarse salt
1/2 cup sugar
1 teaspoon vinegar (preferably rice wine vinegar)
3 whole star anise
3 cups raw cashews

In large saucepan, boil water, add salt, sugar, vinegar, and star anise. Add cashews and boil for 2 minutes.

Remove from heat and cool nuts in liquid. After 5 minutes, drain nuts and spread on cookie sheet, along with star anise; leave to dry overnight.

Roast in 350° oven for 10 minutes; stir. Reduce oven to 250° and bake another 15 minutes.

Remove from oven and let cool on the cookie sheet for a few minutes, till nuts become crisp. Store in tightly covered container.

Makes 3 cups.

❧ Malaysian Spiced Rice ❧

The whole is greater than the sum of the parts. In this flavorful rice, you cannot identify any one spice, only a deep, rich taste.

1/2 cup (one stick) butter or margarine
2 tablespoons minced shallot
2 cloves garlic, minced or pressed
1 tablespoon minced fresh ginger
1 teaspoon ground coriander
1/2 teaspoon ground cumin
1/2 teaspoon ground cloves
2 or 3 whole star anise
1 cinnamon stick (2 inches long)
3 whole cardamom pods, cracked open
4 cups long-grain rice
8 cups water

In a large saucepan or Dutch oven, melt butter. Add shallots, garlic, and spices. Cook, stirring constantly, for 4 to 5 minutes.

Add rice and water. Increase heat to high and bring mixture to a boil; cover, reduce heat, and cook until rice is tender (about 20 minutes). Stir lightly with a fork; remove whole spices and use for garnish.

Makes 8 to 10 servings.

❧ Molokai Ribs ❧

5 to 6 pounds pork spareribs
3 medium onions
6 tablespoons soy sauce, divided
1/4 teaspoon pepper
6 whole star anise
1 tablespoon salad oil
1 tablespoon grated or minced fresh ginger
1/2 cup honey
2 tablespoons brown sugar
1 tablespoon Worcestershire sauce
1 tablespoon lemon juice

Cut the ribs apart into individual pieces. Peel and slice 2 of the onions. In a large kettle or Dutch oven, combine ribs, sliced onions, 4 tablespoons soy sauce, pepper, and star anise. Bring to a boil, then cover, reduce heat, and simmer until ribs are tender (1 to 1 1/4 hours).

Meanwhile, finely chop remaining onion. Heat oil in a wide frying pan over low heat and sauté onion until rich golden brown. Add ginger, honey, sugar, Worcestershire, lemon juice, and remaining 2 tablespoons soy. Mix well and cook until blended. Set aside.

Remove ribs from kettle and arrange in a single layer in a large shallow baking pan. Pour sauce over ribs. Bake, uncovered, in a 400° oven, about 1/2 hour; baste often with pan drippings.

Makes 4 to 6 servings.

✂ Spiced Chicken Livers ✄

1 pound chicken livers
1/2 cup water
1/2 cup soy sauce
1/4 cup dry sherry
1 tablespoon sugar
1/2 whole star anise or 1/2 teaspoon anise seeds
1 cinnamon stick (about 1 inch long)
1 slice fresh ginger
*1 green onion (including top), cut into 1-inch
    lengths*
1/8 teaspoon cayenne

Rinse livers, remove any gristle or fat, and cut into smaller pieces. Place in skillet over high heat and cover with water; boil for 1 minute, then drain off water. Add all remaining ingredients to pan, and simmer for 15 minutes. Place livers and cooking liquid in container and refrigerate for at least 1 hour. At serving time, remove livers from liquid and arrange on serving dish. Or reheat and serve hot, if you prefer.

Makes 6 to 8 servings.

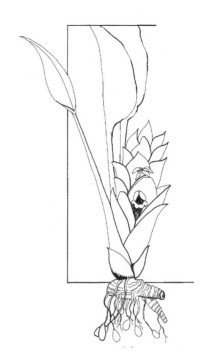

Turmeric

Botanical name: Curcuma longa
Part used as spice: Root
Available as: Ground powder

Turmeric is in the same botanical family as ginger, and the family resemblance is striking: Both are tall plants with large, strappy leaves and fragrant blossoms. Like ginger, the part of the plant that produces the spice is its root. Actually, it isn't literally a root in either plant, but a very fat stem that runs underground more or less horizontally, called a rhizome (pronounced *rye*-zohm). However, most people in the spice trade call it the root, and so shall we.

The turmeric plant is native to southern India, but commercial operations have been successfully established throughout tropical Southeast Asia and in some parts of Central America as well. However, more than 90 percent of the world's supply is still produced in India, and most of it is consumed there.

In commercial plantations, small chunks of rhizome saved from the previous season are planted; each rhizome grows several new "fingers," each one sending out aboveground stalks. During the growing season, the stalks grow tall and flower and the underground part gets fat. About ten months later, when the stalks begin to die back, the much-enlarged rhizomes are dug up, sorted, and cleaned. "Seed" rhizomes are set aside for the next year, and the rest are dried and ground to a fine powder.

This brings us to one way in which turmeric and ginger are dissimilar. You can find fresh gingerroot in the produce section of just about every supermarket in the country. Not so with turmeric. In small shops featuring ethnic Asian foods you *may* occasionally be able to find whole dried pieces of turmeric root. Everywhere else, what you will find for sale is the powdered form of this spice.

Where these two cousins really part company, however, is in the taste. You already know what ginger tastes like (think of gingersnaps); turmeric is nothing like it. The other obvious quality they do not share is color: The flesh of gingerroot is a neutral beige; turmeric is bright yellow-orange inside. That color, and the deep yellow it imparts to everything it touches, is one of turmeric's most important characteristics, and has been throughout its history.

History and Legend

Turmeric is one of the spices known to the ancient civilizations; it was used as a flavoring, as a dye, as a cosmetic and perfume—all uses that remain to this day.

The part of the world we now call the Mideast was once known as the kingdom of Assyria, several thousand years B.C. Around 600 B.C., an Assyrian physician compiled an herbal, a book listing all the plants then known and describing how they should be used. Turmeric appears in that herbal as a "coloring plant." So at least twenty-five hundred years ago, the idea of using turmeric as a dye was well established.

In Asia, where turmeric grows naturally, it has been employed as a coloring agent for many, many centuries, often with a component of ritual and magic to its use. For example:

- In ancient Persia, where the sun was worshiped, this spice that turns things the color of the sun was considered sacred.
- Down through the centuries, people have believed that wearing something treated with turmeric would protect them from evil spirits.
- Buddhist monks have long used turmeric to dye their robes yellow; in Buddhist countries, the color has religious associations.
- In Indonesia, a special rice, colored with turmeric, is served as part of the wedding celebration. And the bride and groom bathe their arms in turmeric water, turning the skin golden for this special occasion.
- In Malaysia turmeric has long been part of the childbirth ritual. The woman's abdomen is painted with turmeric as labor begins. Then the umbilical cord, when it is cut, is treated with an ointment made of turmeric. Both these practices were believed to protect mother and child from evil spirits.
- In India, women rubbed turmeric water on their face to give their skin a golden glow; some used it all over their body, believing it would prevent the growth of body hair, considered unsightly.
- In Southeast Asia, older generations of rice farmers planted pieces of turmeric along with the rice, for luck.

- In India, where the spirits that reside in trees are thought to sometimes leave the trees and take over hapless humans, special exorcists got rid of the spirits by burning turmeric root near the victim. The theory was that the spirits cannot tolerate the smell of burning turmeric.

Medicinal and Other Uses

Knowing what we know of human nature and history, we might imagine that a substance with such a strong visual appearance would be considered powerful medicine. And indeed, in Asia, turmeric has been used extensively to treat several disorders: ulcers, sores on the skin, liver disease, and gastric ailments.

In many Asian countries it has been, and still is, a home remedy for the common cold: A soothing brew is made from milk and honey, laced with turmeric. Beyond this, however, turmeric is not much used today as medicine, even by herbalists.

The Doctrine of Signatures

We know that many plants have constituents that are beneficial with certain diseases; this has been confirmed over and over again by modern laboratory research.

We also know that in the days before test tubes and chemical analysis, medical practitioners had to rely largely on trial and error to determine which plants in which form and formulation were helpful with which conditions. Many patients got better; many died. Physicians kept careful records, and continued to refine their treatments.

One theory that had many supporters in the Middle Ages was known as the Doctrine of Signatures. The basic idea was that some physical aspect of the plant held a clue to its curative properties; by looking at the plant itself, a trained herbalist could deduce what to do with it.

For instance: If a plant had red stems or flowers, a potion made from it would surely be good for reddened eyes. A flower that had several wrinkled lobes, vaguely resembling the brain, was considered good for headaches or any of the many "ailments of the nerves." Any plant that had roots or stems echoing the shape of human limbs might be used to treat broken bones. And so on.

The Doctrine of Signatures was followed for a long time, and indeed still has its believers, but today most medical practitioners view it as a historical curiosity. Common sense seems to align itself with the latter view.

It was not always so. In the Middle Ages, herbal physicians who followed the Doctrine of Signatures (see box on page 303) prescribed various formulations of turmeric (which is yellow in color) to treat jaundice (which turns the skin yellow). As was so often the case, the patients either got well, or died, on their own; turmeric had no real effect.

In fact, it probably made matters worse. We now know that turmeric is one of that class of substances called a choleretic, which means that it acts as a stimulant on the liver. This would be detrimental to anyone already experiencing liver problems.

In ancient times, turmeric was used as a perfume and a cosmetic. In some parts of the world, it still is. In India, women make a paste from it and use it on their face as a beauty mask. In rural areas of the Far East, young women still dip their fingers in turmeric water and scrub it over their cheeks to give their skin golden tones.

Crafts and Household Uses

Fabric dye

Here's the situation: Your daughter wants to be "Big Bird" for Halloween, and you're worried about the cost of all that fabric. Solution: Pick up some used white sheets from a thrift shop or secondhand store, and dunk them in a big tub of dye made by dissolving turmeric in hot water (approximately two tablespoons for each quart of water).

Of course you can use turmeric to dye any fabric, for it is inexpensive and nontoxic, but it is not colorsafe, so you probably wouldn't want to use it on a garment you intend to keep for a while and launder often. Even Buddhist monks no longer rely exclusively on vegetable dyes for their yellow robes.

Project: Easter eggs with natural dye

Have you ever tried making natural dyes for coloring Easter eggs? It's a great deal of fun for adults and children. Everyone seems to get a kick out of observing the alchemy of producing a dye from ordinary kitchen products. You may already be aware that you can make dyes from certain vegetables (onions, beets, spinach); instructions are often found in consumer magazines around Eastertime. But since this is a chapter about turmeric in a book about spices, I'm going to tell you how to use that spice for coloring eggs.

Start by cooking your eggs: Place the eggs in a pan with cold water covering them; bring the water to a boil, turn it down to simmer and cook the eggs for 10 minutes. Remove and cool the eggs. Make sure they are thoroughly dry before you begin your coloring session.

Meanwhile, dissolve 1 tablespoon of ground turmeric in 1 cup of boiling water. Remove from heat. Dip the cooled eggs in the dyebath. In just a few seconds, they turn a rich golden yellow. You can also use commercial curry powder as a natural dye. It contains lots of turmeric plus other spices, and colors the eggs a pale buttery yellow.

All these, as well as the dyes made from vegetables, will produce colors that are softer, more mellow than the kindergarten-bright primary colors you get from commercial dye tablets. They are subtle and quite lovely, and I think you will like the look.

Cooking with Turmeric

Marco Polo, in the famous diaries of his travels throughout the East, was largely responsible for introducing thirteenth-century Europe to the mysteries of the Orient, including the ordinary elements of everyday life. He wrote this about turmeric: "There is also a vegetable which has all the properties of true saffron, as well the smell as the color, and yet it is not really saffron." Later he noted: "Though it is nothing of the sort as real saffron, it is quite as good as saffron for practical purposes."

Marco, we agree. We still use turmeric as a substitute for saffron, when our main goal is color. Turmeric and saffron both color foods a wonderful golden yellow, but the flavor is not so close as to be interchangeable. Turmeric has its own taste, and while you may like it just fine, it is not a real substitute for saffron, any more than parsley is a substitute for spinach. You can use turmeric in recipes that call for saffron, in other words, and you will get a comparable color but a somewhat different taste.

Turmeric Tricks
Add a sprinkle of turmeric to the water in which you cook spaghetti noodles for children. Since you drain the water away, the taste is not appreciably affected, but the noodles turn bright yellow; kids think they're fun to eat.

Turmeric deserves respect on its own merits, and any recipes that feature this spice are worth exploring. But even if you haven't done that yet, chances are good you have still experienced turmeric.

If you ever cook with commercial curry powder, you are getting acquainted with turmeric. It is one of the prime ingredients in this blend, and is wholly responsible for the yellow color. Cooks who prefer to make up their own spice blend for curries also depend on turmeric; while the blend may have as many as twenty or even thirty different spices, nearly everyone agrees that turmeric must be included.

Not especially fond of curry? I'm willing to bet you have some turmeric on hand right now, in the refrigerator. It is part of the formula for all prepared mustard (the kind you put on your hot dogs), so if you have used mustard, you have eaten turmeric.

Food manufacturers also add turmeric to margarine (for the color), to cheese, and to many pickles and pickle relishes, such as the old-fashioned relish called piccalilli. Any food product of that category that is yellow undoubtedly has turmeric in it.

> Turmeric is very sensitive to light; even more than most spices, it's important to store it in a dark space, to preserve its quality. The same is true of commercial curry powder, which contains a large percentage of turmeric.

⁕ Corn Relish ⁕

2 quarts corn (20 fresh ears or 6 10-ounce frozen packages, defrosted)
1 pint diced red bell pepper (2 large or 3 medium peppers)
1 pint diced green bell pepper (2 large or 3 medium peppers)
1 quart chopped celery
1 cup chopped onion
1¹/₂ cups sugar
1 quart vinegar
2 tablespoons salt
2 teaspoons celery seed
2 tablespoons dry mustard
1 teaspoon turmeric

First, prepare the corn. If using fresh corn, remove husks and silks. Cook ears of corn in boiling water for 5 minutes; remove and plunge into cold water. Drain; cut corn from cob. Do not scrape the cob. Set aside.

Combine peppers, celery, onions, sugar, vinegar, salt, and celery seed in pan. Cover pan and heat until mixture starts to boil, then boil uncovered for 5 minutes, stirring occasionally. In a small bowl mix dry mustard and turmeric and blend with a small amount of liquid from boiling mixture; add with corn to boiling mixture. Return to boiling and cook for 5 minutes, stirring occasionally.

This relish may be thickened by adding ¹/₄ cup flour blended with ¹/₂ cup water at the time the corn is added for cooking. Frequent stirring will be necessary to prevent sticking and scorching.

Pack loosely while still boiling hot into canning jars, seal, and process in boiling water for 15 minutes. (See page 165 for canning instructions.)
Makes approximately 12 pints.

❊ Zucchini Chowchow ❊

This spicy relish, so good on hot dogs and hamburgers, is a good way to use up a bumper crop of zucchini.

10 cups ground zucchini
4 cups ground onions
2 green bell peppers, finely chopped
5 tablespoons salt
4 cups vinegar
7 cups sugar
1 teaspoon cornstarch
1 teaspoon nutmeg
1 teaspoon turmeric
1 teaspoon dry mustard
2 teaspoons celery seed

The zucchini, onion, and peppers should be finely ground. Use an old-fashioned food grinder, with the fine blade, or a food processor fitted with a steel blade.

Toss the vegetables with the salt and turn the mixture into a large colander. Cover and let it sit overnight.

Rinse thoroughly with cold water. Press the mixture against the sides of colander to squeeze out all the moisture; this is critical.

Place vegetable mixture in large kettle and add vinegar, sugar, cornstarch, and spices. Bring to a boil, then reduce heat and simmer 30 minutes.

Pack hot mixture into hot sterilized pint jars, seal, and process in boiling water bath for 15 minutes. (See page 165 for canning instructions.)

Makes approximately 10 pints.

⤜ Egyptian Eggplant ⤛

1/2 cup olive oil
3 cloves garlic, minced
1 large onion, chopped coarse
1 green pepper, chopped
1 cube vegetable bouillon
1 teaspoon ground coriander
1 teaspoon turmeric
1/4 teaspoon cayenne
1 teaspoon fresh ginger root, minced
1/2 teaspoon powdered ginger
2 bay leaves
1 medium eggplant, cut into 3/4-inch cubes
1 can (15 ounces) tomatoes, diced, including juice
1 tablespoon brown sugar

Preheat oven to 325°. Heat oil in large skillet. Add garlic, onion, green pepper, vegetable bouillon, and all the spices. Cook over low heat until onion becomes transparent and bouillon cube is dissolved. Discard the bay leaves. Fold in eggplant, stirring well. Mix sugar into tomatoes, and add to eggplant. Transfer to casserole dish and bake for 1 hour.

This is even better made ahead and reheated. Serve with hot rice. Plain yogurt is a traditional topping, and helps mitigate the spiciness.

Serves 8.

⤜ Carolina Rice and Shrimp Supper ⤛

This is one of those wonderful party dishes that allows you to do most of the preparation ahead of time.

2 cups long-grain rice, uncooked
2 pounds shrimp
16 strips bacon
16 small link sausages
4 eggs
1 teaspoon paprika
1/2 teaspoon turmeric
1/2 cup butter
chopped parsley
black pepper (in grinder)

Cook the rice in 4 cups of lightly salted water. Meanwhile, cook the bacon until crisp; drain. Sauté the sausages until well done; drain. Cook the shrimp in their shells in boiling water just until the shells turn pink; drain and cool. Remove shells and devein. Hard-cook the eggs. You can do this much ahead of time; keep ingredients chilled until ready, then warm the bacon and sausage in 325° oven.

When it is time to assemble the dish, place a large platter in a 200° oven to warm while you reheat the rice. Heat the butter in a large frying pan and sauté the spices for 30 seconds. Quarter the eggs and add them, along with the shrimp, to the butter. Stir and simmer until the eggs and shrimp are heated through; remove from heat.

Pile the rice onto the warm platter. Surround the rice with cooked bacon and sausage. Pour the shrimp-egg mixture onto the rice. Sprinkle chopped parsley over all, then a generous grinding of fresh pepper.
Serves 8.

⁕ Madras Mixed Vegetables ⁕

This very colorful vegetable mixture goes well with simple roast chicken or lamb.

> *1/4 cup butter (half a stick)*
> *1 medium onion, sliced*
> *1/4 teaspoon ground turmeric*
> *1/2 teaspoon dried summer savory*
> *1 large potato, peeled and cubed*
> *1 1/2 cups water*
> *1 small head cabbage, shredded*
> *1 small cauliflower, cut in small pieces*
> *1 cup fresh or frozen peas*
> *2 fresh tomatoes, peeled and cut into wedges*
> *1 bunch spinach, washed, with stems removed*
> *about 2 teaspoons salt*

Melt the butter in a large saucepan; add the onion, turmeric, and savory. Sauté until the onion is soft. Add the potato and water; cover and cook on low about 5 minutes. Add the cabbage and cauliflower and cook another 5 minutes. Finally, add the peas, tomatoes, and spinach; cook 3 minutes. Add salt to taste and stir gently before serving.
Makes 12 servings.

⚕ Persian Beef Patties ⚕

1 large potato
2 pounds lean ground beef
2 eggs
1 teaspoon salt
¹/₂ teaspoon pepper
¹/₂ teaspoon onion powder (or 1 teaspoon finely chopped fresh onion)
¹/₂ teaspoon turmeric
2 tablespoons flour
vegetable or olive oil

Grate the potato (or use food grinder) and mix with meat in a large mixing bowl. Beat the eggs and mix thoroughly with the meat. Mix this very well. Add the salt, spices, and flour, and mix again. If the mix is liquidy, add a bit more flour.

Spread a thin coat of oil in large skillet or griddle; heat it gently. Shape meat mixture into flat, thin ovals; you should have 15 to 18 patties. Cook patties until done and crispy-brown on both sides, adding more oil as necessary.

Serve with plain yogurt and sliced radishes.

Makes 4 to 5 servings.

For Other Recipes Featuring Turmeric, See:

Vanilla

Botanical name: Vanilla planifolia
Part used as spice: Pod (called the bean)
Available as: Whole beans or liquid extract

From the viewpoint of modern history, the story of spices is the story of Europeans' exploration and conquest of faraway lands. The race for economic dominance of the spice trade produced some ironic twists. Columbus, searching for a route to the Spice Islands in the Far East, discovered instead the islands of the New World and *their* native spices (see the chapter on Allspice).

The Europeans who followed Columbus to the New World, especially the Spanish, discovered hot chilies and brought this new "pepper" home to Europe (see chapters on Cayenne and Chili Peppers).

But the most important spice discovery was the long, wrinkled, brown "bean" that the Aztecs used to flavor their hot chocolate drink. The Spaniards called it vanilla, and so do we, and it is hard to imagine the world without it.

It is perhaps fitting that this exotic taste, the ultimate in luscious sweetness, comes from an orchid, that most exotic of flowers. As orchids go, this one does not produce an especially noteworthy flower, but that doesn't matter, for it is what comes after the flower that we care about.

You probably remember from high school science (and if not, refresh your memory by reading about the sex life of plants in Part I) that, in addition to the pretty petals, flowers have two critical parts: the stamen, which produces the pollen, and the pistil, which contains an ovary. The stamen, in other words, is the male part and the pistil the female part. The flowers attract bees, which brush against the pollen, and transfer it to the pistil, thus fertilizing (pollinating) the embryo. In a moment you will see why the pollination process is so important in the vanilla story.

Once pollinated, the vanilla orchid produces its fruit—a green pod about as thick as a pencil and six to ten inches long; although it's not literally a bean, it certainly resembles one, which is probably why the fruit is called the vanilla bean.

It is harvested when it is full size but still green, at which point it has no flavor. After a lengthy process of curing, which takes several months, the bean becomes dark brown and wrinkled. During the curing, tiny crystals of a chemical constituent called vanillin develop all along the bean, outside and inside. The taste we know as vanilla comes from this vanillin.

History and Legend

The orchid that produces the vanilla bean grows wild in Mexico and Central America, the land of the Aztecs. For centuries before Europeans came, the Aztecs had been using vanilla to flavor their food and drink, having figured out a way of fermenting the beans to bring out the sweetness.

> The Aztecs called it *tlilxochitl*, meaning "black pod." Cortés and his men named it *vainalla*, the diminutive of the Spanish word for "pod," *vaina*. So our word vanilla means "little pod."

Then came the Spanish conquistadors, under the leadership of Hernando Cortés. Over a bloody three-year period, 1519–1521, the Aztecs and their ruler, Montezuma II, were defeated by Cortés, who claimed Mexico for Spain.

One of Cortés's lieutenants was a soldier who was also a historian: Bernal Diaz del Castillo. Diaz kept extensive records of his time in Mexico, later published as a three-volume eyewitness account of the military campaign and his many observations of Aztec culture. And so we come to vanilla.

In his *Historia Verdadera* [True History], Diaz describes a beverage that Montezuma was fond of: powdered cocoa beans and ground corn, flavored with honey and ground vanilla pods. The drink was called *chocolatl*. It would appear that the Spaniards tried this drink as well, for on their return to Spain they brought vanilla with them.

European chocolate factories imported a great deal of vanilla during the next decades. Before long, vanilla became popular in its own right, to add flavor to foods and fragrance to a wide range of products, including tobacco.

All of this vanilla had to be imported from Mexico, because no one could find a way to grow vanilla beans anywhere else. Not that they didn't try. European nations at that time, remember, invested much time and money in their attempts to control the sources of all the spices they used.

Undoubtedly sales of vanilla jumped considerably in Europe after 1762, when a well-known German physician published the results of a study on male sexuality. He had prepared a medication based on vanilla extract, and given it to 342 men who were impotent. All 342 were magically cured, as 342 women soon attested.

Or so they all claimed. Aphrodisiacs, which purport to affect the sexual organs, actually work mainly on the mind.

Orchids need certain climatic conditions to grow, but those conditions are not restricted to Mexico; after all, orchids are found in tropical rain forests throughout the world. So European entrepreneurs took cuttings from the Mexican orchid plants and tried to establish commercial plantations in several places in the Far East. The plants lived, grew, and blossomed—but no vanilla pods.

Finally, in 1836, a botanist from Belgium by the name of Charles Morren solved the puzzle: The flowers were not getting pollinated.

Remember the female pistil and the male stamen, side by side in most flowers? In vanilla orchids, there is a tough membrane separating the two, and normal pollinating mechanisms like wind are not strong enough to push the pollen through. It turns out that in their native land, the orchids attract a particular species of insect and certain very small hummingbirds, and they could pierce this membrane. In the Far East, these insects and birds were not present.

To produce pods, some substitute for the natural action of these creatures had to be found. Morren knew that pollinating by hand was the only answer, but there was another problem: Each flower is in bloom for only one day, and so whatever procedure man devised had to be something that could be accomplished quickly.

The solution came a few years later, in 1841. A former slave on the island of Reunion, in the Indian Ocean near Madagascar, devised an efficient way of pollinating the flowers. He used a very slender piece of bamboo to lift away the membrane and, with the thumb of his other hand, pressed the pollen-bearing stamens against the pistils.

And that is the way it is still done today. An experienced worker can pollinate up to 1500 flowers in a day, lifting the little flap with a bamboo pick and using his thumb to smear the pollen on just the right spot. Romantic, isn't it?

When that new pollination process proved successful, the Mexican monopoly in vanilla, which had lasted more than three centuries, was broken.

But then a new problem appeared: vanilla rustling. In an economic clash of classic proportions, poor residents of the Asian islands where European entrepreneurs had set up the orchid plantations began to steal the valuable commodity that was growing right under their noses. The owners solved this problem by branding each bean, just like cattle. As the beans began to develop on the vine, a sharp pin was used to prick the outline of a distinctive brand on the bean, and those pin holes would remain as scars on the surface of the pod as it matured.

Today, most of the commercial production of culinary vanilla is still centered in Madagascar, although Mexico continues to produce beans of high quality and is responsible for about one-third of the world's supply. Other countries in Central America and French Polynesia (principally Tahiti) also produce vanilla, although some of it is from other species of orchid and of inferior taste.

Medicinal and Other Uses

In the days of the Aztecs, vanilla was considered an aphrodisiac. Europeans, when they found it, added it to their list of beneficial plants; it was thought to be a good antidote for poison, and also a good general tonic. During the eighteenth and nineteenth centuries, physicians gave it to patients suffering from hysteria and other nervous disorders.

None of those treatments survives in modern medicine. We do know that vanilla is a choleretic, which means that it stimulates the liver to produce bile. People experiencing liver problems can be adversely affected by choleretics, but there's not enough vanilla in normal recipes to cause any problems.

The sweet fragrance of vanilla can be used to perfume you, your clothes, and even your house.

- Put a few drops of vanilla extract on a cotton ball (never directly on your skin), give it a few minutes to soak in, and tuck it into your bra (either in your lingerie drawer or on your person).
- To counteract musty odors, keep a vanilla cotton ball inside the glove box of your car; in shoe boxes; in empty luggage; in clothing storage boxes.
- Every real estate salesperson knows this trick to make the home smell inviting: Place a teaspoon of vanilla extract in a shallow pan of water, and bake in a low oven. The whole house smells like cookies baking, triggering all sorts of positive impulses in prospective buyers.
- You can use that same trick to dispel unpleasant kitchen odors, or to spread a holiday fragrance throughout the house just before a party.

Today, in addition to cooking, vanilla is used in the manufacture of chocolate, in tobacco products, in liqueurs, in soaps and other cosmetics, and in the perfume industry.

Cooking with Vanilla

You are probably most accustomed to using vanilla in liquid form, in those familiar little brown bottles of extract. But is it pure vanilla?

Remember that what gives vanilla its distinctive taste is a chemical compound called vanillin. In a vanilla bean, vanillin develops naturally during the long curing process. But synthetic vanillin can also be produced in a laboratory, by a complex process involving any of a number of other substances; sucrose, oil of cloves, tree resins, wood fibers, waste paper pulp, even coal tar have been used at one time or another.

This man-made vanilla is used in many commercial products (both food and nonfood items), and is the main element in "Imitation Vanilla." This inexpensive form of vanilla flavoring is found in your supermarket, where it must be marked as imitation.

Pure vanilla extract, on the other hand, is made from vanilla beans and alcohol. The product cannot be labeled "Vanilla Extract" if it contains any artificial or synthetic material.

> In case you were wondering why genuine vanilla is so expensive, remember the labor-intensive process of hand-pollinating the orchids, and also remember that the curing that brings out the vanilla taste takes several months.

Vanilla extract—the real thing—is made from dried, cured whole beans. The beans are chopped into small pieces, and then a mixture of alcohol and warm water (at least 35 percent alcohol by volume) is percolated through them, rather like making coffee. The liquid is recirculated back through the beans several times, until all the flavor has been extracted. The liquid is then strained, aged, and bottled.

Most people, including tasters who do this sort of thing for a living, believe that the flavor of true vanilla extract is superior to artificial vanilla. Even though both contain vanillin and therefore have the same basic component of taste, true vanilla has, in addition, several secondary layers of flavor that are missing from the synthetic. These other tastes combine to produce a complex, satisfying, sensual blend with none of the bitter aftertaste of the artificial vanilla.

Two sniffs, side by side, will convince you.

And what will really knock your socks off is a sniff of a whole bean.

Using Whole Vanilla Beans

Whole vanilla beans are sold in supermarkets and spice shops (and by mail order; see Appendix). They may be packaged individually in glass vials or, where spices are sold in bulk, you may find the beans in large containers.

If you are choosing beans from one of those large containers, here's what to look for: The surface should look moist, not dull; the bean should be flexible (like leather), not stiff; the overall texture should be firm and relatively plump, not completely dried out.

Those small vials are usually clear glass or plastic, probably because manufacturers assume consumers want to see what they're buying. They do accomplish that purpose, but they are very poor for long-term storage. Exposure to heat and light will destroy the vanillin in the bean.

Therefore, whether you have purchased a single bean in a glass jar or selected one from a large container, the first thing to do when you get home is store it correctly. Place it in a dark-colored glass container that has a tight lid, and keep it in a closed cupboard, away from light and heat. Incidentally, this light sensitivity is the reason commercial vanilla extract comes in dark brown bottles.

The very best way to store whole beans is to bury them in sugar. Use a container that has a tight-fitting lid and will hold about one pound of sugar. Bury the vanilla bean so that it is completely covered and no light can reach it. In a couple of weeks, the sugar will take on the taste of vanilla; the longer the bean is stored, the stronger the flavor of the sugar.

Now you have vanilla in two forms: the bean itself, and vanilla sugar. You can use the sugar in tea or coffee, or in recipes, in place of regular sugar. Replace what you use, to keep the bean covered. Whenever you want to cook with the vanilla bean, remove it from the sugar and follow the instructions in the recipe (but first see box below about recycling).

Recycling Vanilla

Whole vanilla beans are not cheap, so treat them carefully. Store them properly, and recycle whenever possible.

Often a recipe calls for you to simmer the bean in some liquid (milk, juice, or water), which takes on the vanilla flavor, and then to discard the bean. For heaven's sake, don't throw it away—recycle it.

Wash off the simmering liquid, let the bean dry thoroughly, and then put it right back in the sugar container, and start all over. You can do this half a dozen times before the flavor weakens.

Inside the bean are extremely tiny black seeds. Many recipes call for slitting the bean lengthwise and scraping out some of the seeds. That's what those little black specks are in the premium brands of vanilla ice cream—seeds of the real thing.

⤳ Spicy Banana Nut Bread ⤳

For afternoon tea, toast slices of this bread and spread with raspberry butter or softened cream cheese.

¹/₃ cup butter or shortening
²/₃ cup sugar
2 eggs
1 teaspoon pure vanilla extract
1³/₄ cups all-purpose flour
2 teaspoons baking powder
¹/₂ teaspoon salt
1 teaspoon cinnamon
¹/₈ teaspoon cardamom
¹/₈ teaspoon mace
1 cup mashed bananas
¹/₂ cup chopped nuts

Preheat oven to 350°. Butter bottom and sides of a 9 × 5 × 3-inch loaf pan.

Cream shortening and sugar together until light and fluffy. Add eggs and vanilla and beat well.

In a separate bowl, sift flour, measure, and sift again with baking powder, salt, and spices. Add the flour mixture alternately with bananas to butter mixture. When thoroughly mixed, stir in nuts.

Pour batter into pan and bake approximately 1 hour.

Makes 1 loaf.

Raspberry Butter
Mix equal parts butter and raspberry jam; melt in microwave, blend completely, then chill for about an hour, until firm. Substitute any other fruit preserves, if you like.

⚜ Sweet Potato Casserole ⚜

half a large lemon
2 eggs
1 cup sugar (see note)
¹/₄ cup melted butter
1 cup evaporated milk
1 tablespoon vanilla
¹/₂ teaspoon salt
¹/₂ teaspoon nutmeg
1 teaspoon ginger
¹/₄ teaspoon pure vanilla extract
2 cups grated raw sweet potatoes (about 1¹/₂ pounds potatoes)

Preheat oven to 350°.

Grate rind from lemon; measure ¹/₂ teaspoon. Juice the lemon and measure out 1 teaspoon juice. (If it is small, you may need to use the entire lemon.) Reserve peel and juice.

Beat eggs with sugar until light. Add melted butter, lemon juice, lemon rind, evaporated milk, and spices. Fold in sweet potatoes.

When well mixed, pour into buttered casserole dish. Bake for 25 minutes, stir, bake 20 minutes more.

Note: You can use granulated white sugar, brown sugar, or a mixture of both.

Makes 6 servings.

⚜ Gingered Peach Snap ⚜

¹/₄ cup packed brown sugar
1 tablespoon lemon juice
2 teaspoons vanilla extract
1 teaspoon ground cinnamon
¹/₄ teaspoon ground ginger
3 cans (16 oz. each) sliced peaches in juice, drained (or 4 cups sliced
   fresh peaches)
¹/₂ cup raisins
1 tablespoon melted margarine or butter
2 tablespoons packed brown sugar
³/₄ cup crushed gingersnaps

Combine first 5 ingredients in a large bowl. Add peaches and raisins; toss to coat. Spoon into an 8-inch square baking pan.

Combine margarine and brown sugar in a small bowl. With a fork, mix in gingersnap crumbs until well blended. Sprinkle over peaches. Bake in 375° oven 35 to 40 minutes or until bubbly.

Serve with ice cream or frozen yogurt, if desired.

Makes 8 servings.

—McCormick/Schilling

⊰ Vanilla Mousse ⊱

1 piece (3 inches) vanilla bean
2 cups heavy cream, divided
1/2 cup sugar
2 egg whites
1/8 teaspoon salt

Split vanilla bean lengthwise and scrape out seeds and black pulp. Add pod, seeds, and pulp to 1/2 cup of the cream. Heat just to simmering; simmer for 2 minutes. Add sugar and stir until dissolved. Remove from heat, cool, and remove vanilla pod.

Whip remaining cream until very soft peaks form. Stir in the cooled cream mixture.

In a separate bowl, combine egg whites and salt; beat until soft peaks form. Fold into whipped cream. Pour into shallow pan. Freeze until ice crystals form around edge of pan, about 30 minutes. Scrape out into bowl; beat until smooth and creamy. Pour back into tray; continue freezing until firm, at least an hour.

To serve, remove from freezer, thaw slightly, and spoon into chilled dessert bowls or tall stemmed wine glasses.

Makes 1 quart.

⊰ Cinnamon-Vanilla Milk Shake ⊱

1 pint vanilla ice cream
1 cup cold milk
1 teaspoon vanilla extract
1/4 teaspoon cinnamon
nutmeg

Set ice cream out on counter to soften. Using a hand mixer or blender, combine ice cream, milk, vanilla, and cinnamon; mix thoroughly, until light and fluffy. Pour into chilled glasses and grate nutmeg on top.

Makes 2 milk shakes.

⋅⟨ Vanilla Liqueur ⟩⋅

2 vanilla beans
2 pints brandy
1 pint vodka
1 pound sugar
1 pint water

Split vanilla beans lengthwise. In large glass jar that has a tight lid, combine brandy, vodka, and vanilla beans. Store in a cool, dark cupboard for 2 weeks (longer doesn't hurt).

Strain out vanilla bean. Either discard the vanilla, or leave pieces out on counter to dry and then pack in small jar with sugar; the vanilla probably still has some flavor left.

Combine sugar and water in saucepan. Boil hard 5 minutes, then remove from heat. When completely cool, add syrup to brandy mix and blend well. Pour into attractive bottles and close securely.

Makes 4 pints.

For Other Recipes Featuring Vanilla, See:
Anise Cookies, p. 50
Cardamom Butter Cookies, p. 72
Jasmine Tea Bread, p. 112
Mincemeat Refrigerator Cookies, p. 142
Mace-Blueberry Muffins, p. 216
Raspberry Sauce, p. 218
Nutmeg Butter Cookies, p. 243
Pfeffernusse, p. 262
Fresh Fruit with Poppy Lime Topping, p. 272
Sesame Pecan Pie, p. 291

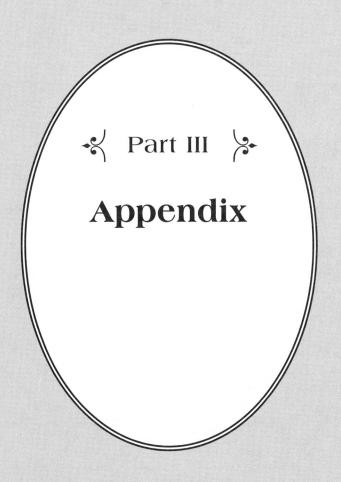

Part III

Appendix

SPICE	APPETIZERS	SOUPS	PASTAS & RICE	MEATS
ALLSPICE	Liver Pâté	Fruit Soup		Pork Chops
ANISE	Marinated Shrimp	Fish		Veal Stew
CARAWAY	Cheese Spread	Cabbage	Caraway Noodles	Pork or Veal Stew
CARDAMOM	Cottage Cheese Dip	Fresh Pea	Indian Rice	Marinade for Pork
CHILI PEPPER & CAYENNE	Seafood Cocktail Sauce	Seafood Bisque	Italian Tomato Sauce	Chili Con Carne
CHILI POWDER	Bean Dips	Corn Chowder	Spanish Rice	Oven-Fried Chicken
CINNAMON	Sugared Nuts	Pumpkin	Noodle Pudding Couscous	Greek Lamb Stew
CLOVES	Fruit Juices	Split Pea		Beef Stew with Dumplings
CORIANDER	Cheddar Cheese Spread	Lentil	Indian Rice Pilaf	Pork Kabobs Curried Chicken
CUMIN	Guacamole Dip	Bean	Brown Rice	Chilis & Curries
CURRY POWDER	Deviled Eggs	Mulligatawny	Tomato & Meat Sauces	Shrimp Curry
DILL SEED	Sour Cream & Yogurt Dips	Cream of Vegetable	Egg Noodles	Lamb Stew
FENNEL	Pickled Shrimp	Pasta & Bean	Italian Tomato Sauces	Baked Fish
GINGER	Oriental Shrimp	Carrot	Chinese Fried Rice	Pot Roast
MUSTARD	Pork Pâté	Cheddar Cheese		Baked Ham
NUTMEG	Chicken Kabobs	Cream of Onion	Risotto	Veal Meatballs
PAPRIKA	Baked Stuffed Clams	Potato-Onion	Red Rice	Beef Paprikash
POPPY	Cream Cheese Spread	Cream of Potato	Butter Sauce for Noodles	Broiled Fish
SESAME SEED	Herbed Biscuits	Sprinkled over Carrot-Orange	Chinese Noodle Salad	Sesame Burgers
TURMERIC	Deviled Eggs	Fish	Yellow Spaghetti	Curried Lamb

Adapted from *American Spice Trade Association*

SPICE	BREAD	VEGETABLES	SALADS & DRESSINGS	DESSERTS
ALLSPICE		Honey Glazed Winter Squash	Creamy Fruit Salad Dressing	Baked Pears
ANISE	Coffee cake	Vegetable Curry	Fruit Cup	Cookies, Cake
CARAWAY	Rolls, Bread	Sauerkraut Roasted Potatoes	Potato Salad	Spice Cookies
CARDAMOM	Waffles	Cabbage, Carrots	Citrus Fruit Salad	Cardamom Bread Cookies
CHILI PEPPER & CAYENNE	Cheese Crackers	Stewed Tomatoes	Tomato Salad Dressing	
CHILI POWDER		Baked Beans	Sour Cream or Yogurt Dressing	
CINNAMON	Cinnamon Rolls	Mashed Yams	Sugared Sliced Tomatoes	Fruit Pies, Cakes, Puddings
CLOVES	Coffee Cake	Beets with Orange Sauce	Fruit Salad Dressing	Poached Apples
CORIANDER	Danish Pastry	Coriander Butter for Winter Squash	Yogurt Dressing for Fruit	Coffee Cake
CUMIN	Cornbread	Black Beans	Vinaigrette	Sugar Cookies
CURRY POWDER		Baked Winter Squash	Fruit Dressing	
DILL SEED	Rolls, Bread	Green Beans New Potatoes	Marinated Cucumbers	
FENNEL	Rye Bread	Braised Celery	Seafood Salad	Apple Pie
GINGER	Ginger Toast	Carrots		Poached Winter Fruits
MUSTARD		Potatoes Au Gratin		
NUTMEG	Breakfast Pastries	Creamed Spinach	Waldorf Salad	Spice Cake
PAPRIKA		Corn Pudding	Macaroni Salad	
POPPY	Rolls, Bread	Mashed Sweet Potatoes	Sprinkle on Sliced Oranges	Poppy Seed Cake
SESAME SEED	Rolls	Topping for Vegetables	Toasted, over Fruit Salad	Baked Bananas
TURMERIC		Curry Sauce for Steamed Veggies	Corn Relish	Cake Batter for Color

ABOUT BLACK PEPPER: So versatile is the flavor of our most important spice that it can be added to most dishes, including some desserts like spice cookies and cakes, strawberries and poached pears. Pepper can also be used as a seasoning corrector, just before serving.

Substitutions and Other Miscellany

Often in this book you are encouraged to use whole spices wherever possible. The taste is always superior, but there are instances where the whole spice is either (1) not available, (2) not convenient, or (3) not the right texture. You cannot, for instance, use whole cloves in an apple pie without running the very real risk of causing someone to choke.

Much the same is true when cooking with onions and garlic. In terms of taste, the fresh version of each is preferable; in terms of texture or convenience, you may want to use the dehydrated or powdered commercial product. If so, the following substitution information may come in handy.

Onions
1 tablespoon onion powder = 1 medium fresh onion
1 tablespoon dried minced onion = 1/4 cup minced raw onion
1 tablespoon dried onion flakes = 1/4 cup chopped raw onion
1/4 cup dried chopped onion = 1 cup fresh chopped onion

Garlic
1/4 teaspoon garlic powder = 1 average-size clove fresh garlic
1/4 teaspoon dried minced garlic = 1 clove fresh garlic
1/2 teaspoon crushed or minced garlic (in oil) = 1 clove fresh garlic
1/2 teaspoon garlic salt = 1 clove fresh garlic

And while we're at it . . .
1 measure dried herb = 3 measures fresh herb
1 stick butter or margarine = 1/2 cup
1 tablespoon = 3 teaspoons
1 pint = 2 cups
1 quart = 4 cups
1 gallon = 4 quarts or 16 cups

Mail-Order Resources

Everyone knows that you can buy spices in jars in supermarkets, and those are very fine products. If you're in the middle of making a cake and discover you don't have any ground cloves, you'll be glad that, at your local grocery store, the big spice companies are ready to come to your rescue.

But that is not the only way to buy spices. There are a number of smaller businesses that sell spices, herbs, and related products via mail order, often in bulk quantities.

It's good to know about these companies for several reasons:

- If you live in the country, making a midnight trip to the store for those missing cloves is not, so to speak, a piece of cake.

- If you are making a craft project that calls for a large amount of spices (the cinnamon stick trivet on page 106, for instance), you'll find it much more economical to buy by the pound from one of the companies that sell spices in bulk.
- Browsing through the catalogs is a heck of a lot of fun. Many of them have some of the same quality as an old-fashioned general store. You'll find things you never knew existed, along with many old favorites.

Here you will also find addresses for the Spice Trade Association and for the big commercial spice companies; they don't sell mail order, but they do offer a wonderful information resource for consumers.

This appendix is—I admit it—opinionated. And it is certainly not a complete list of all the companies that sell spices by mail order. I included only those whose product mix is tilted toward spices, and only those who responded to my requests for information. Also, while all the information here is correct at the time of writing, you should remember that, the world being what it is, things change.

American Spice Trade Association
560 Sylvan Avenue
Englewood Cliffs, NJ 07632
This is the professional organization for commercial spice companies. Most of its publications are rather technical, but not all. Ask for a list of current consumer information materials and their prices.

Clement Herb Farm
19690 Clement's Lane
Rogers, AR 72756
501 / 925-1603
Catalog $1
This small family operation sells a limited number of spices and herbs, and premixed spice blends that look very intriguing.

Sample price, 1999 catalog: Whole coriander seed, $1.35 per packet (approximately 1 ounce).

Frontier Herbs
3021-78th Street
P.O. Box 299
Norway, IA 52318
800 / 669-3275 (customer service, orders)
800 / 717-4372 (fax orders)
Catalog free (be sure to ask for the consumer catalog)
Frontier Herbs sells a line of bottled herbs and spices and related products in natural food stores around the country, but if you do not have such a store in your community, you'll want to study their mail-order catalog. Actually, even if you do have retail access to Frontier products, you'll want their catalog, for the bottled spices are only the tip of the iceberg.

The catalog is the size of a fat magazine, and little space is wasted on pretty pictures and flowery descriptions—just listings of all the products they sell: bulk herbs and spices (in 1-pound units), spice blends, coffees, medicinal herbs in capsules, packaged herbs and spices in glass jars and refill packets, flavorings and extracts, essential oils, kitchen accessories, and an extensive array of health and beauty aids from other manufacturers. Friendly people, fast service, a wide range of products—all in all, a most impressive operation.

Sample prices from 1998 catalog: Whole allspice, $5.95 per pound in bulk.

MarketSpice
P.O. Box 2935
Redmond, WA 98073
425 / 883-1220
Catalog free
If you have ever visited Seattle, you have surely spent time in the Pike Place Market. And everyone who goes there is irresistibly drawn, as if by a magnet, to the MarketSpice shop; the aromas seep out the door and down the hallways and pull you in. There is always a pot of the famous MarketSpice tea, ready for sampling. This shop also has two walls of large jars of bulk herbs, teas, spices, and spice blends, so you can buy as little or as much as you need.

If you can't get to Seattle, you can order through the mail everything they have in the store. The tricky part is, they don't have a mail-order catalog in the usual sense. What they do have is one small flier describing the most popular items—teas, tea gifts, and a few spice blends—and a second flier that lists all the products you can buy by mail: spices, seasoning mixes, teas, and coffees. It's only a listing—no description, no prices. Write or call for specifics if you wish to order something. Better yet, come see this remarkable shop in person.

McCormick/Schilling
211 Schilling Circle
Hunt Valley, MD 21031-1100

A major supplier of bottled spices and herbs, in supermarkets around the country. Look for their free recipe leaflets in the spice section; write to the company with questions on specific spices.

Renée's Garden
7389 W. Zayante
Felton CA 95018
888 / 880-7228
831 / 335-7228
831 / 335-7227 (fax)
www.garden.com/reneesgarden (information and orders)

Renée Shepherd, a mail-order nurserywoman well known for her expertise in gourmet vegetables and heirloom flowers, in 1997 launched Renée's Garden, which sells its specialty seeds direct to consumers through garden centers. Call toll-free for the nearest retail location, or order on-line from garden.com.

Renée is also the author of *Recipes from the Garden* and *More Recipes from the Garden*, two cookbooks featuring herbs, spices, and fresh vegetables. Consumers can order the cookbooks direct or on-line ($11.95 plus 10 percent for shipping).

The Rosemary House, Inc.
120 South Market Street
Mechanicsburg, PA 17055
717 / 697-5111
Catalog $3

A very comprehensive collection: Herbal teas, herb plants, books, craft supplies, essential oils, gift items, and much more. If you become interested in making potpourri, this is a fine source for the materials. Over two hundred types of spices, herbs, and floral botanicals, by the ounce or pound. In business since 1968.

Sample price, 1999 catalog: Whole allspice, $2.00 per ounce. (With a few exceptions, all bulk spices here are $2.00 per ounce.)

San Francisco Herb Co.
250 14th Street
San Francisco, CA 94103
415 / 861-7174
415 / 861-4440 (fax)
800 / 227-4530 (orders)
Catalog free

This is an excellent source for larger quantities of spices; most of the bulk spices are sold by the pound, rather than the ounce, and there is a

$30 minimum for mail orders. A fine selection of items: many spices and herbs, spice blends, teas, and dried flowers for crafts. Unique feature: 36 recipes for potpourri, using materials sold in the catalog. In business since 1973.

Sample price, 1998 catalog: Whole allspice, $1.08 for 4 ounces; $3.25 per pound.

St. John's Herb Garden, Inc.
7711 Hillmeade Road
Bowie, MD 20720
301 / 262-5302
301 / 262-2489 (fax orders)
Catalog $5

The catalog of this company is the most expensive in this Appendix listing, but when you see it you'll understand why: It's a whole book. They have an astonishing array of products, far too many to list here, including many items I've never seen anywhere else. The catalog category named "Spices" is nine pages long, and includes spice blends, dried mushrooms, dehydrated vegetables, orange peel, popcorn seasoning—and many, many spices.

Sample price, 1999 catalog: whole allspice, $2.66 per ounce.

Spice Islands
Specialty Foods
222 Sutter Street, P.O. Box 7004
San Francisco, CA 94021-7004

This well-known company has produced a series of colorful recipe cards and booklets featuring their spices. Write to them directly for further information concerning new recipes or your questions about specific spices.

Tom Thumb Workshops
14100 Lankford Highway (Route 13)
P.O. Box 357
Mappsville, VA 23407
757 / 824-3507
757 / 824-4465 (fax)
800 / 526-6502 (orders)
Catalog free

This deceptively small catalog is jam-packed with wonderful items for potpourri and other crafts, including an amazing list of essential and fragrance oils and handy accessory items that are hard to find elsewhere. Spice selection is limited to those that can be used in potpourri, but all the spices are culinary quality. Send for the catalog anyway; you'll love it.

Sample price, 1999 catalog: Whole allspice, $3.63 for 4 ounces; $8.50 per pound.

Wonderland Tea & Spice
1305 Railroad Avenue
Bellingham, WA 98225
360 / 733-0517
Catalog $1

This small catalog is packed with a wide selection of spices and herbs, along with no-salt spice blends, herbal teas, potpourri mixes, essential oils, and gift items. Owner Linda Quintana searches out suppliers who use organic gardening methods. In business for twenty years.

Sample price, 1999 catalog: Whole allspice, 70 cents per ounce.

⋇ Index ⋇

Page numbers of illustrations are set in bold print